MURDER
IN THE
HEARTLAND

Book One

HARRY SPILLER

MURDER
IN THE
HEARTLAND

Book One

TRADE PAPER
PRESS

To Kathy Jo

Trade Paper Press
An imprint of Turner Publishing Company

4507 Charlotte Avenue, Suite 100
Nashville, TN 37209
Phone: (615) 255-2665   Fax: (615) 255-5081

www.turnerbookstore.com

Library of Congress Control No. 2003095194
ISBN: 978-1-59652-797-3

Printed in the United States of America

10 11 12 13 14 15 16 17—0 9 8 7 6 5 4 3 2

Contents

Acknowledgments

I would like to thank the city and county police departments and the Prosecutor's offices in Kentucky, Illinois, and Missouri for their cooperation in researching these cases. Without their help this book would not have been possible.

Prologue

It was about midnight on June 5, 1974, in Marion, Illinois, when I arrived at the crime scene. Four squad cars were bumper-to-bumper in the middle of the street. Detectives were darting back and forth, taking photos, marking off the scene with yellow crime scene tape, and jotting down notes.

I got out of the cruiser and walked quietly toward the floodlights that the fire department had set up to light the crime scene at the end of Union Street. My heart was beating quickly as I approached the edge of the scene.

I looked down at the thirteen-year-old girl lying naked and spread-eagled in the gravel. Her head was turned to one side with a purplish tint covering her face and neck. The summer breeze slightly brushed her reddish hair back and forth across her cheek.

A trail of ants busily ran across the corpse's smooth, pale skin from her lower torso to the corner of her mouth, then down her neck to the ground. Congealed blood was visible in the vaginal area. My stomach churned and my mind raced. Adults are murdered, not kids; what kind of pervert would do something like this? But one thought kept coming back over and over—this isn't supposed to happen here.

I had lived in Marion all my life. Our county had gotten the name "Bloody Williamson" from a couple of historical vendettas in the 1850s, gangster activity and a mining massacre in the early 1900s, but murder wasn't supposed to happen in Marion now. It happened in mystery books, at the movies or on television, or in the city or somewhere else, but not in Marion.

For sixteen years, I worked as a deputy sheriff, investigator, and sheriff in a place where murder isn't supposed to happen—Southern Illinois—investigating murder cases mainly in Williamson County, but assisting in other counties, too. I learned the hard reality: murder is all around us. It is swift for the victim and can happen to anyone—rich, poor, old, young. It can happen anywhere, day or night. It doesn't matter if you live in a big city or an area like my county, with brick-front towns, small farms, white church houses, lakes and ponds, the Shawnee National Forest, and the muddy rivers. All too often, victims fall prey in places that we think are safe to raise our families, places where we take walks on hot summer nights, where our children play in the park without concern, where we fish in the local pond to land the big one, and where we leave our doors unlocked at night.

A couple of hours after I arrived at my first homicide scene, the body was bagged and moved to a local hospital. The sheriff told me that he thought the girl was Francis June Buckner. Her father had reported her missing three days before, on Saturday, June 2, 1974.

The victim's father said that Francis and her sister were visiting him at his apartment on the Public Square in Marion. At 4:50 on Saturday afternoon, the trio started to walk to a local grocery store on East Main Street.

The sister left her father and Francis so she could pick up a pair of tennis shoes at a friend's house. She was to meet them later. Francis and her father walked about five of the eight blocks to the store before his emphysema got the best of him. He stopped, gasping for air, then told Francis to go on without him. She was to wait for her younger sister at the store, then meet him at the post office steps upon their return. Francis continued while her father watched her walk the remaining three blocks to the store. A few bushes along the way, coupled with the sun's brightness, obscured his view. But confident that Francis had made it to the store, her father returned to the post office steps and waited.

About fifteen minutes later, the other daughter returned alone. She told her father that Francis was not at the store. The father and daughter returned to his apartment and called the store. The store owner said that she hadn't seen Francis. Her father immediately called the police and reported that Francis was missing.

Three days later, neighbors were awakened by a rock being thrown through their window. When they looked outside, they saw a body lying in the street. They reported it to the police. I got the call.

We went to the victim's father's apartment. We told him that we had found a dead body and asked if he would go with us to see if it might be his daughter. He agreed, and minutes later we were at the hospital. A nurse unzipped the body bag and the father's face tightened. He turned and looked at us with tears filling his eyes. "I want the son of a bitch that did this!"

Two days later, a twenty-year-old man was arrested for Francis Buckner's murder. The youth had spotted the girl on Saturday walking alone. He abducted her and took her to his East Main Street apartment, where he strangled her and then raped her corpse several times over the next two days, before placing her body in the street.

I had been a police officer for two months when I had that first experience with murder. Since then, I have learned a lot about the myths of murder. I learned that the sensational murders like John Wayne Gacy or Jeffery Dahmer, whose names become part of the folklore, account for only a small percentage of the homicides that occur in the United States.

The most common type of murder usually occurs when parties are given and alcohol is involved. The altercations often involve matters trivial to anyone but those involved—quarrels over money, over girlfriends, and bars are common. A large percentage of homicides usually involve one spouse killing the other.

One morning, I was in the office at about 6:30, trying to catch up on paperwork, when a woman walked in and stood in front of my desk. She didn't say anything; she just looked at me with glassy eyes.

"Can I help you?" I asked.

"Sheriff, I think I killed my husband," she responded.

There was no thinking about it. We responded to the scene. The victim's brains were spattered against the wall next to the bed. We later found out that the woman and her children had been battered by her spouse for years. His moods became predictable over the years—he was in another abusive period. The wife couldn't take it anymore, so she got the shotgun and shot her husband while he was asleep.

Another case I worked made me realize how vulnerable the American family in small communities can be. On Sunday, November 16, 1987, the Dardeen family—Russell; his wife Ruby Elaine, who was seven months pregnant; and their three-year-old, Peter Sean—returned home from a family get-together. Their trailer was located outside the small town of Ina, near the Franklin and Jefferson County lines. Their closest neighbor was a quarter of a mile away.

Russell had the next couple of days off, but on Wednesday when he did not show up for work, his employer became concerned. Russell was a good employee, and he never missed work. The employer called the

Dardeen home and got no answer, so he called a neighbor and asked him to check on the family. The neighbor noticed that the family car, a late-model Dodge Colt, was missing. The truck was parked in the driveway. No one seemed to be at home, but, otherwise, things seemed normal. The neighbor reported the findings, but the next day, Dardeen relatives who lived seventy-five miles north became concerned and called the sheriff's department. They went to check out the Dardeen home. They cautiously entered the residence and were overwhelmed by the mayhem.

Elaine and Peter Dardeen lay side by side in the bedroom, partially clothed. They had been beaten to death with a blunt instrument. Further investigation revealed that Elaine's seven-month-old fetus had been born, and the dead baby had also been placed in the bed.

Russell Dardeen was missing. He immediately became a suspect. Police contacted his employer and found out that he had last been to work on Saturday and failed to pick up his paycheck on Monday. So, the search for Russell Dardeen was on.

The next shock came when they found the Dodge Colt in the parking lot of a local bank in Benton, Illinois. A large amount of blood was found in the car. Later that day, Russell Dardeen was no longer a suspect. He'd become a victim. He was found in a field by hunters. Russell had sustained bullet wounds to the head and had been badly beaten. His pants and underwear had been pulled down to his knees and his body had been badly mutilated.

I remember a murder case that occurred at a local business on the corner of Main and First Streets in Marion where chiropractor Dr. Don Ripley had a thriving practice. I was summoned to his office on the morning of December 5, 1975. Walking into the waiting room, I saw his patients sitting quietly with blank stares. The radio in the doctor's office played soft music. I stepped through the doorway into the hall. Dr. Ripley was lying face down. He had been shot seven times with a .45-caliber pistol. There had only been a fifteen-minute period between the time the doctor was seen dropping his son off at school and the time his body was found by his patients.

I remember a murder at Westernnaire Estates where Virginia Witte and her husband had just returned from their vacation in May 1978. The husband attended a luncheon for about an hour while Virginia went to get groceries. When he returned just an hour or so later, he found his wife lying on the bed in their bedroom. She was nude, her body had a large slash across the abdomen, and she had a knife protruding from her chest. The groceries were still in their bags on the kitchen counter.

I remember a case in 1985, when I was summoned to a local motel after Tag Anderson was found dead near a shed at the back of the motel. He was lying on the ground grasping a rifle. He had been shot once in the side with a shotgun. Just thirty minutes before, he had spoken to his wife at work and was getting ready to settle down for the evening and watch a movie. We theorized that the victim heard someone browsing around his property out back and went to check it out. Evidently, his inquisitiveness resulted in his murder.

And I remember the Wildlife Refuge on Route 148 where most people see the beauty of the lake, the green fields, and the wildlife. I, however, saw Ladonna Cooper, a mother of three, lying at the edge of the lake with a slashed throat and mutilated body. She had been abducted from a local restaurant, robbed, and bludgeoned to death with a knife. Minutes before she was abducted, she called her husband to tell him that she would be home shortly. She was laughing with him as she hung up the phone. Ladonna's husband sat back in his chair and dozed off. A few minutes later, he awoke, startled that his wife wasn't home. It was 12:15 a.m. He rushed to the restaurant and found the door wide open. A small amount of blood was in the room. Three days later, we found Ladonna at the refuge.

These murders all have similarities: they were all unsolved murders that occurred in places where most people think murder isn't supposed to happen.

In September 1989, I resigned as sheriff to take a position as associate professor of criminal justice at John A. Logan College. I thought the immediate presence of murder would be something of the past, something for discussion in the classroom—until one morning when I turned on the television.

I watched the morning news and learned that the decapitated body of Michael Miley had been found in his car trunk. His hands were bound behind his back, and the car had been burned. It was a shocking and gruesome murder, but what was even more shocking was learning that the two people that had committed the murders were a husband and wife, both students in my criminal behavior class. Convicted of the crime, one of those students is serving a life term and the other is on death row awaiting execution.

The classroom gossip about the headless murder victim has quieted down now, but I still have daily reminders of murder and how swift it can be.

In this book, *Murder in the Heartland,* there are twenty case files. They are cases from the Heartland that, as Sheriff, I participated in the investigation of or that I have researched as a writer. It is my hope that in reading these murder cases people will become more aware of our vulnerability as citizens. Rural America isn't immune to the bizarre and unpredictable human behavior that leads to murder. As much as we like to think of ourselves as safe, murder can happen here. Too often it does.

Case 1

Serial Murderer John Paul Phillips

Theresa Clark
January 26, 1975

Kathy McSherry
July 13, 1976

Susan Schumake
August 17, 1981

Joan Weatherall
November 11, 1981

Carbondale, Illinois

At about 8:20 on Monday morning, January 27, 1975, two Southern Illinois University students pulled into the parking lot of the Ambassador Apartments on Danny Street in Carbondale. The couple had just returned from a weekend trip in Pana, Illinois.

Both students grabbed their luggage and climbed the stairs of the two-story apartment building and stopped in front of apartment 20. The girl set her luggage down. When she'd left the apartment on Saturday for the trip to Pana, her roommate "Theresa Clark" had been sitting there writing letters dressed in a blue robe. Now, the letters were scattered all over the floor. The books that normally sat on the coffee table were on the floor. She scanned the room and noticed the hanging plants had been moved off of the picture window curtain rod so the curtains could be closed.

The couple slowly walked to the girl's bedroom. As they walked down the hall, they saw large brown spots in the rug. Was it dirt? But a rag was lying to one side of the hall soaked with something red. The bathroom door was shut and had smears of brown on it. The couple walked into the bedroom and set the luggage down.

They looked at each other and without saying anything walked into the kitchen. Broken glass was everywhere—on the table, the floor, the counter top. Theresa's eyeglasses were lying on the floor; one lens was popped out. A cutting board that had been hanging on the wall was on the kitchen table broken into three pieces.

The couple's stomachs churned and their minds raced with thoughts of horror as they noticed the still quiet of the apartment. "Terri! Terri!" the male student called out. No answer.

He walked slowly back down the hall to the bathroom, his girlfriend close behind him. He opened the door and stepped inside. "Oh my God! Oh my God! She's dead," he screamed as he spun, grabbed his partner, and bolted from the apartment.

The Carbondale police logged the call at 8:34 a.m. "There's a dead body at Ambassador Apartments, number 20," the frantic college student blurted.

Minutes later the police arrived at the apartment and met the students at the front door. "She's in the bathtub," the male student said, sobbing.

The Carbondale officer entered the apartment and carefully made his way to the bathroom. Floating face up was the nude body of a white female. The officer noticed that her blue eyes were open and dilated. She had several wounds in her chest, one breast was mutilated, and her throat had been cut. He quickly secured the scene and called for the detective unit.

Detectives arrived and began to process the crime scene, one room at a time. In the living room, they found a stick to aid the growth of plants knocked out of the pot and lying on the coffee table.

The female roommate told the police that a plant stick found on a shelf in the living room had been moved; a model car that normally sat on the television had been moved onto some books on the same shelf; and speaker wires from the stereo were also on the top of the shelf, and they usually were on the floor.

Smeared blood was found on the couch along with the victim's notebook and some crumpled papers.

Under the coffee table, several blood-soaked papers were found with hair fibers matted in the blood. A footprint of blood was underneath the chair in the living room and a large amount of blood was found on the rug near the couch. The wall next to the large blood spot was splattered with blood. Several bloody footprints led off in different directions from the large blood spot. A blood-soaked dish rag lay on the floor near the couch.

From the major area of blood in the living room, drag marks of blood led across the room, down the hall, and into the bathroom. Scratch marks were on the bathroom door. Inside the bathroom, the trail of blood led to the bathtub where the body was found. Police found blood on the table and on the counter top and bloody footprints in the kitchen.

The officers discovered pry marks on the back door, a bloody footprint just outside the back door, and then a trail of blood leading down the stairs.

While detectives were completing the crime scene process, other police officers were scanning the area around the apartment. A tenant from apartment 9 approached one officer and gave him a set of keys. The officer examined the two-key ring, seven-key combination. The tenant told the officer that shortly before noon on Sunday, January 26, he went to empty his tray in the dumpster at the southwest corner of the apartment building. He noticed the set of keys and picked them up. He said that he figured someone had accidentally thrown the keys away. Then when he saw the police at the apartment, he decided to give them to the police.

The officer immediately took the keys to apartment 20 and tried the key in the front door lock and the back door lock. Both fit.

About that time, another officer scanning the area reported finding two keys, two double-edge brass keys, and one Chrysler key on the south corner of the driveway. The roommate identified the keys as belonging to Theresa.

The crime scene examination was completed and the body was transported to the local hospital for an autopsy.

The investigators continued the on-scene investigation with a canvass of the apartment complex where the murder took place. The resident of apartment 18 told police that on Saturday, January 25, she was washing dishes when, sometime between 8:30 and 9:00 p.m., she saw a white male pass by the kitchen window. She said that it startled her because he was so quiet. He was about five feet, seven inches tall, had dark brown hair, and was about twenty-five years old. He was wearing a dark coat and a light shirt with an open collar. She said that a short time later she heard a screen door open and close.

Another neighbor said that about 9:30 p.m. she heard a scream and someone hit the floor. About twenty minutes later, a man walked down the stairs in front of the neighbor's bedroom. "He was wearing quiet shoes, a dark jacket, and possibly gloves," she reported.

The police continued the door-to-door canvass. One by one, however, the remaining neighbors told the detectives that they had not seen or heard anything that aroused suspicion.

At 5:00 p.m. on January 27, A. S. Thompson, M.D., performed an autopsy on the body of Theresa Clark. The doctor concluded that the victim had sustained multiple stab wounds: four in the back penetrating the lungs and liver. As a result, there was massive hemorrhaging of the lungs and liver. In addition, the victim's throat was cut, exposing the larynx. The right breast had been mutilated extending into the mammary gland tissue. There was blunt force injury to the scalp causing hemorrhage of the brain lobes. There were defensive wounds to the right hand, thumb, and finger. The victim was raped, but the doctor was unable to find any sperm. However, the most distributing finding for the police was the condition of her skin. Although she had died from the stab wounds inflicted, she had still been alive when she was dragged into the bathroom and placed in the bathtub. Her killer had placed her in scalding water.

Meanwhile, police interviewed the couple who found the victim. According to her friends, Theresa was a career-oriented grad student in speech pathology who had no boyfriends because she did not want to become involved. She would go out with a few guys to dinner on occasion, but nothing else.

The friend said that Theresa wasn't expecting anyone to visit on Saturday, the day they left. "There was never any company or anything like that. I want to say one thing. There's…about two nights before, you know, this guy kept coming in and using the phone. He used the phone. He used the phone twice. He said he was the next door neighbor. When he came in the first time, you know, he barely made it to the telephone, he was staggering," she said. "He was the next door neighbor or the one downstairs. He said to come down. He said his name was Jack."

Another witness came forward and told the police that a man named Jack Wells, twenty-seven; five feet, eleven inches; and 185 pounds, lived in the area and was on parole. Wells had a long record of assault and sexual crimes against women that dated back several years.

Meanwhile, the citizens in the community were becoming frightened after hearing the news of the murder. Police received a number of calls about suspicious activity. One lady told the police that a man had been following children at a local church. The lady said that the first time she saw the man, on Saturday, January 25, he was standing on the front steps of the church watching the kids play. The second time he was on the steps leading to the basement. He came into the church once and walked up to the display board for a few seconds then walked toward the area where the children were playing on a trampoline. "I asked him if he was there to pick up one of the girls. He said no, smiled, and walked off."

On Sunday, January 26, the man saw one of the girls walking up to the church. He pulled to the curb and asked her to get in the car. She wouldn't and continued to walk toward the church. He got out of the car and followed her to the church. He asked her, "How many times have you shit today?"

The girl was terrified and began to cry.

"What kind of bowel movements do you have? Runny?" he asked, laughing uproariously. Then he turned and walked away.

Further investigation revealed that Wells had confronted several women about having sex with him. One woman in particular said he wanted her to have anal sex with him. She told him that she was not up to it and allowed him to perform oral sex on her. He then asked her to defecate and urinate on him. She said that she refused to do that and soon broke off any relationship with him.

Police took a group of six photos that included one of Jack Wells to all the people who had reported information in the case. In every case, the people identified Jack Wells as being the one they had seen or who had approached them.

On January 28, police arrested Jack Wells on a parole violation and took him in for questioning. He was read his Miranda rights and questioned for several hours. He claimed he knew nothing about the murder or the victim. Then police took fingernail scrapings, scalp hair, pubic hair, and blood samples from the suspect. They turned them over to the lab for analysis.

At about 8:00 p.m. that same day, police received a call from a lady that worked at a department store in the local mall. She said that a man by the name of John Paul Phillips with an address of apartment 5, Ambassador Apartments, had just returned a knife, serial number 110. The lady told the police that the man was in the record department of the store.

Police confronted the twenty-one-year-old Phillips, who told them that he received the knife as a Christmas present from his dad. He said that he used the knife to skin deer. He told the police that because of the neighborhood that he lived in, he frequently stuck the knife in his bedpost at nighttime to be used as protection in the event of a break-in. Recently, he told police, he had removed the knife from the post and the point of the blade had broken.

Police learned that Phillips was a heavy drinker and lived close to work because his driver's license was suspended. Probing further they found that he did now wear a size twelve shoe, the size calculated to have produced the bloody footprint in apartment 20.

The knife was submitted to the lab for serology testing.

A few days later, the evidence collected from all suspects was analyzed. Polygraphs were given. All the suspects were cleared. The police were back to square one.

The Carbondale Police Department worked day and night for weeks on the case, but their efforts were fruitless. Months passed and then a year. Then, in the middle of 1976, there was another murder in Jackson County, and once again it was brutal. At about 6:00 a.m. on July 13, 1976, a young woman pulled into her driveway on Allyn Street in Carbondale. The Southern Illinois University student had just returned from a weekend with her family and was looking at another Monday morning of classes at the university.

The student opened the door and took one step inside. The house cat darted between her legs and shot out the door. *What's wrong with her,* she thought. She noticed a lamp lying on the floor in the living room. A chair had been moved slightly from the angle at which it normally sat.

The house was quiet. Too quiet.

"Kathy? Kathy?" She called out.

No one answered. She walked down the hall toward the bathroom. *Kathy should be up by now,* she surmised. The hall was dark, but the college student could see smears of something dark brown on the walls. She walked into the bathroom and found more smears on the wall. The bathtub contained about five inches of colored water. She took a closer look. *It's blood,* she thought. Her stomach churned and her mind raced with thoughts that she might find Kathy dead. She started walking toward the bedroom and immediately saw two feet on the floor sticking out from between the bed and the wall. Her heart pounded hard in her chest as she walked to the opposite end of the room and she screamed as she got close enough to look. A nude female body was on the floor with a bloody rag covering the face. A mass of congealed blood covered the chest and a large area of the floor on both sides of the body. Several severe stab wounds were visible in the chest and stomach of the victim. The student tore out of the room screaming.

The call came into the police dispatch at 6:12 a.m. "I found Kathy! She's been murdered!" the frantic roommate yelled over the phone.

Carbondale police hurried to the crime scene and checked the house to verify the reported crime. Then the lawmen secured the crime scene and put in a call requesting the assistance of the detective unit and the crime lab technician.

Next, the patrolmen interviewed the roommate who told him that she and Kathy McSherry had shared the house for a little over a month. The roommate said that she left the house on Saturday to visit her family and returned at about six that morning to prepare for classes. "That's when I found Kathy," she said sobbing.

The student told the police that the twenty-four-year-old victim was a transfer student from Western Illinois University. She was majoring in administrative science and this was her first semester.

She did not have a boyfriend, but did go out on occasion and went motorcycle-riding with a male student that she met right after she moved in.

Meanwhile, the crime scene technicians arrived at the crime scene. Upon entering the residence, they found blood smeared on the walls in the hallway, bedroom, kitchen, and bathroom. There were obvious signs of a struggle, with several items overturned in different rooms. Investigators photographed the scene and dusted for prints. They collected numerous samples of blood, hair fibers, and other trace evidence at the scene, but there was no knife. They checked all the entrances to the home and discovered that there had been no forced entry. Nothing was missing from the home. Then police made another puzzling discovery. In the midst of what appeared to be a struggle—a kitchen chair turned over, broken dishes in the floor, blood smears on the wall—a neatly stacked pyramid of beer cans stood in the center of the kitchen table. There was not a single fingerprint on the stack of cans.

Police began a door-to-door canvass of the neighborhood. Several neighbors reported that they had heard dogs barking about 4:30 a.m., "They were barking fierce," one neighbor said. "I looked out the window but I didn't see anything so I went back to bed."

"I heard the dog across the street cause all kinds of ruckus right after I heard what I thought was a scream," another neighbor said. "I looked out the window, but I didn't see anything so I went back to bed. When I heard what happened, I about died myself, I felt so bad. If only I could have helped," the neighbor said as tears begin to well in her eyes.

The neighbor's young daughter came running to the door crying, "Mommy! Mommy! I know who done it. I know! It was Helter Skelter!"

An autopsy was performed on the body of Kathleen McSherry. The pathologist concluded that the victim had sustained ten stab wounds in the chest, stomach, and back. The size of the wounds indicated that a knife with a four- to six-inch blade was used, and the cause of death was one stab wound which pierced the heart. She had also been raped.

Police questioned the victim's friends and acquaintances. All of them were eliminated as possible suspects and were unable to give the police any information that could help them solve the case.

Then police got a call from an employee of the Human Sexuality Services Program who had read about the murder. She told the police that she knew a Jim Burns who might be a possible suspect. She said that he was always hanging around the girls' dorm on campus. Once he came up to her and told her that he needed to have sex to stop his uncontrollable body tremors. He said that if he didn't have sex he might do something violent. He rambled on, asking her if he raped someone if it would give the same feeling as a normal sexual encounter. He then told her that he could communicate with other planets. She said that he stared at her breasts the whole time he talked.

Police checked Burns out and interviewed him, but he was quickly eliminated as a suspect.

Police compared the similarities between the Theresa Clark and Kathleen McSherry murders—the stab wounds were the same, both were young white females, both had been raped, and no signs of forced entry or burglary were found. They strongly suspected that they were looking for the same person in both homicides.

The investigators continued the investigation, questioning friends and students and following up on phoned-in leads of suspects and suspicious behavior. Police contacted the local parole officer for a list of possible suspects. A list was obtained from the area prisons of newly released prisoners. The old suspect list in the Clark murder was rechecked. One by one, however, the leads dwindled and no killer had been found.

Rumors ran rapidly through the university town of Carbondale and spread over to Williamson County, as well.

Six homicides had occurred since January 1975. Three men were found shot to death in a trailer in November 1975: Terry Eanes, twenty-three; Robert T. Gilmore, twenty-one; and James Williams, twenty-two. Three defendants had been arrested and convicted in those crimes. Just three blocks from where Kathy McSherry was murdered, Cary L. Reisher, seventy-nine, was found in her home in January 1975. She had suffocated when she was bound and gagged during a robbery. Police had solved that case, too.

The similarities between the unsolved murders of Theresa Clark and Kathy McSherry, however, would lead a person to believe that someone was preying on young women. The murderer was still out there, but there was little indication of concern in the community. Just thirty-six hours after the brutal murder had taken place, Allyn Street was almost motionless except for a few children playing.

All that remained to suggest something had happened on the block was a Carbondale police car passing by regularly, pausing at number 521, where Kathleen McSherry had been murdered.

Most of the neighbors had not known her. "We've been here more than forty years, and it's been a while since something like this happened," said a neighbor who lived directly across from the murder scene. "I'm concerned about the violence, but I'm not going anywhere."

A couple of murders occurred in 1975 and 1976 in Williamson County, also, and there were rumors of a connection, but no one seemed to take them as a serious threat.

Six days after the murder, Carbondale lawmen received a call from a Chicago police investigator. He asked the Southern Illinois police if they had two unsolved homicides in 1975 and 1976 involving the stabbing of young females, one in a bathtub and the other on North Allyn Street. After Carbondale police confirmed that the murders did take place, the Chicago police investigator said that he had arrested a twenty-seven-year-old white male for threatening another white male, twenty-three years old. According to the Chicago police, the suspect stopped by his parent's house and dumped several knives down the sewer before he was arrested. Then, after he was in custody, he said that the man he had threatened had murdered two girls in Carbondale, Illinois, while he was a student. The suspect said that one girl was placed in a bathtub and the other was murdered in the bedroom of her home on Allyn Street. He described the scene on Allyn Street as very bloody, saying that the murderer had cut off the girl's breasts, put them on the bed, and mutilated her privates. He said that the assailant had hidden the knife under a junk lawnmower in a dump halfway up a slope in a strip pit near Desoto, Illinois. The Chicago investigator told the Carbondale police that he didn't believe the man being accused was involved in the murders, but the twenty-seven-year-old male that had been arrested was weird enough to do the murders himself. He described him as "a schizophrenic paranoiac."

The next day, Carbondale police officers arrived in Chicago and questioned the suspect. He told the police that he had a vision. He claimed that he sometimes got visions when he smoked Marlboro cigarettes. He said that he saw the man he threatened stabbing a girl with long brown hair. He said that he cut off her breasts and placed them on the bed. He said he saw the murderer cutting her vagina.

"Could you explain in a little more detail what things you saw in reference to this vision about the murder on Allyn Street? Where the victim was lying?" The detective inquired.

"The victim was lying on the bed. Her–her body was lying vertically along the horizontal side of the bed. Her legs were hanging over the edge of the bed and her arms were resting somewhere. And one of the sex organs was next to her body and the other sex organs were taken. The whole room was bloody, there was broken glass somewhere, maybe in the living room," the suspect explained.

"Do you remember if the victim had any clothing on?" detectives asked.

"Maybe some panties and a slip."

"Do you remember where the wounds were on the body?"

"Well, the chest was all dug up. Something might have happened to her eyes and her nose, but I'm not sure about that," the suspect said.

The police had knots in their stomachs as they realized that what they hoped would be the break in one case was leading nowhere; the man was disturbed, but definitely not a suspect in the murders in Carbondale.

In short order, the frustrated lawmen stopped the interview, thanked their Chicago colleague for his help, and began the five-hour drive back to Southern Illinois.

Three weeks after the McSherry murder, another crime occurred, this time in Williamson County. On August 6, 1976, John Paul Phillips, the young man that had been questioned in connection with the murder of Theresa Clark, went to the Little Grassy Lake area where he met a couple that he claimed owed him money. John Paul, by his own admission, was highly intoxicated, having drunk a large amount of tequila and injected an undetermined amount of morphine. After he and the couple were at the campsite for a short period of time, John Paul pulled a pistol on the male at the site, took eighteen dollars in cash, and then handcuffed him to a tree. He hit the man in the head several times with the pistol and knocked him unconscious. He then forced the girl into the truck at gunpoint. John Paul forced the girl to drink beer and ingest three capsules of a drug. He forced the girl to remove her clothing and continued to threaten her life. After a period of time driving around the area, John Paul returned with the girl to the campsite where he had left her companion handcuffed to the tree. The man was screaming for help and John Paul jumped out of the truck to stop him from yelling. As he did, the girl, groggy from the drugs and still nude, jumped out of the truck and ran for the road. A passing fisherman stopped her. John Paul, realizing that he was about to be caught, fled through the woods. In a short time, Williamson County officers were at the scene.

The officers called for ambulances and took the victims to the hospital. After taking statements, they found out the couple recognized the suspect as John Paul Phillips from Carbondale. The Williamson County state's attorney filed charges of one count of attempted murder, one count of aggravated kidnapping, one count of armed robbery, and two counts of aggravated battery.

John Paul turned himself in a few days later and was brought to the Williamson County jail. John Paul went to court and entered negotiated pleas of guilty to the offenses of aggravated kidnapping, armed robbery, and two counts of aggravated battery. He received two concurrent three-to-ten-year sentences for aggravated battery, a seven-to-twenty-four-year sentence for aggravated kidnapping, and another seven-to-twenty-four-year sentence for the armed robbery, all to run concurrent. A couple of weeks later, he was in Menard prison to do his time.

It was three years before another brutal murder of a college student would occur. The call came into the Carbondale police dispatch at 3:05 a.m. on August 18, 1981. An SIU student reported her roommate, Susan Schumake, missing. She said that Susan had left for a meeting at the SIU Student Center at four thirty the evening before and had not returned nor had she called. "It wasn't like Susan to do that," she insisted.

She described Susan as twenty-one years old; five feet, one inch tall;

with dark brown hair, wearing jeans and a long-sleeved, hooded top of rust, brown, and beige Indian design.

The dispatcher filled out a police service report and checked a box on the form that read, "Attempt to Locate Subject." The officer then informed the caller that she would have to wait for forty-eight hours before she could file a missing person report. If they located her, they would call; if she returned home, the roommate was to call the police.

That evening at 7:42 p.m. the roommate called the police once again. She told the police that Susan had still not returned. She also told the police that she was wrong about the location of the meeting that Susan attended. The meeting was at the campus radio station located on Wright Hall on the campus. She said that she had gone to the radio station and found out that Susan had been leaving the building around 5:30 p.m. on August 17. According to witnesses, she went up the hill behind the building and that was the last time she was seen.

Police questioned the roommate further and found out that Susan did not have any serious problems, was not depressed, and didn't have any boyfriends or other friends that she might by staying with. "As far as I know," the roommate said, "she doesn't have a bicycle or a car."

At approximately 8:00 p.m. that same day, police searched the path north of the radio station. The path, nicknamed the Ho Chi Minh Trail, was a shortcut for the students. The trail began north of Wright Hall, ran west across Illinois Central Gulf Railroad tracks, and ended at Route 51 directly in front of the main campus. Detectives checked the brush along the trail and the woods in the immediate area. The search was fruitless.

That evening an officer reported for the third shift at 11:30 p.m. He read the report about Susan Schumake and decided that he would make a search of the path since it was the last place she had been seen. At 11:45 p.m. the lawman began his search down the path. The light beam from his flashlight moved along the dirt path and against the weeds on both sides of the trail. Suddenly, the officer stopped. On the left side of the trail he discovered trampled weeds. A closer look revealed the weeds were trampled for about ten square feet. The officers followed, then discovered another path leading to a small group of trees. He shined his light toward the trees. A partially-nude female body was lying under the trees. The officer cautiously approached the body and took a pulse. The victim was obviously dead. Using his pack radio, he called for assistance and, while waiting, roped the crime scene off.

At about 12:34 a.m. Carbondale police, SIU Security police, and Crime Scene Technicians (CSTs) from the Illinois State Police arrived and began processing the crime scene.

The victim was lying on her stomach with her feet pointed north and her head pointing southeast. She was wearing a rust, tan, and brown multi-colored pull-over top and a pair of wedge shoes. Lying near the victim's head were a pair of blue jeans with legs turned inside out and a pair of pink panties on the legs of the jeans. Her head was covered with congealed blood.

The crime scene was photographed and processed for physical evidence. The investigators collected, packaged, and marked cigarette butts, blue jeans, panties, and miscellaneous items found in the grass near the victim. From the body they collected fingernail scrapings, head and pubic hair samples, and one hair recovered from the back of the victim's right hand.

About ten feet southwest of the body, the officers discovered a shallow grave. The police strongly suspected the perpetrator began digging a grave and stopped short of completion because of being detected. The officers collected soil samples from the area and completed the crime scene process. At that time, the Jackson County Ambulance Service transported the body to the local hospital morgue for an autopsy.

Next, officers interviewed the victim's roommate. She told the police that she had been friends with Susan for about five years. Police learned that on August 17, Sue had worked on papers dealing with her job at the local radio station. Sue had a 5:00 p.m. meeting at the radio station. She left around 4:30 p.m. wearing a hooded shirt, jeans, and a yellow backpack with black straps. Sue carried sales material from the radio station, a hairbrush, sunglasses, contact lens case, and a pair of glasses.

The roommate told the police that she knew of no one who would want to kill Susan. "She has never experienced any trouble with anyone in the past," she said.

Police learned from another friend that she had driven Susan to the Student Center and dropped her off at about 4:40 p.m. on August 17. The friend corroborated Susan's roommate's description of the clothing Susan was wearing when last seen and said that when she got out of the car she was carrying a yellow and black backpack. That was the last time she saw Susan.

Susan's work supervisor told the lawmen that she had last seen Susan standing outside the door after a sales meeting at about 5:45 p.m. on August 17. Susan walked west around the building and up the small hill toward the Ho Chi Minh Trail.

The supervisor said that she had known Susan since November 1980, when Susan joined the staff at the radio station as a commercial copywriter. Susan had been involved in some sales and promotion work and had been promoted to assistant sales person in June 1981.

The radio staff had sales meetings once a month and the meeting on August 17 was one of those regular meetings. The meetings were normally held at the Student Center, but this meeting had been changed to the Wright building at the last minute because the Student Center did not have room for the meeting.

After the meeting, everyone had stood around and talked. The supervisor thought that Susan had been the first one to leave. She did not make any comments about where she was going.

"She just said goodbye to everyone and walked around the building and up the hill," the supervisor remembered. Meanwhile, Dr. Steven Nuernberger performed an autopsy on the victim's body which was positively identified as that of Susan Schumake. The pathologists found superficial abrasions and bruises on both thighs, the backs of both hands, both knees, and the lower stomach. There were abrasions on the lower lip, left side of the face, and the right eye.

The doctor discovered three large hemorrhages on the head. Two wounds two centimeters by three centimeters were located on the right side of the head. The third wound was two centimeters by one centimeter and was located in the right frontal area of the forehead. The neck had hemorrhages to the right lower sternocleidomastoid muscles, right and left sternohyoid muscles, left omocyoid muscles, and the soft tissues overlying the trachea. Examination of the vaginal and anal area revealed that the victim had not been sexually assaulted.

The doctor did find a rare lighter-colored pubic hair when he had a combing of the pubic hair.

Upon completion of the autopsy, the pathologist concluded that Susan Schumake had died of strangulation.

Continuing the investigation, police began contacting fellow students of Susan Schumake in hopes of finding anyone who might give them information leading to a suspect in the homicide. They found out that Susan was an excellent student as well as a friendly and outgoing person. On occasion, she and several other students would go to the local lounge for a drink; she always had a good time. However, one by one the friends told the police that they knew of no one that would want to kill her.

Police contacted the prisons in the area and obtained a list of prisoners who had recently been released on parole. Each person was checked out without providing any leads.

Phone calls begin to bombard the police department from citizens reporting individuals that might be suspects. One woman reported that on the day of the murders a white male approximately twenty-four years old approached her in a parking lot on the corner of Grand Avenue and Illinois Avenue. He made a lewd remark, but the woman wasn't sure what he said. She "just knew it had to be lewd."

One woman called in crying hysterically, claiming to have undergone a psychic experience in which she witnessed Susan Schumake's murder. She gave the police a profile of the would-be murderer. Later, police learned the woman had recently been released from a state mental hospital.

A woman from Murphysboro called the police and reported that a man came into the restaurant and ate breakfast the morning after the murder. He was acting strange. He had a suitcase and a pair of sunglasses. A bus ticket was sticking out of his back pocket. After he ate, he came to the counter to pay for his meal. He wouldn't look at the lady and he spoke in a low voice.

"What was he doing that was strange?" police asked.

"That's it!" the caller replied.

Next, the police canvassed the campus area where Susan worked and was last seen alive. The canvass was going nowhere until police learned that John Paul Phillips had recently been released from prison on a mandatory release and was working in the communications building next to the radio station on the day of the murder.

At 8:15 a.m. on August 19, police officers located John Paul at his father's business and began questioning. The police asked John Paul about his activities from Sunday, August 16, through Tuesday, August 18. John Paul told the police that on Sunday he, his wife, and a friend Bill Walker went to a local lake from about 1:00 to 6:00 p.m. and then returned to his house for dinner.

On Monday, August 17, he worked for his father from 6:30 a.m. to 4:30 p.m. After work, he said he drove to Desoto, Illinois, and visited with his friend Bill Walker for a while, then went home. He said his wife got home about 6:00 p.m. and later that night they went to visit friends, returning home about 10:30 p.m.

Then John Paul changed his story and told the police that he and his wife stayed home and Bill Walker came for dinner.

John Paul then told the police that on Tuesday he got off work about 4:30 p.m. and went home. His wife arrived at about 5:30 p.m. and they went to visit friends in West Frankfort. "I don't want to give their names, but I will if I have to," he said.

While John Paul was telling his story, lawmen noticed scratch marks on his right forearm, the inner part of his left forearm, and his forehead. "How did you get the scratch marks?" they asked.

"I got these from playing with the dog at the lake," John Paul said, pointing to the scratches on his forearms. "I got the scratches on my forehead from fixing a lamp at home," he explained.

The police completed the interview and walked outside. John Paul shot out the door and was face-to-face with the police. "I didn't go to West Frankfort," he whispered, glancing at the door. "I visited some other friends. I didn't want to tell you in there because my dad doesn't approve of them and I didn't want him to know it." Before police could say anything, John Paul's father walked outside and the conversation ended.

At noon the same day, police went to John Paul's residence to question his spouse. John Paul was nervous and blurted out, "Don't give them any names of our friends. I don't want them bothered."

The officers asked John Paul to step outside while they talked with his wife. He glanced at both police officers, then walked out of the apartment. Police asked her to explain her activities from August 16 through August 18. She said that on Sunday, she, John Paul, and Bill Walker went to Little Grassy Lake. They were at the lake from about 12:15 p.m. to around 6:00 p.m.

They returned home and John Paul went to the grocery store. He was gone about thirty minutes. Sue said she phoned Bill Walker's girlfriend and she came over. They ate and the couple left about 8 p.m.

On Monday, August 17, she worked all day and arrived home around 5:15 p.m. John Paul either was home or got home a short time later. "No more than five minutes later. I can't remember if John Paul left the apartment on Monday night or not, but if he did I went with him." On Tuesday, she returned home about 5:45 p.m. and she and John Paul went to visit friends out of town. They returned home about 10:00 p.m.

"Who were your friends?" the officers asked.

"I can't tell you. John Paul doesn't want them bothered."

"Do you know how John Paul got the scratches on his arms and forehead?"

"Yeah, he got them on Saturday. We were roughhousing and I scratched him."

About that time John Paul came back into the apartment. "We have some conflicting stories," the officers told him flatly.

"Oh!" John Paul said, "Monday night was the night we went to West Frankfort, not Tuesday."

Police strongly suspected that John Paul was lying. They asked him to come to the police station for another interview. John Paul agreed. The questioning began and the policemen asked John Paul to explain his activities from August 16 through August 18 once again. Again his story changed. He said that the three went to the lake on Sunday and returned about 5:00 p.m. He and Bill Walker went to the apartment of a guy by the name of Mike—he didn't know his last name—in Christopher, Illinois.

They shot a .270 caliber rifle with a scope on it. While they were shooting, the recoil caused the rifle to hit John Paul on the forehead and between the eyes. He said that he and Walker left Mike's about 7:00 p.m. and returned to Phillips's apartment. After dinner about 8:00 p.m., John Paul left the apartment and went to the local high school for a while and then returned to his apartment about 10:00 p.m. Bill and his girl friend left at that time.

On August 17, Phillips said, he went to Bill Walker's house after work but returned home about 6:30 p.m. and ate dinner. At about 8:00 p.m., he left and went to Bill Walker's again. He returned a couple of hours later. He said that his wife did not go with him.

"John Paul, we would like to have some head hair and pubic hair samples. Would you give us those samples?" the police asked.

"Sure!" he said grinning. "What do I do?"

On August 25, the police received the results from the crime lab. Nothing of evidential value was found from the fingernail scrapings. The hair recovered from the back of the victim's right hand was a Caucasian body hair yellow-brown in color. There was Caucasian pubic hair discovered in the vaginal area which was not the victim's and was also yellow-brown in color.

Traces of semen were found in the vaginal area. The blood found on the body was the victim's. A comparison between the hair standards found on the victim's right hand and vaginal area and those of John Paul Phillips revealed that the hairs were not those of John Paul Phillips.

The lab suggested a comparison of semen and blood samples from the suspect and victim, but John Paul refused to give the samples voluntarily. Unless they could find probable cause, there would be no comparison. The police found no probable cause.

On November 4, 1981, a Susan Schumake Memorial Committee was established to assist the Carbondale police, who had exhausted all their leads. There was a reward for anyone who provided information that would lead to the arrest and conviction of the murder of Susan Schumake. A few days later, flyers were printed with a bold headline reading "RE-WARD $2700," details of Susan's activities when she was last seen on August 17, a photograph of Susan, a list of police department phone numbers, and a promise that all information would be kept confidential. Students and police distributed the flyers throughout the area. The police hoped that someone would call, anyone who could give them a lead.

Seven days after the flyers were distributed on November 11, the Carbondale police got a call—a dead body had been found in a pond in Elkville.

At about 10:30 a.m. on November 11, 1981, a Jackson County couple arrived at a strip cut located three miles east of Elkville, Illinois, for a morning of fishing. The wife started down the bank of the strip cut first. She was almost to the edge of the water when she looked up and shouted, "My God! Get down here! There's a body in the water!"

The husband scurried down the bank. "Jesus!" he said as he reached the water's edge. A nude white female was floating face down in the water.

The couple shot up the side of the hill and ran for the blacktop road a short distance from the strip cut. The man waved down a passing motorist. "We've found a dead woman in the strip cut! Call the police."

The call came in to the Jackson County Sheriff's Department at 10:45 a.m. "A lady stopped me on the road and told me they found a dead body in the strip cut. It is three miles east of Elkville on Vergennee Blacktop. I'll go back and wait on you there."

Jackson County deputies arrived at the scene at 11:16 a.m. They came across a grassy shoulder of the gravel road, down a narrow path on the embankment to the edge of the water, and found a nude white female floating face down in about eight inches of water next to the bank of the pond. Her long, dark hair made a snaking motion on the surface of the water as the water gently moved the five foot four, 110-pound body back and forth with each wave. The officers immediately scrambled back up the embankment and called for the detective unit.

Police arrived at the scene and began the crime scene process by photographing the body and the crime scene area. Lawmen began a search of the area and located a set of tire tracks that left the gravel road on a trail between and parallel to the strip cut embankment and the gravel road. The tracks were in a U-shape and it appeared that a vehicle had stopped almost directly in front of the narrow path leading to the location of the body. Police also found a seven-ounce Miller beer bottle with the cap still on it, and a sandwich wrapper near the tire tracks. There was no sign of the victim's clothing.

At 12:13 p.m. that same day, the Jackson County Coroner arrived at the scene. Assisted by a number of lawmen, the coroner removed the body from the water and placed it on a backboard provided by a local ambulance service. The hands and feet of the victim were bagged and the body was transported to the local hospital for an autopsy.

Police combed the area one more time, but their effort was fruitless.

At 1:40 p.m., Dr. Pamela S. Gronemeyer performed an autopsy on the body. There were three large lacerations on the scalp. The largest wound was five-and-a-half centimeters in length and located on the left side of the head. A one-centimeter wound was located on the right side of the crown of the head. Beside this wound a two-centimeter laceration was also found. The pathologist determined that all the head wounds were made with a blunt instrument. There were contusions on the checks and around the right eye. The upper lip was swollen. These wounds were a result of the victim falling after receiving the fatal wounds.

Both wrists had abrasions and contusions which were a result of being bound with rope or cord. There was a six-centimeter abrasion on the right side of the neck. There was a fracture of the hyoid bone with hemorrhage into the soft tissue around the thyroid and carotid artery. The vocal cords were also hemorrhaged. The vagina had some contusions in the lower region, but no semen or blood was found. No foreign hairs were found on the body. As a result, the doctor could not determine whether the victim had been sexually molested.

Dr. Gronemeyer determined the cause of death was asphyxiation, secondary to strangulation. Now the authorities had to find the identity of the victim.

At 11 p.m. on the same day, November 11, the sheriff's department received a call from the manager of a local motel in Carbondale. The manager wanted to report an employee missing. According to the manager, Joan Weatherall had not shown up for work nor been heard from since the night before when she left work. The manager said that he had called Joan's residence, but there was no answer.

Detectives went directly to the motel and met with the manager. They showed him two photographs of the unidentified female homicide victim. "My God! It's her!" he gasped, raising both hands to his face.

When the manager had control of himself, he gave the police the phone number and address of the victim's family. They called the family and asked to talk with them. The family agreed.

Detectives arrived at the residence at 11:45 p.m. The police explained that they were investigating a homicide and needed the help of the family in identifying the body. The officer showed the photograph to Joan's relative and she immediately identified her. She was asked to accompany the police to the morgue for positive identification. At 12:30 a.m. on November 12, the family positively identified the victim as Joan Weatherall.

Detectives interviewed Joan's relatives who told the police that she last saw Joan on Tuesday, November 10, between 10:30 p.m. and 11 p.m., at the local motel in Carbondale. Joan was leaving work and asked her to go with her to a local night club. She refused and Joan left with a friend, Bob Johnson. When Joan did not show up for work, the relative called a friend who was at the same local night club the night before. The friend told Joan's relative that he saw Joan leave between 12:30 a.m. and 1 a.m. on Wednesday morning, November 11, with a girl named Lisa Walton. Police found out the names of Joan's former boyfriends and additional friends that Joan socialized with.

Police then told the relative that they had not found Joan's clothing and asked the relative if she could recall what Joan was wearing the night of November 10. She remembered that Joan was wearing a blue crushed velvet sweater, bluish-gray corduroy slacks, and either a three-quarter length raccoon fur stadium coat or a gray full-length artificial fur coat. Her shoes were maroon or red with pointed toes and stacked heels. Joan's purse was vinyl, seven-by-seven inches, maroon, with a long, narrow shoulder strap. The contents would be a green leather wallet with Indian designs, a white plastic makeup bag with blue flowers, a white hairbrush with small mother of pearls on the back. Joan was also wearing an eighteen-inch gold chain with an oyster shell-styled pendant and a twenty-four-inch gold chain with a gold locket. The relative said that Joan drank very little, but when she did she drank either scotch and water or beer.

The probers continued the investigation with an interview of Lisa Walton, who had left the club at the same time that Joan had left. Lisa told the police that they left at the same time that she had but that she and Joan went separate ways. Joan walked west on Illinois Avenue and Lisa went the opposite direction. She said that she never heard anything unusual.

Police also questioned all of Joan's former boyfriends and close friends. The police were in hopes that they would have some information that would give them a lead to a killer. One thing police did find out was that Joan was very independent, and her friends found it hard to believe that she would get into a car with anyone. But, there was little information that was helpful to the police.

Police were coming to dead ends with the investigation. They contacted the Federal Bureau of Investigation's Behavioral Science Unit, whose analysts concluded that Joan Weatherall was tortured physically as well as psychologically by her assailant. She was not assaulted for sexual motivations, but rather to teach her a lesson.

The victim knew her killer and the killer knew her very well. Her personal background made it easy for the killer to take her life. In the killer's eyes, she had degraded herself on numerous occasions by her personal behavior—behavior that offended the killer.

The evidence found at the crime scene showed that the victim was in all probability bound and tied "spread-eagle" to trees. This indicates that a considerable amount of control had to be exerted and utilized by the killer to keep the victim quiet and still. Blunt force trauma to the victim's head would have rendered her unconscious; however, the killer did not want her dead until she was taught a lesson. The crime scene area was fairly isolated, but the killer had a complete familiarity with this location. He had been there before. The killer's disposal of the victim in the water would indicate that he was trying to get rid of evidence. If the offender was cognizant of evidence collection, he might have a criminal history. He probably intended to torture and kill other victims in the future, probably in the same area.

The offender would be anywhere from mid-twenties to early thirties and be of the same race. He probably would be masculine or macho, working perhaps as a laborer, truck driver, or general construction worker. His employment record would indicate multiple employments as he would have difficulty maintaining a permanent job routine. He would have difficulty relating to the opposite sex and would consider them as being a threat and evil. He would have a poor self-image. He would be a native of the area.

The killer did not plan to kill the victim, the FBI unit concluded, but once he got involved in what he was doing ,he reached a point of no return and elected to kill her to save himself.

The killer in all probability took pictures of the victim in various stages of the assault. A search warrant would find these photographs as well as sadomasochistic pornography and cartoon drawings by the killer depicting bondage and torture.

Since the murder, the killer had probably attended the funeral and burial or returned to the crime scene, or periodically visited the grave, or turned to heavy drinking and drugs. He might also have moved or sold his vehicle, afraid that there was some evidence remaining even after he thoroughly washed his vehicle.

On Tuesday, November 18, a woman named Arnie Glisson called to file a complaint with the police. Amie had parked in the Kroger parking lot at Carbondale. She went into the grocery store and began shopping. On two occasions she noticed a man in green coveralls in the aisle where she was shopping. She finished shopping, paid for the groceries and started pushing a cart full of groceries toward the door. She noticed a person walking very rapidly up behind her. At first she thought it was just a shopper in a hurry, so she pushed her cart a little faster. Just as she stepped on the mat for the automatic door, she felt a touch on her right side just above her wrist. She looked back over her shoulder and realized the man in green coveralls was right behind her. She didn't think the touch was accidental, so she turned and said, "Pardon me. If you are in such a hurry, let me get out of your way." He said that he wasn't in a hurry, he had just seen that Amie wasn't wearing a ring and wanted to meet her before she left. Amie kept walking out of the store and toward her car as the man followed her and kept talking about her not being married.

The man was about a half a step behind Amie when he said, "You know, those shoes make you walk real nice—why don't you give me your phone number and address and let me call you."

"I'm not interested and I don't give my name to strangers," she replied.

"Well, you aren't married," he muttered.

"I don't believe in marriage or dating or giving my name to strangers," she snapped. Amie unlocked the passenger side of the car and started loading the groceries into the front seat. When she finished, she shut the door and locked it, then turned with her back to the car and faced the man in coveralls. The white thirty-year-old had straight, dark brown, mid-collar length hair and a trimmed moustache. He was five-eleven to six feet tall and weighed about 175 pounds with a medium build. He had piercing eyes and what she described as an evil grin. With her car to her back, a light colored car on one side, and the grocery cart on the other Amie panicked with the realization that she had no way to get away from him.

Amie took one step back and he moved one step forward. He paused for a moment, then said, "Come on, why not tell me your name and give me your phone number. I'd really like to call you."

"You can't call me and if you don't step back you may not be able to walk either," she threatened.

His grin turned to a frown. "Well, you don't have to get crazy about it. I'd just like to take you out."

"No! I'm getting scared and if you don't want to be embarrassed you better back off. I will yell for help."

"Well, you don't have to go crazy about it," he repeated as he turned and walked down three parking stalls and climbed into a light metallic-colored car.

Amie climbed into her car and noticed that the man had not started his car. He was just sitting there with that grin and his hands on top of the steering wheel watching Amie.

Amie started the car and pulled out of the parking lot. As she pulled to the stop sign, she noticed that he was behind her. She continued east of town with the man following her a few cars back. When she got to the spillway road, she turned right and he followed. Instead of going to her house, Amie went past the house and turned on old Route 13. By now, he was eight or ten cars behind. She was going about forty-five miles an hour and, without giving a turn signal, she quickly made a turn. All the groceries fell to the floorboard. He didn't turn. She had lost him and she hadn't seen him since.

On Sunday, November 29, the Williamson County detective unit found some clothes that they believed belong to the murder victim in the strip pit in Elkville. Police had received a call on the evening of November 28. The man calling told the police that he had been in the Crab Orchard Lake area parked when he got out of his car to throw away some trash and found several pieces of women's clothing. He thought they might be related to the recent murder.

Police hurried to the scene and found a partially burned Illinois driver's license belonging to Joan Weatherall. They sealed the area off and decided to wait until daylight to process the scene.

At 6:38 a.m. the following morning, police began a search. They found rope on the ground and some tied to a nearby tree, a flowered change purse, a flowered cosmetic purse and contents, a Miller beer bottle, credit cards belonging to Joan Weatherall, blue angora socks, a blue hooded sweater, panty hose, a bank check endorsed by Joan Weatherall, and a library card issued to Joan Weatherall. They tagged the evidence and submitted it to the lab.

Other detectives continued the search, and over the next several days they located a red bra and several blue threads on the Elkville Blacktop west of the strip cut area and a rope, sunglasses, and a comb at another location at Crab Orchard Lake. Soon the results of the evidence were given to the police. There was nothing that could help them in solving the case.

In the middle of December, the police were at a dead end. The murder had taken its toll on a former boyfriend as well. He told the local newspaper that people needed to change their attitudes toward crime because "it can happen to your wife, your husband, or children." He said that he had lived with Joan for a year and that she knew better than to get into a car with someone that she didn't know. "When it all comes out, it will probably be someone we both know."

"Someone must have seen something on Illinois Avenue," he said in desperation. He stood on a street corner and handed out flyers with Joan's picture on them asking for information and telling people to be careful. Each day he became more depressed as no one seemed to know anything that would help. Then one day in mid-December, he walked to the street corner. Joan's flyers were lying on the sidewalk and in the street gutter. He left in tears.

The day after Christmas there was another abduction. About 6:30 p.m. on December 26, 1981, Linda Young, an SIU student, left a friend's apartment on University Avenue in Carbondale to go to the movies. Linda opened her car door and started to climb in. Suddenly, she was pushed through the door and to the passenger seat of the car. The assailant grabbed her around the neck with his right arm and shoved a four-inch buck knife in her face. "I need a ride!" he demanded. "Don't look at me. Don't look at me!"

The husky man tightened his grip as he started the car. Linda had lost her glasses in the struggle and couldn't see well. She was trying to think, but things were happening too fast. He drove down East College Street, then through some curves with a lot of trees. "Don't look at me," he snapped, again.

Linda was trying to concentrate on where they were. She strained her eyes looking over the top of his forearm and out the passenger window. She recognized the houses along the street and knew she was on Oakland Street. Then he turned right on Chautaqua Street. "The car doesn't have much gas. Uh, since you need a ride and I haven't seen your face, maybe you could just stop and let me go," Linda pleaded.

He said nothing as the car went over a bridge and stopped. Linda strained to look and could see the ground was clear. "Don't look at me. I have this knife," he ordered. "Take off your coat."

As soon as Linda took her coat off he grabbed her hands and tied them behind her, then looped the rope around her throat. Then he put a mask over her head and tied it with a piece of rope. "Lay down," he ordered.

Linda lay in the front seat. He began driving again. The ropes on Linda's wrists were loose. She began to work them back and forth slowly so he wouldn't notice. Four or five minutes passed and he stopped the car and got out. Linda had the ropes loose enough that she could get rid of the rope. She had to hurry and get away. Just as she freed herself she heard the passenger door open. He grabbed her wrists and tied them once again. Then he pulled her up and out of the car. He opened the trunk and put her inside. She laid quietly, listening. He started driving once again. She pushed the trunk lid with her feet, then her hands. It was no use. The trunk was locked. She tried to determine where he was going. There were many turns. Then he stopped. There was a lot of noise. She decided he was at a gas station. She could hear the gas pumping in. Then he took off again. Linda could feel the wires that lead to the taillights. She pulled and twisted them. If the taillights didn't work maybe the police would stop him and she could scream when they were near the car. Soon the car stopped again. The trunk opened and the assailant lifted Linda by the arm. He walked her to a building and opened a door. She could see light through her mask and realized the room was small. Then he led her into a second room and untied her hands. "Take off your clothes," he ordered.

Linda began to undress. When she took the last piece of clothing off he pulled her mask off. She could see a dim light in the room—a window.

But she wouldn't look at him out of fear that he would kill her.

"Lay down," he ordered. Linda lay on the carpeted floor. He begin to caress her more gently and less violently. He began to kiss her breasts, then her genitals. Linda's heart pounded with fear. He stood and kissed her as if he were having a normal sexual relationship. She did not resist for fear of death. Then he crawled on top of her and entered her in a traditional sex position. He moaned and became excited. "I feel good," he said softly. Then he turned her over and entered from the rear. He seemed to be more excited now. "You're so good, you make me feel so good, you make me feel so good. I just want to love you. Don't be scared. I just want to love you." Ten or fifteen minutes passed as Linda tried to block out her fear and disgust of the situation. He ejaculated, then rolled to the floor beside Linda and lay their for a moment. "You make me feel good," he said. He stood and pulled Linda to her knees. He pushed his penis in her face and tried to push it in her mouth. Linda turned away, but he pulled her face back and the second time put it in her mouth. Linda felt nauseated, wanted to vomit. It seemed an eternity before it was over. When he finished, he turned and began to gather her clothes. Linda's heart pounded as he handed her one piece of clothing at a time and told her to put her clothes back on. After she finished, he put the mask back on her head, tied her hands behind her back, and told her that he would guide her back to the car.

"Will you take me back?" Linda asked.

"Yes," he said, "I will."

He guided her back to the car. "You can stay in the front seat this time," he offered.

They started to drive again as Linda lay in the front seat. "I'm sorry I wasn't good," he said. "I shouldn't have done that to you. I didn't mean to scare you. I will take you back to your apartment."

This guy is really crazy, Linda thought, but since he was talking, this was her chance.

"Did you know me before?" she asked.

"No," he answered.

"So you were just passing by and decided to do that? Why did you do that if you didn't mean to hurt me, you had that knife around my neck?"

"I just saw you and you were what I wanted," he said. "I didn't mean to hurt you, you are so sweet."

He pulled into a parking lot and stopped. Linda's heart pounded hard in her chest as he pulled her toward him. He untied her hands, then she heard a car door open. She waited for a minute then quickly pulled the mask off. He was gone. She was in the parking lot where she was abducted. Her body relaxed, but she was in disbelief that he had taken her back to her apartment. She looked around, then got out of the car, and ran for her friend's apartment. She pounded on the door. Her friend opened the door and she rushed in, crying. "I've been raped!"

Her friend's smile turned to an expression of shock. "We have to call the police!" he said.

"No! They won't believe this story. The guy was crazy—he apologized, then brought me back. They won't believe it."

"If we don't call, then it can happen again," he argued.

A short time later the police arrived at the apartment. Linda told her story as the officers listened and carefully took notes. When she finished, they questioned her for clarity.

"To the best of your ability describe the person that attacked you," they urged her.

"He was real strong, really strong."

"Was it a white male?"

"I think so, it is a white male."

"Okay, go ahead and describe him."

"Um, he was very strong. He was drunk, really drunk, I could smell that easy."

"What kind of alcohol did you smell on his breath? Was it beer, could you tell?"

"It didn't—I don't think it was beer. I think it was stronger than beer."

"Did he have any facial hair?"

"No. No, he didn't have a mustache or beard."

"Could you tell me about how tall he was?"

"About six feet tall."

"Did you notice anything about his weight? Was he fat?"

"He was not fat and he was not thin. He was strong."

"Did you notice anything about his hair?"

"It was a light brown, about collar length."

"What about his voice?"

"He had a deep voice. I don't think he was a student either."

After the interview, Linda went to the hospital for an examination. Blood samples and hair samples were taken and seminal material was identified.

Meanwhile, detectives canvassed the neighborhood and the bars on the strip in hopes of finding someone who could identify a suspect fitting the description of the rapist. One by one the bar owners, patrons, and neighbors told the police that they had no idea who the suspect could be.

Police checked their files for known sex offenders in the area and put together a group of photographs. Linda was contacted on January 2, 1982, seven days after the rape occurred, and police met with her at the police station. After looking at the photos, she told the detectives that none were the man who raped her.

Then six days later, an attempted abduction occurred in Williamson County. About 6:30 p.m. on Friday January 8, 1982, Jan Murphy left her home on Virginia street in Carterville, Illinois, to make a bank deposit. It was unseasonably mild for a winter day in the small rural town and Jan, living only a few blocks from the bank, decided to walk. She stepped off the curb on Virginia Street when suddenly a brown and tan pickup truck turned off Division Street and moved toward her. "I better get across the street quick," she thought. Jan darted across the street, and the truck rushed past her. Jan looked at the driver as he gave her a nasty glare. Jan watched as the truck turned at the corner of Virginia and Pine Streets and disappeared. "He must have had a bad day," she said to herself. She continued walking down Pine Street, across the parking lot behind the police station, up the sidewalk beside the bank and through the front doors. Jan made her deposit and in a few minutes was on the way back home. She decided to circle the block and left walking north on Division Street. One block from the bank, she crossed a grocery store parking lot and headed west on Pine Street. At the corner of Virginia and Pine Streets, just one block from her home, Jan heard a vehicle come to a sudden stop. The door slammed and she heard a man's voice, exclaim, "Shit!"

Jan walked across the street and the man followed. He stepped in front of Jan, saying, "Excuse me. Is that where the preacher lives?" He was pointing to the house at 204 Virginia Street.

"No," Jan told him.

"Well, the church is locked. Are you sure that's not where the preacher lives?"

"No, I know who lives there. Maybe there's a number on that thing over there," Jan said, pointing to the bulletin board by the church.

"Well, it's locked," he snapped, glaring at Jan once again with nasty eyes.

He shrugged his shoulders and acted like he was going to step off the curb and head toward his truck. So Jan continued toward home. Suddenly the man had his left arm around Jan with his hand over her mouth. With his right hand, he pulled a knife out and held it to her chest. "You're going with me! You're going in the truck with me! If you scream, I'll stab you."

"Oh Lord," Jan gasped, her voice muffled.

He dragged her across the street and the gravel church parking lot to the truck. Leaning Jan up against the truck, he reached for the door of the truck with his right hand. Jan's mind raced. "I can't get in the truck with him. I have to do something," she thought. She could see the back of the police station but couldn't call for help. She glanced down and saw the bottom of his zipper. She freed her right hand and hit him as hard as she could in the crotch. He moaned and bent slightly. With her left hand she pulled his hand off of her face, then turned quickly and broke free. Jan ran around the back of the truck and down the middle of Virginia Street toward the police station screaming. "Help! Help! A man attacked me with a knife!" Finally, she shot through the door of the police station to safety. Patrolman Bob George was at the desk.

"A man tired to attack me! He has a knife! He's driving a light colored tan truck!"

Officer George looked out the window and saw the truck cross the railroad tracks at Olive Street. "Is that the truck?" he asked.

"Yes, yes it is!"

The lawman ran for the squad car and pulled out of the parking stall, watching the truck stop at the intersection of Grand and Olive. He sped to the intersection and was behind the truck as it turned onto West Grand Street. Officer George turned on his red lights and attempted to stop the truck, but it continued. Officer George turned the spotlight on and waved it back and forth in the rear view mirror of the truck, but the truck still continued. Officer George called for backup. At Green Briar Road, the truck turned, drove about three hundred feet, and pulled to the side of the road. George quickly exited the vehicle at the same time the driver of the truck did likewise. "Turn around and put your hands on the bed of the truck," Officer George ordered.

The man turned and placed his hands on the bed as ordered, asking, "What's the problem officer?" and smiling at Officer George.

"Do you have a knife or any other weapon with you?"

45

"I don't have any weapons on me, but there is a knife on the dash in the truck," he responded.

Officer George cautiously approached the man and searched him. The suspect was clean.

About that time, Officer Michael Spruell arrived at the scene.

George asked Spruell to stay with the truck while he took the suspect to the police station for questioning. When they arrived, George asked the suspect for some identification. He reached into his back pocket and pulled out a black plastic folder and a brown plastic garbage bag and laid them on the desk. He followed with a registration to a Datsun 280Z in the name of John Paul Phillips.

"Is your name John Paul Phillips?" George asked.

"Yes," Phillips replied.

"Mr. Phillips, you have the right to remain silent, if you decide to make a statement, the statements can and will be used against you in a court of law. You have a right to have an attorney present during questioning. You have a right to consult an attorney before questioning. If you cannot afford an attorney, one can be appointed. Do you understand these rights?"

"Yeah, and I don't want an attorney."

"Did you talk to anyone while you were in town?" George asked.

"Yeah, I stopped at the church down the street and asked some chick for directions and she got scared and ran off."

"Did you threaten the girl in any way?"

"I don't think so," Phillips answered.

"I'll be right back," George told Phillips as he walked into another room. Jan Murphy sat in a chair with shaky hands rubbing a Kleenex across the red welts surrounding her mouth.

"Jan, can you identify the man that attacked you?" George asked.

"Yes, I can. He was about five-eight, five-nine, slim build. He was wearing jeans, a dark-colored lightweight jacket, and a plaid shirt."

"If you saw him again, would you recognize him?"

"Yes, yes I would."

George escorted Jan outside the police station to a location where she could see inside through the front window. Phillips was sitting in a chair in front of the window. Jan stood on weak legs and fell into the policeman's arms, exclaiming, "That's him! That's him!"

Meanwhile, Officer Spruell searched the truck. He found a Rugar .22 caliber rifle, a buck knife, a roll of masking tape, rope, brown plastic bags, a bag of marijuana, and a pair of rubber gloves. He finished the search and called for a tow truck.

Officer George continued with the questioning of Phillips. "I am going to ask you one more time what happened," George started.

Phillips sat silently looking at the floor.

"Mr. Phillips, you're under arrest for aggravated battery, aggravated assault, armed violence, and attempted kidnapping."

"Can I call my wife?" Phillips calmly asked.

"Yes," George replied.

Phillips dialed the number, "Hon, I'm at Carterville Police Station. They're going to take me to the county jail in Marion. Call dad and tell him we won't be out to dinner with him. I got in trouble over some chick."

The next day, police put together a photographic lineup of black and white photos. Linda Young looked at the photos. "That's him! That's him!" she shouted pointing to John Paul Phillips' photo.

State's Attorney Randy Patchett prosecuted the case. Rather than complicate the case by having two trials, Patchett got a conviction on John Paul for the abduction in Williamson County. During sentencing he was able to have SIU students testify that there had been multiple abductions. John Paul received forty-five years for the crimes.

For the next three years, John Paul served his time at Menard Prison in Chester, Illinois. Then one day, John Paul walked through the cell door at Nine Gallery Cell 23. Tom Mocaby, a fellow inmate, looked at John Paul and said, "Hey, man, come on in and have a cigarette."

John Paul turned and looked at Mocaby for a moment with glassy eyes, then stood and walked into the cell.

"Here," Mocaby said, handing John Paul an open pack of Kools.

"Thanks, man," John Paul said as he settled onto the bunk across from Mocaby. He lit the cigarette and took a deep breath.

"What happened, man?" Mocaby asked.

"The judge is going to throw the book at me. But, they don't know the half of it," he said starting to laugh uproariously. "They don't know about the girls I killed."

"What?" Mocaby responded, startled.

"They don't know about the murders. I picked up a girl that works at a local motel—Joan Weatherall. Took her to my dad's office. I beat the shit out of her, choked her, raped her, and killed her," he said, still laughing. "I beat the man. They can't ever prove it. I took a water hose and washed her off. Stuck it up her cunt and washed out the evidence."

Mocaby watched as John Paul's eyes seemed to gaze into another world. Phillips laughed once again, then puffed on his cigarette, giggling like a small child. "I like the ones that fight back. If they don't resist, I don't like them. That bitch fought back," he said.

"You said 'murders.' Is there more than one?" Mocaby asked.

John Paul looked past Mocaby as if he wasn't there, "I broke into a house and stole some marijuana. Shit, man, I was feeling good. I followed this couple out to Grassy Lake. Cuffed this guy to a tree and beat the shit out of him. Made this chick take some pills. Then I raped her—made her suck my dick."

"Another cigarette?" Mocaby asked, handing his pack again to John Paul.

John Paul took a cigarette, lit it, and took a deep breath. "I killed two other girls, too. Clark was her name. I stabbed her and put her in scalding water. I had bib overalls on. There was blood all over them. I couldn't remember what I done with them. Damn, I was paranoid for a while. The man didn't catch me, though," he said giggling.

"Then I did McSherry. Stabbed that bitch with a butcher knife. I liked looking at the expression on their face when I was killing them. They looked scared, man, real scared," he said laughing all the time. "I liked listening to them scream.

"I used to go back after I killed them. There was a cat in the house. He was eating on the body.

"I did some work for Dad down in Louisiana. I was coming home one night and picked this black guy up. I was in my dad's van. I picked this guy up and we stopped at a rest stop—had a couple of beers and a joint. I had a new .357 mag under the seat. I got to thinking about it and I decided I wanted to try it out. I wanted to see what it would do. I pulled it out and made this nigger get out of the van. He had the damnest look on his face," John Paul said, starting to giggle once again. "There wasn't anybody around so I took him behind the restrooms. Made him get down on his knees and eat sand. He wasn't saying anything. Just looking at me with big eyes and following orders. I got tired of messing with him so I shot him right below the right eye. Killed the damn nigger dead with one shot. There was a swamp in the bayou by the restrooms so I dumped him in the swamp. He just slowly sank. Damn one shot!"

Mocaby wasn't sure if John Paul was telling the truth, but after his release he decided to contact the police.

On June 5, 1984, Detective Robert Burns, Special Agent Gary Ashman from the Illinois State Police, and Tom Mocaby met at the Randolph County jail. Mocaby told the detectives that he had been a cellmate of John Paul Phillips in Menard Prison. They were assigned to Nine Gallery Cell 23. Mocaby told the police what John Paul had told him and he mentioned the names Joan Weatherall, Katheen McSherry, and Theresa Clark.

Mocaby remembered that Phillips had said he stabbed McSherry and Clark. "I get kind of mixed up on these two 'cause he just talked and rambled on about both these two," Mocaby said. "I don't know which. I know one of them, I believe it was in 1975, and he lived right downstairs from her apartment. He went upstairs one night and knocked on her door and asked to use the phone. She come to the door, he just kicked himself the rest of the way in and he raped her. I don't know which one of the two, but he said he tried to rape her in the ass and she kicked out a window or something and that's when it all started. He said she went into hysterics and went into the bathroom to clean up, and when she came out, he stabbed her. He said that he had a butcher knife about ten or twelve inches long. He stabbed her in the abdominal area, then he kept stabbing her. She kept telling him that she ought to call an ambulance 'cause she was dying. And the other one, he took a sheet, soft soaked the blood up, and wiped blood on the walls and shit, but I don't know which one of the two.

"He put one of them in a bathtub, the one that lived upstairs. He says he come back a couple of days later, sat at the dining room table at her house and drank some beers. He said they were baby Millers. After he drank the beers, he wiped the bottles off and set them in a stack on the table. He took her cigarette lighter as a souvenir. He had the lighter for a long time.

"He said the one in the bathtub had a rag over her face. He come back a couple of days later. He went in the bathroom and pulled the rag off her face and most of her face came off with the rag, it stuck to the rag, peeled off. She was all gray and starting to fall apart."

Continuing his story, Mocaby told the lawmen that John Paul said he was bitter toward women. "He said he cut one of their throats. The first time he cut her, it didn't go all the way through, it just like pops down, there is strands and shit holding it together, but then the next time, he cut the rest of the way through."

"How did he pick his victims?" the policemen asked.

"He told me he'd go out for three or four months and he lets all that shit build up inside of him, all these little different things that have happened to him. One day he just can't handle it no more. He just goes off and finds one of these gals and waxes them. One of the first murders he did, he rode a bicycle to it, a ten-speed bike. He rode over there and killed her. He said when he left, he came right back a couple of hours later and, when he got there, the police was already there. He started cutting up, how the criminals always returns to the crime, the sight of the scene of the crime. He said he always went back."

"Did he say why he did that?"

"He's nuts, man. He don't know why he does it. He says a lot of things. He—he'd say sometimes just for the thrill, you know. He said ever since he was little, he used to have the Carbondale Police just chase him all around. He would get into a little shit just to get them to chase him. They chased him out in a corn field."

"Was he bragging?" the detectives asked.

"Yeah. He'd laugh about it the whole time he was talking about it. How smooth he did all this, and the police ain't got nothing on him. How they come questioned him and he wouldn't even talk to the police. That's his whole thing, just try to outsmart the police."

"Did he ever mention Joan Weatherall?" the lawmen asked.

"That's who he talked to the most. He said one night he was driving his old lady's car 'cause his car was being worked on. It was a light blue Monte Carlo. He said he was parked in the parking lot at the back around the area where there were some bars. He was waiting for someone to come out the back door. Once there were two girls came by, but there were too many witnesses so he waited. Then Joan came out the door. He came up and snatched her. He dragged her away and choked her until she passed out, then carried her over by this house that's got a driveway beside the house, right back behind these parking lots. He put her back there and went and got his car. He opened the trunk and put her in the trunk, then took her out to his dad's warehouse. He took her and raped her repeatedly. He said after he raped her he was going to tell her he was going to take her back to town and he needed to tie her hands up. He kept saying she was real sloppy and real drunk. She kept telling him he was an animal, an animal, she was real wild. He said that was the reason he killed her, 'cause she was so sloppy. He said he did several rapes, all kinds of rapes. But he says the only reason he kills these broads is he is afraid they will tell. Anyway, he said he was going to tie her hands up and take her back to town, and he tied her hands up and hit her in the head with a hammer, just to try and knock her out, and he slipped this noose around her neck. He had some kind of knot that would tighten. When he hit her she fell to the floor and was spinning around in circles. Blood was shooting out all over the concrete floor. She was spinning on her back with her hands tied behind her and he stood and waited for her to die. He said that he hosed all the blood off, hosed her insides out, then took her out to the loading docks and raped her again. He said he raped her in the ass, then cleaned her out again. He said he didn't want to leave any sperm. He said he wrapped her up in plastic, put her in the trunk, and took her to Elkville to some strip pits and dumped her in the strip pit. He said she rolled down the hill and when she got in the water, the first time the water wasn't very deep, she wasn't full submerged so he climbed down the hill and pushed her the rest of the way in the water.

"He said he went home; the sun was almost coming up at the time. He had on a pair of bib overalls. He told his wife he had been burglarizing, that's how he got all muddy. So he threw his clothes in the washer and washed them two or three times. Then he jumped in bed with his old lady for a while. When he got up, he got his clothes and he said that all the blood didn't come out of the overalls. He said he put them behind the file cabinets at his old man's office.

"He said that he went back to the strip pit a couple of months later, just reminisced."

"Did he talk about raping anyone else?" the policeman asked.

"Yeah, he raped a girl from South America. He said he was sitting in a parking lot by some apartments and this girl come out. He thought she was damn beautiful so he kidnapped her, stopped and got gas, took her out to his old man's office and raped her.

"He talked two or three different rapes. He said up around Mt. Vernon some young fifteen- or sixteen-year-old was hitchhiking and he picked her up. He took her out and raped her and just took her back to where he got her.

"He said that around St. Louis someone carved 'good rape' in this broad's stomach. He would laugh every time he talked about it. He was always saying they carved 'good rape' in her stomach. 'A good rape, the bitch is dead—it's a good rape 'cause she ain't gonna tell.'"

"Is there anything else you can tell us?" the detectives asked.

51

"Yeah, I got out in May '83, and when I got out, I was supposed to screw this broad up—Sue, his wife. I was supposed to break her arms and legs and burn her car. He didn't want me to kill the broad because he wanted to save it for himself. He said he's gonna skin her like a frog.

"He said he would pay me, but the only way I would get paid was when he read it in the papers. He said he would pay me $1500."

"Where would he get the money?"

"From his father. I asked him one time what his father thought of all this. He told me that his father had much love for him. His father can understand why he does it. He has talked to his father about the murders."

"His father knows about him murdering the girls?" the detectives questioned.

"Yes, he said he had talked with his father about it. Shit, man, his dad gives him $100 a week every time he visits him. They're real tight.

"When we were in the cell he used to draw me a map of, not the route he took to the warehouse, but the route around the parking lot. He hung it on a clipboard in the cell and I told him, 'man, you better throw that away 'cause it might fall into the wrong hands.'

"I asked him from time to time why he would do that to women. He would start laughing uproariously and point his finger at me. Just stand there and laugh. He's damn crazy, man."

"Is there anything else you can tell us?" the detectives asked.

"He has a girl he did a bunch of home invasions and shit with. She's a mean broad, Joan Smith. She knows some shit about him, but he says he ain't got nothing to worry about 'cause she won't talk. She knows some shit about him."

This information sparked an intensive investigation by police. Detectives were able to find the car that had belonged to John Paul Phillips' ex-wife—the car he was supposed to have placed Joan Weatherall's body in and transported it to the strip pit in Elkville—and process it for evidence. The crime lab technician found twenty-eight hairs in the back seat and trunk of the vehicle. Three head and one pubic hair could have come from the victim. Five years after the murder, this evidence, along with testimony by Thomas Mocaby, was enough to bind John Paul Phillips over for trial.

John Paul Phillips went to trial in October 1986, after a change of venue to Massac County. The prosecution called their key witness, Thomas Mocaby. The other physical evidence found in the car was not linked to the murder victim. After several days of trial on October 9, 1986, John Paul Phillips was found guilty of the murder of Joan Weatherall. His sentence hearing was set for November.

During the sentence hearing, Thomas Mocaby was brought in to testify that John Paul had told him in detail about raping and killing two other girls: Theresa Clark and Kathleen McSherry. The purpose for this testimony was to show that John Paul had been involved in multiple murders, which made him eligible for the death sentence. As Mocaby was leaving the witness stand, John Paul leaped from the table and attempted to attack Mocaby. He had a small metal tube in his hand. It did not fire and John Paul threw it at Mocaby. Then, he tried to get around the defense attorney to attack Mocaby with his bare hands. John Paul's father stood and applauded as John Paul attempted to attack Mocaby. The assault failed, but Mocaby's testimony did not. On November 12, 1986, John Paul Phillips was on his way to Menard's death row.

On May 2, 1991, I wrote to John Paul Phillips at Menard to see if he would let me interview him. He wrote me back on May 9, 1991, saying that he would talk to me, but that we needed to set up a code so the prison administration wouldn't know what we were talking about. I researched the Weatherall murder case and several others that John Paul was involved with before contacting him again. Then, in early October, I wrote him again for a meeting date. The meeting was never to take place. A week after I wrote, John Paul Phillips died of a heart attack at the age of forty.

Update

Since the Susan Schumake murder in 1981, there has been some disagreement among detectives about who committed the murder. Some argue that it was John Paul Phillips. They support their theory based on the fact that John Paul was in the area when the murder was committed, he had scratches on his face and arms, and he lied to the police. In addition, the victims' backpack was missing, which is common among serial murders as they often take something from their victims as souvenirs. Those who disagree say that the murder did not meet the MO of John Paul Phillips. At the time of the murder, the technology did not allow for DNA testing. However, in October 2001 John Paul Phillip's body was exhumed to obtain DNA samples to test with sperm found on Susan Schumake's body. The results indicated that the DNA did not match.

Author's Note

Amie Glisson, Bob Johnson, Jan Murphy, Sue, Bill Walker, Lisa Walton, Jack Wells, and Linda Young are not the real names of the persons so named in the foregoing story. A fictitious name had been used because there is no reason for public interest in the identity of these persons.

Case 2

The Deadly Nightcap

Sherry Byerley
September 19, 1981

Marion, Illinois

"No, man, I'm tired. I'm going home," the friend muttered as he looked at his watch. "It's two-thirty in the morning already."

Byerley reached over and turned the car off. "Come on, man, one more beer won't hurt you." The two men exited the vehicle and walked up to the mobile home.

As they stepped inside, Byerley called for his wife. "Sherry! Sherry! Where are you?" He walked to the back of the trailer while the friend waited in the living room.

"My God, Sherry, what's wrong? What has happened to you?" he yelled. He ran to the living room. "Something is wrong with Sherry! She won't wake up! What shall we do?"

As the friend started out the door, a neighbor pulled the front door of the mobile home open. "You need an ambulance?"

"Yes, there's somethin' wrong with Sherry!"

"I'll call," he said, turning and running for his home.

The ambulance hurried down the dark streets of Marion, Illinois, to the trailer court. It was now 3:00 a.m., September 19, 1981.

The ambulance attendant rushed into the bedroom and at one glance knew the girl was dead. He knelt down by the partly-nude body and saw a large amount of blood on the back of her head, neck, and shoulders. He returned to the ambulance and called the Marion Police Department.

Marion Sergeant Jack West arrived at the scene and went into the bedroom. He scanned the room, noticing the blood on the body, the sheets on the bed, and the carpet at the foot of the bed.

"Did you look at the injury?" he asked the ambulance attendant.

"Yes, but I didn't touch the body. I think she's been shot."

Sergeant West hurried for the radio and called for the detectives, then guarded the crime scene until their arrival.

Detective Les Snyder arrived and proceeded to the master bedroom at the back of the trailer. The girl was lying on her back on the floor at the end of the bed. She was dressed in a plaid maternity top, white bra, and underpants. The corpse was bare-footed. Her head was lying in a large puddle of blood. Detective Snyder wasn't sure what he had, but he wasn't going to take any chances. He would treat the investigation as a murder until evidence proved otherwise. Synder called the Illinois Department of Law Enforcement and asked for a Crime Scene technician.

The technician arrived at 4:15 a.m. and met with the detectives. He photographed the scene, then began to collect, package, and mark the physical evidence. He collected hair from the floor, the victim's left hand, and the floor beneath the victim's right hand; cigarette butts from the ash-tray; brown slacks from the bed; a gold-colored bedspread; a blue roller-skate case against the east wall in the bedroom; a red spot in the sink in the bedroom; two latent prints from the west closet door; two latent prints from the wall trim of the northeast portion of the bedroom; and possible blood from the kitty litter box in the bedroom. The technician then re-quested that the body be moved to the local hospital for an autopsy.

Meanwhile, the detectives began an interrogation of the victim's hus-band. Detectives read Clyde Byerley his Miranda Rights and provided a waiver of rights form. He read the information and signed the waiver to talk with them about his wife's death.

Byerley told the police that a friend picked him and his wife up at about 9:00 a.m. on September 18 and took them to the friend's home in Creal Springs. The husband worked on the friend's car and then on his own car until about 6:30 p.m. At that time, he and Sherry left the home in his 1964 Plymouth Valiant.

The car broke down at the intersection of Old Route 13 and New Route 13. They both began to walk toward Marion, when a woman in her forties picked them up and drove them to the square in Marion. The couple walked to a friend's house, but the friend was not at home. A local bar was nearby, and Clyde decided he wanted a beer. They went into the bar, and he had a beer. Sherry drank one Vodka Collins. Her dad picked her up a short time later and took her home.

Clyde told the police that he stayed at the bar until about 8:00 p.m., when a friend took him to another bar. He said that he stayed at that bar until closing time and then went to the truck stop. Clyde drank a couple of cups of coffee, then asked a friend if he would give him a ride home.

At about 2:30 a.m., they pulled into the driveway. When they went into the trailer he noticed that the door was unlocked and all the lights were on. He said that he yelled for Sherry, but she didn't answer, so he walked to the back of the trailer. Sherry was lying on the floor at the foot of the bed. Clyde kicked her leg and shook her. When he looked at her face, he saw that it was purple. He yelled for his friend.

"What was she wearing?" the police asked.

"She just had on underpants and maybe a blouse. Damn! My head is screwed up!"

"You have been through a lot, Clyde. We understand."

Clyde sat quietly for a moment, then continued with his story. He and his friend had gone to a neighbor's house and asked them to call an ambulance. He called some people but couldn't remember who.

"I do remember grabbing Sherry and hugging her. She was very cold!"

The husband explained that he did not have a gun but had owned a nine shot, .22-caliber pistol at one time. He had sold it for $30.

Clyde told detectives that he did not kill his wife, but he had hit her in the past. "She fought like a man, but we were getting along fine. She was three months pregnant. I don't know why anyone would want to kill her, but I did run a guy off a few days ago that had been staying with us. His name is Jack. He lives near Cobden. I don't know any reason why he would have killed her. Was she stabbed?"

"No, she was shot in the back of the head."

"I don't own a gun."

"How much have you had to drink?"

"About twelve beers."

The interview ended. Clyde had smoked an entire pack of cigarettes during the questioning. The detective took the ashtray and dumped it, then requested that Clyde sign a consent-to-search form for a 1964 Plymouth Valiant that was stalled at the intersection of New and Old Route 13. Detective Snyder made arrangements for the husband to receive clean clothes, then took into custody the clothes that Byerley was wearing.

The results of the autopsy confirmed that the victim was three months pregnant and that the cause of death was a gunshot wound to the back of the head. There was penetration of the brain and intracranial hemorrhage.

The crime scene technician, who was present at the autopsy, collected for evidence a lead slug, samples of blood for toxicological study, a pink and white maternity top, a hair standard from the victim's head, and inked fingerprints of the victim. He then went to the Marion Police Department and took sealed bags containing the clothes of Clyde Byerley. All of the evidence collected was then submitted to the Illinois Department of Law Enforcement Crime Laboratory in Springfield, Illinois.

The probe continued with an interview of a friend of the Byerleys. The friend said that on September 18, Clyde, accompanied by a male and woman whom he didn't know, came to the friend's residence. Clyde was driving a gold-colored Grand Prix belonging to an acquaintance.

According to the friend, Byerley wanted to go to a local bar but told him that first he wanted to stop by home and pick up some money. They drove to Clyde's mobile home, and he and Clyde went inside. The friend said he waited in the kitchen while Clyde went to the rear of the mobile home and returned shortly thereafter with a .38-caliber Colt pistol placed inside a brown leather case. The friend said he looked at the gun and gave it back to Clyde. Clyde then took the gun back to the back of the mobile home and returned. Byerley told his friend that he had more guns, a .44 magnum and two 9mm pistols. The friend said that they then got back in the car and went to a local lounge.

While they were in the lounge Byerley told his friend that the gun that he had shown him was hot and not to tell anyone. They drank a couple of beers, Clyde picked up a girl, and they left the bar. They drove to a liquor store, bought a six-pack of beer, and consumed it.

Then Clyde told him that he wanted his friend to take him to his mobile home, but if there was a blue truck there not to stop. They arrived at the mobile home about 11:00 p.m. Clyde went inside, and his friend waited in the car. The friend said that he heard what sounded like a door slamming, and he saw Byerley run out the door and around the back of the mobile home. About ten minutes passed and Byerley came back around the mobile home and stood at the corner with his head cupped in his hands. The friend ran to Clyde.

Clyde was crying and said, "I think I have killed my wife! I shook her and can't wake her up! She's done this to me before. What should I do?"

"We need to call the ambulance and the police. We better not leave."

"No, take me to my sister's."

They got into the car, and, as they left, Byerley started laughing and said, "I'm just kidding; I didn't do anything. She ran out the back door and ran to her dad's."

"We went to another local bar, and Clyde laughed all the way." At about 1:00 a.m., the friend left the bar and Clyde was still there with some friends.

Detectives were onto something. Either Clyde or his friend were lying to police. Detectives suspected it was Byerley.

They continued the interview with yet another friend of the Byerleys. He said that he picked the Byerleys up at around 8:00 a.m. on September 18 and took them to his home in Creal Springs. Byerley was to work on his friend's car.

At about 6:00 p.m., the couple left in Byerley's car. The friend cleaned up and went to Marion to a local lounge. He met Sherry who informed him that their car had broken down. He gave her twenty cents to call her dad, and, while she called, he bought Clyde a beer. When Sherry's dad arrived to pick her up, she told Clyde to stay with the friend because her dad did not like Clyde. She left, and the friend met a girl. He and the girl left the bar and went to Herrin, Illinois, where they stayed at a local bar until closing. He said he did not know where Clyde went.

At about 2:00 a.m., he was at the truck stop when Clyde and a friend of Clyde's came running into the restaurant real excited. They said that something had happened to Sherry. She was on the floor of the bedroom and wouldn't get up. The friend went to the mobile home to check on her, thinking that she had overdosed. He went into the bedroom and saw that Sherry was dead.

Clyde came in and started hugging her, and that is when the friend saw the blood. He said that Clyde was very excited and told him, "Help me get the guy that killed her! He didn't have to kill her! He didn't have to kill her!" The friend tried to calm Byerley down and took him outside.

"Did he own any guns that you know of?" police asked.

The friend told police that about two weeks ago Byerley came to the friend's residence and showed him an old .38-caliber, long-barreled, police special. The friend tried to buy the gun from Clyde just to get it away from him. He said that the gun was in poor condition and that the bullets were old and corroded. He said that he could identify the gun if he saw it again.

Police brought Clyde Berley back for interrogation. The detectives asked the husband if he would explain his activities for them once again.

They wanted to make sure they were accurate when they made out their reports. Clyde told the police the same story he had earlier, claiming that he had not returned to his mobile home except when he found Sherry in the early morning hours. However, he did change his story somewhat. He told the police that he met two friends, borrowed a friend's car, and drove around for a while, although he never went home. They did go to a liquor store and bought a six-pack, which he and the two friends drank while they were driving around, then they returned to the bar. He told the police that he had owned a gun a long time ago but no longer had it.

Detectives suspected Byerley killed his wife, but they were not ready yet to catch him in his lie. They wanted to gather more information.

The probe continued with questioning of an acquaintance of Byerley's. The acquaintance said that he got off work at about 5:00 p.m. and went to a local bar. At about 7:30 p.m., Clyde Byerley came into the bar and told the acquaintance that his car broke down. He offered to take Byerley wherever he wanted to go. Byerley said he was in no hurry and that he never asked him for a ride.

According to the acquaintance, Byerley left the bar about an hour later. The acquaintance then left the bar and went to another local bar where he encountered Clyde once again. Clyde asked him if he could borrow his car for about thirty minutes to go and pick up a friend. Byerley left alone. The acquaintance said that Clyde wasn't gone for very long, maybe thirty minutes. When Clyde returned, his friend was with him and they had a few drinks and played pool.

At approximately 11:00 p.m., Clyde came over and asked if he could borrow the car again. He wanted to go home and get some money. He and a friend left the bar together and returned about 11:50 p.m.

Once again he drank a few beers and played pool. At last call the acquaintance went over to Clyde's table. As they were finishing their beer, the acquaintance asked Clyde where he had gone the second time. He said that he had gone home, and that he and his wife had gotten into a fight. She had run out the back door and had gone to her dad's.

He said that if Byerley did kill his wife he was cold about it because he was clowning around. Byerley told the acquaintance that he was getting a divorce. When the acquaintance left the bar, Clyde Byerley was still in the lounge drinking.

The canvass continued with a statement of another friend who said that Byerley picked him and his girlfriend up in front of a local convenience store at about 9:00 p.m. He then went to a friend's trailer, picked the friend up, and drove to his home. Byerley went inside for about five minutes and returned to the car. He drove off and his friend said that Byerley was wanting to buy a small handgun. Byerley said that he had something to show him and went back to the mobile home. Clyde and the friend went into the house and stayed for about fifteen minutes.

As Byerley was driving back to the bar, he told the friend that he also had a 9mm pistol and a .44 magnum. He told the police that he knew that Byerley used to carry a small .38-caliber pistol on his person. Finally, he said that they all returned to a local bar about 10:00 p.m. which was the last time that he saw Clyde.

Another friend said that he arrived at the local hangout about 12:30 a.m. on September 19. He talked with several friends he knew, then spotted Byerley sitting at a table talking with a girl. He didn't know who the girl was, but he went over to the table and sat with them.

Clyde wanted the friend to drive him home. They left the bar at approximately 1:00 a.m. and went to the local truck stop. They went inside, drank coffee, and ate. Clyde was trying to push the girl off on him. She got tired of it and went to sit with some other people she knew.

"Do you know if Byerley owns a gun?" Snyder asked.

"Yes, he does. He had an old .38-caliber revolver at a friend's in Creal Springs about three weeks ago. We both shot the gun."

Continuing, the friend said that he and Clyde left the truck stop about 2:00 a.m. He drove Clyde to the trailer and Clyde insisted on his coming into the house. When they got to the storm door, he noticed that it was unlocked. The inside door was unlocked also, but lights were on and music was playing. The friend stood at the door and Clyde told him to come on in—it was not going to hurt anything.

Byerley started yelling for his wife. He yelled, "Sherry!" He told the friend he did not know where she was. He went to the back bedroom. The light was on. "Oh God! What have you done?" he screamed. Then he yelled, "Come and help me!"

The friend went to the bedroom and saw that Sherry was lying at the foot of the bed. She looked like she had purple spots on her face. Clyde wanted to know what they should do. The friend said they should call an ambulance and the police. As they started out the door, they were met by the neighbor who hurried home and called both emergency services. Clyde was very agitated and friends had to settle him down. They got him to stay

61

outside until the police arrived.

A canvass of the neighborhood revealed from two separate neighbors that, within the last three days, they had visited Clyde Byerley at his mobile home, and he had showed and tried to sell them a .38-caliber pistol. Neither of them wanted the gun because it was old and in poor condition.

The police knew they had enough information to establish that Clyde Byerley had lied to them about having a gun and about returning home until 2:00 a.m. or later. He had been held over eight hours, and the police had not charged him with any offense. Detective Snyder was worried that they could run into a legal problem if they didn't make a move. They checked with Sheriff Kobler who informed the detectives that they had been watching Byerley. He was very nervous and had not eaten anything while at the Sheriff's office. They decided to make their move.

Sheriff Kobler brought Clyde Byerley into the office. He and Detective Les Snyder began the interrogation. Byerley was jittery, smoking one cigarette after another. The police asked him to sit down and read him his Miranda Rights.

"Do you understand your rights?" they asked.

"Yes," the suspect responded as he began to shake almost uncontrollably.

"Clyde, you're under a lot of pressure. You know me, and you know that I am not going to hurt you. Do you want to talk to me about it?"

Byerley broke down and began sobbing his eyes and saying, "I didn't mean to kill her. I didn't mean to kill her."

"Calm down, Clyde, tell us what happened."

"I didn't mean to kill her."

"Will you give us a written statement?" detectives asked. "Other officers are at the scene looking for the murder weapon. Did you take it with you when you went out back?"

"Yes, I did. I can't tell you exactly where it is. It was dark. I can show you, though."

"We want to get a written statement first, then we will go out to the scene."

The suspect told police that he was with his wife at a local bar at about 7:30 p.m. Sherry's dad had picked her up, and Clyde stayed at the bar. He drank three beers then went to another bar. He drank one beer there then went to another bar where he had three more beers.

He then borrowed his friend's car, picked up three other friends, and they went to the liquor store and bought a six-pack of beer. They went to Byerley's residence, and he and another friend went into the house to look at a gun. The suspect showed the friend a .38-caliber revolver. The suspect said that he wanted to see if his friend wanted to buy the gun. He put the gun back in the bedroom, got five dollars, and they left. It was approximately 9:00 p.m., and Sherry was not at home at the time. They went back to the bar and the suspect drank three more beers.

One of the friends went back to the trailer with him. It was about 10:00 p.m. by now. He stayed in the car while Byerley went inside.

Sherry was home and they got into a fight over his drinking. The suspect got his gun and stuck it in his belt. He told Sherry that he was going to leave and went to the closet to get his clothes. Sherry walked over and pulled the gun from the suspect's belt and started walking out of the room. The suspect walked over, reached over her shoulder, grabbed the gun, and pulled it back over her shoulder. The gun went off, and Sherry fell backwards.

The suspect panicked and ran out the back door, turned to the right behind his trailer and hid the gun and holster under a neighbor's mobile home. He went back into the house and saw that Sherry was dead. He went back out to the car, and they all went back to the bar.

Later that night, he went to the truck stop. He asked a friend to take him home. When he got there he acted like he had just found his wife for the first time.

"We then went to a neighbor's house and asked him to call the police," Byerley said.

After the confession, Byerley took detectives to the neighbor's mobile home where he had hidden the gun. Police watched while Clyde Byerley crawled under the mobile home and returned with a .38-caliber Colt Revolver, serial number 148949. The handgun had one live cartridge. The gun was in a brown leather holster. Police took the gun into custody and submitted it to the crime laboratory for analysis.

On November 18, police received the analytical findings of the evidence. The murder weapon was found to be in good operating condition. The discharged cartridge case submitted was fired from the murder weapon. The spent projectile taken from the skull of the victim was fired from the murder weapon.

After chemical examination, the pink smock revealed the presence of a lead smoke pattern on the left back shoulder area consistent with the murder weapon. The head hair found in the victim's hand was not consistent with the victim's head and the head hair found underneath the victim was not consistent with the victim's head hair. Clyde Byerley was charged with the murder of his wife on September 19. In July 1982, the suspect stood trial in First Circuit Court in Williamson County, Illinois. The twelve-person jury found him guilty of murder. He was sentenced by Judge Donald Lowery to twenty-to-forty years in prison.

His response to the judge was, "I will always love my wife, and I will never touch a drop of liquor again."

He is now serving his sentence in Menard State Prison in Chester, Illinois.

Case 3

The Axe Murder

Madeline Willis
July 14, 1984

Marion, Illinois

A call that a house was burning came in to Illinois's Marion Fire Department at 6:06 p.m. on July 14, 1984. Alert firefighters hurried to their
vehicles and were soon speeding across the city to the smoke-filled home
on Monroe Street.

It was a humid summer evening as they set to work extinguishing
the blaze. As they did so, the fire-fighting team led by Fire Chief Charles
Heyde discovered a black woman lying in the southwest bedroom of the
dwelling. They noticed some wounds in the back of her head and found a
bloodstained axe lying near her.

Believing the woman to be still alive, the firefighters had her transported to a local hospital for emergency treatment. Meanwhile, Chief Heyde radioed the police department to report the suspicious circumstances
surrounding the discovery.

Detective Michael Wiseman arrived on the scene at 6:35 p.m. and got
a rundown on the facts from Chief Heyde. The chief told Wiseman that the
woman had been rushed to the hospital in the belief that she was alive, but
word had been received that she'd been pronounced dead on arrival.

Chief Heyde told the detective that the victim was found on her stomach across the bed. He described the wounds on the back of the head. He
said that the axe had been double-bladed and covered with blood.

Shortly, Detective Mike Snyder joined Wiseman at the scene and the
two police probers roped off the entire area around the house with crime
scene tape. Then, Snyder requested assistance from the State of Illinois
Crime Lab and the Division of Criminal Investigation (DCI) of the Illinois

Department of Law Enforcement. He also asked the State Fire Marshall's Office to send an arson investigator.

Crime Scene Technician Frank Cooper of the State Crime Lab soon arrived at the scene. He inspected the bedroom and the house, which was situated on the east side of South Monroe Street, facing west. Then he took photographs of the single-story wood-frame residence, which consisted of a living room, a dining room, a kitchen, two bedrooms, a bathroom, an enclosed back porch, and an enclosed front porch.

Cooper finished photographing the exterior and then moved inside. The heaviest amount of fire damage was in the dining room area, but the rest of the dwelling had sustained heavy damage.

After the technician was done photographing the crime scene, he began to collect, package, and mark the physical evidence, which included the bedspread from the bed, a curtain from the south window and the southwest bedroom, the double-bladed axe, a hatchet from the couch in the living room, four prescription bottles from the living room floor, a pullover shirt with the brand name "Pro Shop" from the bed in the southeast bedroom, and a pink fitted sheet from the same bed.

Technician Cooper left the scene and drove to the morgue at the local hospital and took inked fingerprints and palm prints of Madeline Willis, the dead woman.

In a coordinated effort with Technician Cooper, State Fire Marshal Barney West investigated the crime scene. He eliminated all accidental causes of fire. Then he determined that there were three separate, unrelated fires—one in the southeast bedroom, one in the dining room, and one in the living room. Each fire had been set with trash and paper. Thus the arson investigator ruled that the fire was arson.

Detectives began to canvass witnesses by interviewing the firefighters at the scene. Fireman Carl M. Kelton, a nine-year veteran, said that he'd received a call from a unidentified woman who reported the house on Monroe Street burning. He and Assistant Fire Chief Paul Barnwell responded, arriving approximately one and a half minutes later.

Kelton approached the residence and saw smoke coming from the dining room window on the north side of the residence. It appeared to him that all the other windows were closed.

The fireman connected and charged a water hose. Barnwell began spraying the fire through the open window while Kelton removed an exhaust fan from the fire truck to place in the front door. While he was getting the fan, Keaton saw the front storm door of the residence closing. As he approached the residence with the exhaust fan, a person wearing hair rollers, who Keaton thought was a woman, came out of the front storm door, went down the steps, and proceeded to the south. Keaton continued toward the door, but he was unable to install the fan in the doorway.

Keaton then entered the burning structure through the front door and went into the living room. He looked toward the southwest bedroom and could see the outline of the bedroom window, as well as the outline of the bed. It appeared to the fireman that some clothes or pillows were lying on the bed.

He then tried to enter the dining room, but he was prevented by the excessive smoke and heat.

Keaton could hear some "popping and cracking" sounds, so he went outside and took the hose from Barnwell. Barnwell went to the rear of the house to open the door, while Keaton attempted to force the smoke and heat out of the rear of the house with the water hose. His efforts were in vain.

Keaton came back out the front of the residence and encountered two black men standing at the bottom of the front steps. They asked the fireman, "Did she get out?"

Keaton told the men that "she" had come out of the house when the firemen had first arrived. He pointed to the woman with rollers in her hair standing about fifty feet away and said, "There she is."

"That's not her!" one of the men explained.

The firemen quickly turned and reentered the house. He yelled out, "Is anybody here!" He got no response. When he went back out the front door, a man standing at the bottom of the steps told Keaton that his mother was in the house and that she was in the first bedroom on the right.

Keaton went back inside but could not reach the bedroom because of the heat and smoke.

Two emergency medical technicians wearing air-packs entered with Keaton and made their way to the southwest bedroom. Keaton could now see a woman's legs and told one tech to call for an ambulance. Assisted by the other tech, Keaton carried the unconscious woman outside. He saw blood on her face. When the ambulance arrived, several firefighters assisted ambulance personnel with placing the victim on the cot.

Keaton said that as they lifted the victim, her head fell back, and when he placed his hand under her head he could feel a large opening or crease in her skull. He removed his hands after placing her on the cot and both of them were bloody.

After assisting the victim, the fireman was advised that her nephew might be in the back bedroom. Keaton entered the house once again wearing an air-pack and made a search. He found no one else inside.

Keaton returned to the woman's bedroom and saw blood and hair at the foot of the bed. A bunch of clothes on the floor was piled almost as high as the bed. Leaning against the dresser was a double-bladed axe. Its blade was covered with blood and hair.

The fireman said that he continued moving through the house by dropping to his knees in order to breathe better.

While he was crawling through the living room he also saw a hatchet on the couch. This hatchet did not appear to have any stains on the blade or the handle.

Local bystanders informed police that one Leo L. Willis was the victim's nephew. He had been seen walking west on New Route 13 at 6:15 p.m. Police began a search for him.

When detectives returned to the police station, they received a call from a Marion resident saying that Willis had returned to the fire-damaged house. Detectives went to the residence and found him hiding in the attic. A friend of his talked him into coming down. He was then transported to the Marion PD for questioning.

At 11:23 p.m. on July 14, Detective Wiseman and DCI Special Agent Greg Geittman interviewed Leo L. Willis. Willis said that he, Madeline, and another relative had eaten together just before noon. Then he'd gone to a local store, picked up some orange juice, and returned home.

He said that Madeline and the other relative started to ask him a lot of questions. Why didn't he eat more? What was he thinking about? Then they began to talk about him, so he went to bed.

He was startled awake by a smoke alarm going off. He got up, changed his pajamas for some street clothes, got some cigarettes, and left the house through the front door. Then he ran across town to a friend's home.

Detectives asked him where Madeline Willis had been when he left the house. He responded, "I don't know."

The lawmen had observed bloodstains on Willis's pants. They asked him where the blood had come from.

"Oh, do I have blood on my pants?" he responded.

Realizing that they were going to get nowhere with the questioning, the detectives placed Leo Willis under arrest and transported him to the Williamson County Jail. While he was being booked, they took his clothes into evidence.

At 8:00 a.m. the following day, Technician Cooper met with detectives at the victim's home and resumed the crime scene processing. Additional photographs were taken of the interior. A white towel and a pink plastic waste basket were collected from the southwest bedroom, marked, and placed into evidence.

At 10:30 a.m., Cooper headed for the hospital to attend the autopsy of Madeline Willis. The postmortem examination was performed by Dr. A. S. Thompson shortly after.

The pathologist determined that death had been caused by the savage cutting wounds to the back of the victim's head and neck—her spinal cord had experienced massive bleeding.

The case investigators continued their neighborhood canvass. One relative told them that he'd had breakfast at the Willis home about nine o'clock in the morning. He said that he and Madeline had spent the morning in the back yard. At about two o'clock in the afternoon, she'd gone back into the house to prepare the next meal. At that time, Leo was just getting out of bed. When the meal was finished, said the relative, Madeline asked Leo if he wanted something to eat. Leo didn't answer. According to the relative, Leo had not eaten with his family for more than a month. He would go to the store, buy food, and return to his bedroom and eat his meal by himself.

The relative told the police that he himself ate dinner and then went back to his own home where he took some required medicine and lay down to rest. He was awakened later by someone knocking on his back door. He went outside, heard sirens, and thought that someone had set fire to a house just north of Madeline's. Then he realized that it was Madeline's house burning and he ran to the back door, but he was unable to get inside.

He turned and ran though the garage to the front door. There was too much smoke for him to enter, so the relative got down on his hands and knees to see if he could spot Madeline. Unable to see her, he went around to Leo's bedroom and banged on the window. There was no response.

Now the kinsman ran to Madeline's bedroom window. He got an old tire to stand on so he could see into her window. He pulled the screen off and could see Madeline lying on the bed with her head near the window. She was face down with her right arm slightly extended above her head. The relative said that he then told a fireman that she was still inside the residence.

He also said that the last time he'd seen Leo was when he left Madeline's residence. Madeline had told him that she had gone to sleep in her chair in the living room on occasions, and when she woke up, Leo would be standing over her. The relative said that Madeline would sleep with her clothes off only when she was by herself. Moreover, he'd heard that Madeline was carrying a pistol for protection against Leo.

The relative said that Leo thought Madeline should take better care of him, and as a result, he did not like her anymore. The kinsman also told police that Leo Willis had a history of mental problems.

Next, the police questioned a neighbor. He said that he'd seen Leo only once during the day—at about 1:30 p.m. Leo was in the garage of the Willis residence. Then he went to a small building near the garage and returned to the residence.

At about 8:00 p.m., the neighbor was sitting in his carport when he noticed smoke coming from the Willis residence. He ran there and tried to get in through both the front and back doors, but the smoke stopped him.

Then he went to Madeline's bedroom window, where he found Madeline's relative standing on a tire and trying to see Madeline. The relative pulled the screen off the window and stood on the tire. Then, he fell back, yelling, "Oh my God!"

A friend interviewed by detectives said that he'd received a call that the house was on fire and that Madeline was injured. He went to the scene where an acquaintance told him that Madeline was dead and Leo could not be found. He decided to drive around himself to see if he could spot the man.

When another friend found Leo before the police arrived, Leo told him the house had apparently caught fire and that he came to the friend's residence because he had no place else to go. Told that Madeline was hurt, Leo said he hadn't seen her before he'd left the residence.

As they walked toward the patio of the residence while waiting for the police, the friend said that Leo was "shaking all over." He told Leo that an axe had been found in the house near Madeline and he asked Leo if he'd hit her with it. Leo replied that he woke up and the house was on fire, so he just ran out of the house. He added that Madeline was mad at him.

The acquaintance then told Leo that his Aunt Madeline did not show any emotion or surprise. Leo just sat and shook all over. The friend told probers he did not believe that Leo understood that Madeline was dead.

Continuing, the witness said that ever since Leo had gone into the U.S. Navy his personality had changed completely. He was very quiet and removed from the rest of his surroundings and frequently would not converse with anyone.

He said that during the fall of 1983, Leo Willis had been arrested and sent to the Alton Mental Health Center. A psychological evaluation had been done on him and Leo remained there from December 1983 to March 1984.

Another neighbor told police that it did not surprise her that Leo had killed Madeline because there had been "bad blood" between the two since 1979. The witness said that Leo and his aunt had a good relationship until other relatives had moved into the area. Leo, Madeline, and the other relatives began having financial troubles, and Leo thought that his aunt was always siding with the others. He even accused his aunt of stealing money from him to give to them.

In the summer of 1982, the woman friend was visiting with Leo, who was in the Navy at the time. On one occasion, Leo told her to watch how people were talking about him and making fun of him. The friend indicated to Leo that there wasn't anyone making fun of him, but it didn't seem to matter. A short time later, Leo went AWOL.

After Leo came home, he had changed considerably. According to the woman, he was no longer a nice, polite person, but a very angry man. He told her that he could hear voices telling him what to do. She said that Madeline was afraid of Leo. She kept a gun for protection from her nephew and was afraid to go to bed because she didn't know what Leo might do to her. As a result, Madeline often slept in a chair in the living room.

The detectives next move was to question a former schoolmate of the nephew's. The man said that Leo was into body language, meaning that if you moved your hand a certain way it meant some type of harm would come to you. According to the schoolmate, Leo had been raised very close to white people and did not seem to accept black culture very well. The man had not seen Leo since Leo had been sent to the mental health center in 1983.

Deputy Sheriff Bill Johnson of the Williamson County Sheriff's Department was questioned next. He had known Leo in high school. The deputy knew of no problems that Leo might have had while in school. Leo seemed to be level-headed and didn't pick fights or cause trouble.

While working on communications one evening in October or November 1983, the deputy recalled an incident involving Leo. According to Johnson, Leo came to the sheriff's office at approximately 1:00 a.m.

He told Johnson that someone in the Navy wanted to kill him and that someone was also going to kill Madeline Willis.

The deputy called Madeline and she told him that she was scared of Leo. Meanwhile, Leo did not believe that the deputy was talking with Aunt Madeline. It was Johnson's opinion that Leo was, or had been, using drugs. Johnson said he thought that Leo needed mental help and, in fact, he said, Leo had requested help.

The deputy contacted a mental health counselor. She talked with Leo over the phone and concluded that he was using drugs.

Johnson said that Leo was bound and determined to go home. While the deputy was getting a blanket for Leo, who was dressed in gym shorts, Leo told him twice that he heard voices. The deputy gave him the blanket and that was the last time he saw Leo.

The investigation continued with the questioning of an old friend of the victim's. According to her, she had last talked with Madeline Willis on Friday, July 13. At that time, the friend indicated, she had taken the victim to a local grocery store. Leo had been with them. As they were returning home from the store, they stopped at a yard sale. Leo got out of the car and started walking down the street. His aunt told him that they would take him home, but he walked on without responding.

As they were returning home, Madeline told her friend that Leo wanted to go to Michigan to see his relatives, but she wanted him to take treatment first. Madeline further explained that her nephew had quit eating for approximately three weeks and would not talk. The friend told police that Madeline had taken Leo to Jefferson Barracks about two weeks ago and that he spoke only one time.

Leo did alright for a while, but then he started walking late at night. On one particular occasion, Madeline had told her, she woke up and Leo was standing over her. She told him to get out of her face. The victim said that her nephew would often just stare at her.

One witness told police that she and the victim were talking about guns one day and that Madeline did own a small hand gun. The friend had noticed the gun in Madeline's pocket of her smock top on several occasions.

Madeline did most of her sleeping in a chair in the living room. She would fall asleep while watching television and wake up early in the morning. The friend told officers that the reason the victim had all her clothes in the bedroom was so that she could separate the summer clothes from the winter clothes.

Another friend of the victim's said that he had probably spoken to Madeline about three weeks ago, when she'd called him and asked if he could furnish transportation to the Jefferson Barracks. The victim told him that she was trying to get a doctor to look at her nephew because she was alarmed at the way he had been acting the last few months.

He told the detectives that Madeline normally kept her personal or family problems to herself. He could never remember a time when she related any of her personal problems to him.

Probers interviewed a neighbor who had spoken with Leo Willis just a few days before the murder. According to her, Leo did not appear to care about anything. He told her during their conversation that his father was the "twelfth devil." She said that she was not surprised at all to hear that Madeline Willis had been murdered and that Leo was the alleged perpetrator.

Police ended their canvass by interviewing a local bartender. He said that, about three months ago, Leo Willis was in a bar drinking. For no apparent reason, he grabbed a customer around the throat and began choking him. Realizing that he was not joking around and about to do great bodily harm to the customer, the bartender pulled a handgun, pointed it at Willis and ordered him to turn the man loose.

Just before the incident took place, said the barkeep, Willis was playing the jukebox and dancing alone, as well as talking to himself while he was listening to the music and dancing. The bartender had not seen Leo since that incident.

Meanwhile, Technician Cooper received the test results of the evidence taken from the crime scene. The bedspread, Madeline's pink top, the curtain from the window in the southwest bedroom, the double-bladed axe, Leo's pullover shirt from the bed in the southeast bedroom, the pink fitted sheet from the southeast bedroom, and Leo's pants taken from him at the police station—all these had been found to have human blood on them.

The blood analysis indicated that Madeline Willis had Type "O" blood and Leo Willis had type "A" blood. As a result, the blood on the bedspread and the sheer curtain in Madeline's bedroom and the pink fitted sheet from Leo's bedroom, as well as his pants, indicated that the blood could have come from Madeline Willis, but not from Leo Willis.

Leo Willis was given a psychiatric examination on September 3, 1984.

A longitudinal study of the material elicited from Leo Willis indicated that, although he was able to relate for brief periods of time in a rational, coherent manner to a question or problem presented to him, he quickly became tangential and irrelevant. His association processes were loosely organized and, in fact, at times, disorganized. He appeared, according to the doctor, to be living autistically. The conclusion was that Leo Willis had a major mental illness present and active. The diagnosis was schizophrenia, undifferentiated and chronic.

The doctor said that Willis knew there were charges against him and was able to list them fairly accurately. In addition, Leo believed the charges were serious and followed the word serious with the words "prison chair." On the other hand, according to the doctor, Willis could not appropriately cooperate in his defense. This was based upon the fact that Willis was found to be largely tangential and producing autistic-type statements that had nothing to do with the issues at hand. There was even an unpredictability about how he would be able to handle himself in a court situation. Therefore, the doctor found Leo Willis unfit to stand trial.

The First Circuit Court in Williamson County, Illinois, found Leo Willis unfit to stand trial and he was transported to a state mental institution. After several months of treatment, however, the court reversed its decision. On September 16, 1985, the First Circuit Court in Williamson County, Illinois, found Leo Willis guilty, but mentally ill, of the murder of Madeline Willis and guilty, but mentally ill, of arson. The defendant received sixty-five years for the murder and seven years for arson. Leo Willis is now serving that time in Menard Prison in Chester, Illinois.

Case 4

Bizarre Sex Murder

Ron Hicks
July 2, 1985

Harrisburg, Illinois

On July 3, 1985, the temperature was a stifling ninety-six degrees and the humidity was close to 100 percent. It was a typical summer day in Southern Illinois, unpleasant though it was.

For the Hicks family, the past twenty-four hours had been anything but typical. In the early afternoon, a relative entered the Harrisburg Police Department and reported that six-foot, 150-pound, thirty-two-year-old Ronald Dean Hicks had been missing since the day before.

He was described as having black hair and brown eyes. The relative reported that one of Hick's children and a neighbor boy saw Mr. Hicks pull into their driveway on West Raymond Street at around 6:00 p.m. and then back out of the driveway and head east. He was alone.

The victim did not report to work on July 3 at the Chevrolet garage and had not been located. He was wearing a light-blue shirt with a cloth name tag over the left pocket, dark-blue pants, and steel-toed work boots.

A family member said that there were no clothes missing from their home, and they believed that he had about $100 on him when he left.

The communications radio logs indicated that a truck registered to Ronald D. Hicks had been located by a city patrolman the night before. The truck was located near the animal control building on Feasel Street. Since there seemed to be nothing unusual about it, the information was logged and forgotten.

The officer assigned to the case, Assistant Chief Dee Pelhank, and several other officers conducted a search of the vehicle, the area around the dog pound, and the city barn near the location of the victim's truck.

75

The keys were missing from the vehicle, but there appeared to be no foul play. The search of the area was fruitless.

Pelhank obtained a list of friends and relatives of the family and began contacting each.

The victim's employer said that the victim had clocked out at 5:18 p.m., hung around the garage until about 5:30 p.m., and then left. He saw nothing unusual about Hick's behavior.

None of the other people interviewed had seen the victim.

The investigator then canvassed all the local bars. A bartender remembered seeing Hicks between 5:30 p.m. and 6:00 p.m. She served him one beer. He drank it and then left. He was alone at the time.

Pelhank was baffled. Hicks had been seen by three different people between 5:30 p.m. and 6:00 p.m. and then vanished! Harrisburg is a small mining town with a population of around twelve thousand. Rumors were rampant. The pressure was on.

Pelhank contacted the Saline County Sheriff's Department for assistance. On July 8, the two departments, using motorized trail bikes and a three-wheeler, conducted a four-hour search of a five-mile area inundated with thick vegetation and strip mines in, around, and south of the location where the victim's truck had been found. Once again, they came up dry.

Three weeks passed and not a shred of evidence hinted at the whereabouts of Hicks. Pelhank decided to contact a psychic. What did he have to lose?

He called a well-known psychic from Connecticut. All he got out of his mouth was, "I have a missing person," and she began to talk.

"There is definitely a truck involved," she said. "I am in the truck. Then I get out. I am talking to a lady here, a lady with light brown hair. The longer I am in my truck, the madder I get. My head hurts, and it feels like I am being taken out of the truck. Uh, I feel like, uh, I keep seeing a, uh, hilly terrain.

"The next thing I know is I am having a hard time breathing, and now I am making the sign of a cross. I hear gunshots. I see a cowboy hat. I see a green car, an older car. There must be an old gate there or maybe some boards there that buffer that water.

"An old building flashes through my mind—an old building, dilapidated, no paint. It smells funny, like someone threw sewage or dead animals or something like that."

The information did not help the detective, but he couldn't shake her comment about the truck and the gunshots. He had not given her any information about Hicks; yet, her first comment was about the truck.

After a week passed and he still had no knew information, Pelhank called the psychic again. Again, before he could give any information about the victim, she began to ramble.

"There is a railroad track or trestle close by there. About a hundred yards. Go there. There's where the coon hunters always run their dogs. There's a path. Go down that path, right along there is where—there you ought to smell something. There's where we ought to come up with something."

The detective meditated. Even if she were right, it would be like looking for a needle in a haystack. There were hundreds of miles of railroad tracks and dozens of trestles in the area. The officer felt helpless. With no leads, he had pulled his last card—the deck was now empty, and still he had no clues of the missing man.

Three months passed before the police got a break. It was on November 2, 1985, at 11:35 a.m. Communications Officer JoAnn Schmid received a call from a local resident. He informed her that he had discovered a body in the northeast section of the county.

Directions were given to Schmid and Detective Burgrabe and they met the caller at his residence. The caller took Burgrabe to the scene which was two hundred yards across the Saline County line in Williamson County. As the detective passed an empty wood-frame two-story house with a dilapidated unattached garage, he walked down a deer path and noticed a railroad trestle about 150 yards. He couldn't help but remember the familiar description given by the psychic.

About seventy feet down the path, the detective came upon the body. One look was all it took for Burgrabe to realize it was the skeletal remains of a human being. The remains were scattered along the path for about fifteen to twenty feet. Mixed with the bones was a pair of steel-toed lace-type boots that had been chewed or torn away until all that remain was the sole, heel, and the steel toe covered with the leather-type material. There was a pair of pants and a brass-type metal buckle with an "R" in raised letters. The pants were blue and still on a leg bone. A blue shirt with bloodstains lay among the bones.

Detective Burgrabe requested assistance from Crime Scene Technician Jerry Barnes of the Illinois State Police. He arrived at the scene at 1:10 p.m.

The officers began processing the crime scene by photographing the bones and surrounding area. Burgrabe cataloged three locations on film and marked the bags of evidence as each item was collected. The search turned up two small metal articles to the upper left where the body had apparently been lying. The two slugs were found among bones and finger-nails from one or possibly both hands. The hands appeared to be high on the right side of the body. Both bullets were lying above ground and within inches of each other.

After all the bone fragments were collected, the soil where the body had apparently lain was inspected to a depth of approximately two inches, but nothing else was found. An inspection of the skull showed no damage; however, several other bones appeared to have been chewed by animals. The officers cleared the crime scene at 4:00 p.m.

Burgrabe contacted the Harrisburg PD to inform them about the skel-etal remains found. He also described at length the other evidence found at the scene.

On November 5, at 12:15 p.m., Crime Scene Technician Barnes, De-tective Burgrabe, and Detective Pelhank met at the Williamson County Sheriff's Department. The detectives were sure they had the remains of Ron Hicks, but positive identification had to be made. Pelhank provided dental records to the Technician.

On November 4, at 9:32 p.m., V.A. Beadle, M.D., examined the skull, lower jaw, and dental charts and positively identified the victim as Ronald Dean Hicks.

One of the officers contacted a realty company in Harrisburg to verify the owner of the property. The owner was contacted by phone, informed of the incident, and asked for permission to drain the sewage lagoon for possible evidence. The owner gave permission, and the officers drained the pond for possible evidence. None was found.

On November 4, 1985, police began an elimination process of sus-pects. A close family member to Hicks was contacted first and agreed to take a polygraph examination. Saline County Chief Deputy Miller and Assistant Chief Pelhank conducted the examination.

The officers began by asking about the events that took place on July 2, 1985, the day Hicks was reported missing. The question-and-answer session went as follows:

Were you present when Ron Hicks was shot?
No.
Did you help or plan to have Ron Hicks shot?

No.

Do you know who shot Ron Hicks?

No.

Do you know of anyone who might be mad at Ron Hicks?

None that I know of.

Was he involved sexually with anyone else?

Well. A time or two, I thought he was.

What made you think that?

The relative squirmed slightly in her chair, paused for a moment. She then began to explain that for a period of time she and Ron Hicks had been involved in a swinger's group. She indicated that sometimes she and Ron Hicks had sex with other couples and sometimes she had sex with another man and Ron Hicks at the same time. They had not been involved with the group for about a year, but she provided the detectives with the names of the people and couples she had been involved with at the time. The relative indicated that as far as she knew, the victim had no recent contact with any group members nor did she believe any of them would have had any motive to murder him.

An hour and a half passed. The interview was about to end. "I don't know of anything else tonight. Anything you can think of?"

"Yes! This–what I was trying to figure out was all these things with this psychic—the green car, the little man. How in the world could a little man handle Ron? That's just, you know…"

"The green car, I can think of three people I know who have a green car, and the police department has already got that. They all have older green cars, but Bud Sullivan's car is about a 1978, and the other ones are all older."

"Well, you can't put a whole lot of stock in that. That was just a psychic, you know. Maybe it's valid, maybe it's not," said Pelhank.

"We aren't going to solve this case by that psychic," muttered the relative.

For the next several days, officers interviewed the people the relative indicated were in the swingers' club. One person stated that he and his wife had a marital dispute and his wife moved in with Hicks. While he was visiting his wife and children, a relative brought out nude photos of Ron Hicks and members of the swingers club.

Also on one specific occasion, his wife, several swinger members, and Ron went to Evansville for one evening and rented a motel room. They had sexual intercourse in front of his wife. She had told her husband that she did not participate. The husband indicated that he and his wife had worked out their problems and had not been in contact with the Hicks family for about a year.

The wife was interviewed and verified her husband's story. She also stated that she had not been involved in the sexual activity.

A neighbor was questioned and indicated that she visited the Hicks. She said that on occasion, there were problems; but other than that, things seemed to be okay.

Also, she said that on one occasion Ron had asked her to join the swingers' club. The neighbor declined. According to her, two or three males a day would come by the home. The neighbor stated that she recognized only one of the male subjects who was a regular.

He said that he'd first met Ron Hicks through his car service and that he had met one of the close relatives before Ron was introduced to him by a mutual friend.

Officers had conducted an extensive canvass for the past five days. Although the activities of the Hickses were somewhat bizarre, there seemed to be no motive for the murder of the victim.

They turned to the Division of Forensic Services and Identification of the Illinois State Police. Through visual, microscopic, and chemical testing, the blue-gray shirt did not reveal the presence of any smoke powder residue or lead wipe. Although there were two holes in the side of the back panel, and one in the bottom of the front left panel, the lack of smoke powder residue determination of the bullet were not suitable for microscopic comparison.

The officers were frustrated. They had exhausted all leads. Still no motives. Still no suspects. They were back to square one.

Seven months later, on May 23, 1986, Detective Burgrabe received a call from Chief Deputy Miller. Miller indicated that he needed to meet with Burgrabe because he had possibly come up with some pertinent information in the Hicks case. In mid-afternoon, Burgrabe met with Miller and Pelhank at the Saline County Sheriff's office. The officers told Burgrabe that a reliable source had advised that a local citizen and cab driver by the name of Bud Sullivan needed to be interviewed because he possibly had valuable information about the Hicks homicide.

Miller had already asked Sullivan to come in for an informal interview. During the interview, Sullivan told police that he had dated Myla

Ring from rural Harrisburg for the past year and a half. Further, he was a good friend of Ron Hicks and had introduced Myla to Hicks. Later, the two had dated, he added. Sullivan indicated that Myla told him that she had shot Ron Hicks on July 2, 1985, but didn't say why.

When the interview ended, Miller informed Burgrabe not to put substantial credibility in Sullivan's statement until further interviews could be conducted with Myla Ring.

The officers contacted Myla Ring and told her that everyone with prior contacts with Hicks was being interviewed. Myla readily agreed to be interviewed. Officers informed her that she was in no way compelled to speak with them, but she indicated that she wanted to help in any way she could.

Chief Miller, alert for reactions from Ring, started the interview with the comment, "We have information that you have dated Hicks."

Ring quickly responded, "Bud Sullivan must have told you that."

"Yes, he did," Miller answered.

Myla continued. "I dated Bud for about a year and a half. He introduced me to Hicks. They were good friends. Bud told me about Ron's swingers' group. I never participated with the group. My only dealings with Hicks was when my car was being worked on and usually Bud took the car in and picked it up. He was extremely jealous. Didn't want me around any men, especially Hicks…Bud was so jealous that he has on numerous occasions beat me for just looking at or talking innocently to another man."

"Are you still dating Bud?" Burgrabe asked.

"No, we broke up about two weeks ago," she said with a giggle. "I'm going with someone else now."

"Has that caused any problems?" inquired Miller.

Myla laughed, "It sure has! You should know that. You guys have been out to his home a couple of times when Bud's been causing trouble."

Miller and Burgrabe locked eyes. Then Miller turned and asked, "Do you think that Bud could kill someone?"

"Yes," she responded, brushing her hand through her light-brown hair, "especially if he is in one of his jealous rages!"

The officers realized they were on to something and decided to call Bud Sullivan in for an interview.

At 6:00 p.m., Sullivan arrived at the police station and realized that his statement was to be a voluntary interview and that he was not compelled to say anything.

Bud said that he understood his rights, but needed to get something off his mind that he had suppressed for too long. He said that he had initially met Myla Ring at a party. A few days after the party, he went on, Myla Ring called him and asked him to go out. On their first date, Sullivan picked her up, brought a twelve-pack of beer, and drove to the Shawnee National Forest.

There, Ring allegedly told Sullivan about an armed robbery she and a male friend had committed in Chester, Illinois, at a Clark Station on July 7, 1986. She then told him if he did not consent to sexual relations with her, she would say he was the one with her during the robbery.

Sullivan submitted not wanting to be implicated to an armed robbery. He explained that Myla held this over him during the entire relationship. Further, that because of their age difference and Ring's constant craving for sex, he got to the point that he was unable to handle her sexual needs.

Sullivan introduced Myla to Ron Hicks hoping to take some of the pressure off himself. Sullivan indicated that Myla had at one point had sex with Hicks and said that Hicks was a pig. But she continued to date him. Sullivan told the detectives that the day after Hicks disappeared, Myla came to his home and said that she had killed Ron Hicks.

She allegedly told Sullivan that she parked at the Harrisburg City Park near the swimming pool on July 2, 1985, and that Ron picked her up in his pickup truck. They drove about twelve miles west of Harrisburg onto coal company property, an area Ring knew because her father worked for the coal company and had taken her out there on numerous occasions.

They stopped at an abandoned residence and parked in the driveway. Ring supposedly told Hicks she knew a good place out back behind the abandoned residence. According to Sullivan, Ring told him that Ron and she walked out back. She told him she had to urinate and asked him to look away.

Sullivan said that Hicks turned his back on Ring, who stepped behind a tree. There she took a .22-caliber pistol out of her purse, stepped out from behind the tree and shot Hicks. Hicks ran for about fifty feet and fell.

She then walked up to Hicks who was kneeling with his hands clasped together over his head and emptied her gun into him. Myla walked to the truck, got in, and drove to the county highway garage.

The next day, she related the story to Sullivan and told him if he said anything about it, she would implicate him in the murder as well as the armed robbery.

Officers asked Sullivan, "What was Ring's motive?"

He answered, "She didn't say and I didn't ask."

"Would you submit to a polygraph?"

"I'll have to consult my attorney, but probably not."

He was asked, "Would you meet and engage Myla Ring in a similar conversation on the above admission?"

He replied, "I will."

As Sullivan left the police station, and the detectives informed him that they would be in touch with him again. Meanwhile, officers checked with the Chester Police Department to see if an armed robbery had occurred on the date indicated by Sullivan. Also, the officers began to dissect the statements of Ring and Sullivan to determine whose story was viable.

Officers confirmed that an armed robbery had occurred as Sullivan had indicated, and on May 27, 1985, at 11:35 a.m., they arrested Myla Ring and brought her to the Saline County Sheriff's Department.

Upon arriving for questioning, Myla surprised the officers. Extremely emotional, she turned and looked at the officers and said, "I shot him."

Burgrabe, realizing that she was referring to Hicks, immediately read Myla her rights. Myla then signed a Miranda Rights waiver form and agreed to give a verbal statement of the shooting death of Ron Hicks.

Myla began her story by informing the detective that she had first dated Bud Sullivan on July 16, 1984. Sullivan had not formally introduced her to Ron Hicks. She had known him, she related, because Bud had taken her car to Hicks for repair work on several occasions.

In May 1985, Bud and Myla had a fight. Two friends of hers suggested that she should go out with someone to make Bud jealous. She thought of Ron Hicks because of what Bud had told her and decided to go to his garage and asked Ron to go out with her. Hicks indicated that he would go but couldn't leave until 5:00 p.m. Myla told Hicks to meet her at a store which was only a block and a half from Bud's house. They met and drove to a secluded mine road.

There Myla performed oral sex with Ron Hicks. An hour later, they were back at the store where Ron dropped Myla off and then drove to his house. Myla waited around for fifteen minutes and her friend picked her up and took her home.

Shortly after she got home, Bud called her, and she went back to his house. She felt guilty and wanted to tell him what took place. Although she told him that she had gone out with Ron, she didn't tell him about the sexual relations, partly because she didn't want to hurt him but mostly out of fear of a jealous rage.

Bud was suspicious and decided to talk to Ron about it. He went to Ron's house, then returned home about an hour later. Bud was depressed and told Myla that Ron had told him the whole story. Bud wanted to drive around for a while, so they got a six-pack and went to the lake.

He began talking about how she had done the same things his wife had. He threatened to kill himself and Myla. He said he could not handle the cheating.

"Days passed and Bud's depression got no better," Myla said. She stated that he constantly reminded her about her cheating on him. He finally told her that she had to dispose of Ron so he could live and not have to look across the street at Ron's house knowing that Ron was over there and that Myla had gone out with him.

He began to threaten Myla with a .22 caliber pistol. Bud set a time limit. Ron Hicks had to be dead by July 6. There was no significance to the July 6 date according to Myla. Bud simply conjured up the date in his head. Myla finally agreed to kill Ron Hicks for Bud, and they began to make plans.

They decided that the location would be an abandoned house near the coal company about twelve miles west of town. Myla knew the area well since her father had been an employee of the coal company and had often taken her with him when she was small.

Bud instructed her to get a .22-caliber pistol that had belonged to her deceased father. Following the plan Bud then bought ammunition and practiced for several days with the weapon.

The plan was set! Myla was to ask Ron to go out, coax him to the location, and then shoot him. She said she went to Ron's garage and asked him to go out on July 2. Ron agreed and between 6:30 p.m. and 7 p.m., Bud dropped her off at the nursing home two blocks away from the park. She walked to the pool and Ron picked her up.

Myla told him she had a place for them to go, and they headed west on Route 13. A few minutes later, Myla and Ron pulled into the driveway of the abandoned home. "Let's go out back," Myla allegedly said, and both exited the truck and walked down a path for a few hundred feet. Myla told

Ron to turn around while she urinated. Ron did as he was told, while Myla knelt and fumbled for her gun.

She said she then turned around and fired a shot, striking Ron in the upper right shoulder of his back. Ron took off running and fell to the ground. Myla calmly walked up to him and emptied the gun in Hick's body.

Quickly, she told the probers, she went to Hick's truck and put on a brown wig and glasses as instructed by Sullivan to disguise herself in case anyone saw her driving the truck. She took back roads back to Harrisburg and parked the truck at the county highway department.

Bud picked her up and then drove to his house. Bud took the gun, the brown wig and glasses. He was to burn them, but Myla indicated she had seen the wig and glasses no more than two weeks ago.

The officers ended the interview, charged Myla with murder and immediately prepared to secure a search warrant for Bud Sullivan's residence.

Two hours later, officers arrived at a white trailer located on West Sloan Street in Harrisburg, Illinois, the residence of Charles "Bud" Sullivan. Officers presented him with a search warrant. The residence was cluttered with boxes and stacks of pornographic magazines. In one corner, a jar with a white four-month old fetus floated in clear formaldehyde. Sullivan later claimed his ex-wife had a miscarriage and that try as he may, he could not part with his child.

The officers took a black, three-drawer metal filing cabinet, a brown wig, a pair of eyeglasses, some .22-caliber bullets, and a set of truck keys belonging to Ron Hicks. Officers arrested Sullivan for conspiracy to commit murder.

Myla Ring and Charles Sullivan were arraigned in the First Circuit Court in Williamson County on June 13, 1986. Myla was charged with the murder of Ronald Hicks, and Sullivan was charged with conspiracy to commit murder.

Myla was assigned a defense attorney. Within a month, the attorney came forward to the prosecutor and informed him that Myla had not committed the murder, that Bud Sullivan had pulled the trigger. The crime was committed as she had told the police except that Sullivan was hiding behind the tree when Myla and Hicks walked down the path. Then Myla told Hicks to turn around while she was to relieve herself, and Sullivan stepped from behind the tree and shot Hicks. She told the police that she confessed to the crime because she feared for her life, because she was afraid Bud might kill her.

The prosecutor, Charles Garnati, and the defense attorney agreed to a reduction of Myla's charges to concealment of a homicide and to go lighter on her sentence if she would plead guilty to the charges and testify against Sullivan in his trial.

On November 11, 1986, physical evidence and testimony by Myla Ring was presented at a jury trial of Charles Bud Sullivan for the murder of Ronald Hicks. The twelve-person jury found him guilty.

Charles Bud Sullivan was sentenced to life in prison on April 27, 1987, and is now serving that sentence in the Menard Penitentiary, in Chester, Illinois. Myla Ring was sentenced to five years and served that sentence in the Dwight Prison for Women in northern Illinois.

Case 5

The Spouse Murder

Cathy Hightower
November 21, 1985

Marion, Illinois

At approximately 7:00 p.m. on November 21, 1985, a resident on Chestnut Street in Marion, Illinois received a call from a family member. While on the phone, he heard what sounded like a gunshot.

"Did you hear that?" He asked the family member. "It sounded like some gun went off."

He ended his phone conversation, then walked over to the window and looked out. Everything seemed peaceful and quiet so the resident thought nothing more about it.

The Marion Police Department received a call exactly thirty-six minutes later. The male intoxicated voice reported that a person had been shot.

Patrolman Jerald Kobler was dispatched and arrived at the scene at 7:39 p.m. He walked to the front door and knocked. Billy G. Hightower Jr. opened the door, and Officer Kobler stepped inside.

"She is out back in the van," Hightower muttered.

At that time, Detective Les Snyder arrived, and the two officers walked to the back of the house with Hightower. They exited the back door, and the first thing that the detective spotted was a long barrel automatic shotgun with a light brown stock. The shotgun was lying on the central air conditioning unit with the barrel facing east.

The officers walked to a brown Dodge van parked in the driveway. From the passenger side of the van, Snyder saw a white female sitting in the passenger seat. The victim, Cathy Hightower, had a hole in the left cheek area of her face. The officer went to the passenger side of the van

87

and noticed that the bullet had exited through the right cheek and then through the passenger window.

The officers scanned the scene for evidence while waiting for the crime scene technician to arrive. Officer Kobler found a piece of skull and a small amount of hair on the concrete about twenty feet from the van. Officer Snyder found a hole in the north wall of the residence along with another piece of skull. The officers conversed and then roped off the crime scene for the Illinois State Crime Lab.

Meanwhile, Chief Ronald Swafford arrived at the scene and was briefed by Detective Snyder. The two detectives went into the house while Kobler guarded the crime scene.

Hightower's attorney had arrived, and he and Hightower were both standing in the living room. The room was filled with the odor of alcohol. Chief Swafford, a friend of Hightower, asked what happened. The attorney advised Hightower not to say anything. Detective Snyder immediately read Hightower the Miranda Rights and told him that he would have to go to the police department for questioning. He was handcuffed and Swafford escorted him to the squad car.

Snyder called on the pack radio and requested that the fire department bring their lighting system so that the scene could be processed. The fireman arrived a short time later and set the floodlights in place.

Crime Scene Technician Jerry Barnes arrived and met with the detectives. Snyder pointed to the brown Dodge van bearing Illinois registration 697506B. Barnes walked to the passenger door and looked inside. The victim was sitting in the right front passenger seat of the van with her right ankle resting on top of her left leg. Her chin was resting on her chest and what appeared to be a gunshot wound had entered the left side of the face and exited the right side of the back of her head.

The right front passenger door was shattered from what appeared to be a trajectory of the projectile after passing through the victim. A discharged shotgun shell was lying on the floor between the driver and the passenger seats. The victim was dressed in a brown and white fur coat, blue sweater, blue jeans, white socks, and white Puma tennis shoes.

Head hair and bone fragments from the victim were scattered on the concrete patio between the van and residence and on the north wall of the residence. Also, there was a hole in the north wall, possibly from the projectile. A Browning 16-gauge, semi-automatic shotgun, serial number X24806, loaded with two rounds, was lying on the air conditioner unit between the van and the north door of the residence.

Barnes photographed the crime scene, then collected, packaged, and marked as physical evidence the Browning 16-gauge shotgun, two shotgun shells removed from the weapon, a discharged 16-gauge shotgun shell, hair from the north wall of the residence, and a possible projectile from the north wall of the den.

The local ambulance service arrived to remove the body and transport it to the local hospital for an autopsy, which was scheduled for the following morning.

At the police station, Billy G. Hightower Jr. and his attorney waited in the squad room for the arrival of the detectives. Hightower wanted a cigarette but was advised that he could not smoke because the police were going to administer a breath test to determine the amount of alcohol the suspect had consumed. He laughed and said: "I've been drinking whiskey since one o'clock." Hightower looked through bloodshot eyes at the officer in the room with him, and said, "You're a big boy. Will you help me if I decide to leave the department?"

"No," Officer Barwick replied, "I can't do that."

"Well, I'm not going anywhere, but if I decided to leave, I have a nine millimeter that will get me out of here."

"The police officer that patted you down must have missed the gun. Do you have that gun on you?"

Hightower shrugged his shoulders. "Well, you don't know, do you?"

The attorney interrupted, "He doesn't have a gun!" Then he reached down, took the suspect's cigarettes and handed them to the officer.

"Nobody can stop me from smoking or leaving this place if I want to go," Hightower blurted.

Chief Swafford walked into the squad room and ordered the officer to take Hightower to the detective's office. Snyder was waiting for the suspect. Both Hightower and his attorney took a seat in front of the officer's desk. Synder read Hightower his Miranda Rights, then asked him if he would waive his rights. Hightower refused to waive his rights and informed the police officer that he had nothing to say.

Snyder then filled out a permission-to-search form and asked Hightower to sign the waiver so the police could do a search of his residence. Again the suspect refused to waive his rights. He also refused to take a breath test.

Snyder placed Billy G. Hightower Jr. under arrest for suspicion of murder. While being processed at Williamson County Jail, Barnes collected hair samples, palm prints, and fingerprints from the suspect.

At nine o'clock the next morning, Pathologist Miles Jones performed the autopsy on Cathy Hightower. The results indicated that the thirty-two-year-old white female was shot with a large caliber weapon at close range. The weapon produced powder burns. The path traveled from the jaw, exiting the brain on the posterior aspect, or left side. Toxicology levels of blood, urine, and bile revealed alcoholic consumption prior to death. It is likely that the woman was in a moderately-inebriated state before death. The cause of death was massive cerebral trauma to the head. Death ensued instantly.

Barnes was informed that the search warrant for the residence had been issued by the court. Barnes immediately returned to the residence and began a crime scene search of the interior of the home.

From the lower drawer of the gun case located in the southeast master bedroom, Barnes collected five boxes of Western Super X 16-gauge, two-and-three-quarters-inch rifle slugs. Three boxes were full and two had two slugs missing. He also collected one Cobra telephone answering system machine VOX remote, serial number 83378098, with attached plug-in power supply which was sitting on the top of the kitchen table.

He submitted the evidence from the crime scene, the evidence from the victim, and the evidence from the suspect to the Bureau of Scientific Services in Carbondale, Illinois, for laboratory analysis.

The probe continued as detectives began a canvass of relatives, friends, and acquaintances. A relative told detectives that she was aware of problems which existed between the victim and suspect. The relative told police that the couple had recently separated and that they had had a number of quarrels.

Concerned for Cathy's safety, the relative warned her against provoking him. She also told detectives that she had contacted Cathy on November 20, 1985, at approximately 8:00 p.m. at a local bar and encouraged her to straighten her life up, take care of her kids, and get a job. Although the relative thought that Cathy was still living with Billy G. Hightower Jr., she found out during the conversation that Cathy was living in a local motel.

Continuing, she told officers that on November 21 at approximately 6:45 p.m., she contacted Cathy at the lounge. Cathy informed the relative that Hightower had been drinking. The relative informed Cathy that Hightower had called and said that Cathy's car was washed, repaired, and that he had two hundred dollars for her. The relative thought that this was just an enticement to get Cathy to go to the residence. Cathy told her that she was still living at the motel. The relative told Cathy to be careful and hung up. She then told police that she did not think that Cathy would go with Hightower that night.

She said that Cathy had asked her for $500 for a lawyer. She said that on the night of the shooting, when she last talked with the victim, she asked her if she was going to use the two hundred dollars Hightower was giving her for the lawyer. She told the relative that she was.

The relative explained to the detectives that on one recent occasion, Cathy went to St. Louis, Missouri, for three days with a boyfriend. Hightower thought that Cathy was going with a group of women, but later found out the truth, she said.

While Cathy was gone, the relative said she received two telephone calls from Hightower. He said that when Cathy came home, he was going to kill her.

"Anything else?" the detectives questioned.

"Well, when Bill and Cathy were first married, Cathy's son was having problems with his lessons. The couple was always picking at him about it, and on one occasion the boy told me that Hightower threatened to shoot him if he didn't do better with his lessons.

"And one other thing, Cathy seemed to not be scared of Bill at all, then on some occasions, she seemed to be horrified of him."

The detectives continued the canvass by questioning another relative. She told police that about a week ago, at the request of another family member, she went to Johnston City to pick up Cathy. Upon their return to Marion, they were going to do Cathy's laundry.

The relative arrived at the motel a little after 11:00 a.m. and knocked on the door of room 5. Cathy opened the door and pulled the relative inside the motel room. She was frightened and said that Bill was following her around and was going to kill her. They put Cathy's laundry in the car and drove to Marion. On the way, Cathy talked about Bill's intent to kill her. She said that he had a gun in his van. The relative noticed her hands shaking as she talked. She continued saying that Bill told her that no one else was going to have her.

Another family member told police that Cathy had come to visit her about three weeks ago on Sunday. Cathy explained to the family member that on Saturday evening before, that she went to Vienna, and that Hightower had stolen her purse out of the car and pulled some wires loose from underneath the hood of the vehicle. She then said that Bill told her that he was going to kill her, then kill himself.

She said that the suspect was going around town telling people what he was going to do. Also, the family member was informed that the suspect was carrying a shotgun in the back of the van.

A co-owner of the local bar where Cathy was last seen was interviewed by the police. She said that she became acquainted with Cathy when she worked at the lounge on a part-time basis for about three weeks. She said Cathy worked until about 4:30 p.m., and that she received a telephone call from Cathy at approximately 6:00 p.m. on the night of the murder. Cathy said that a friend was in the bar and wanted to know if the co-owner wanted to go hunting. The last time she had seen Cathy was on November 20. Cathy had worked the 12:30 p.m. to 4:30 p.m. shift on that day.

The employer advised the police the first time she met Bill Hightower Jr. was when she was married. She said that Cathy told her that she had known Bill for a long time, and, during the early stages of their marriage, Cathy was happy to have a home to go to. Cathy subsequently became disgusted and said she was tired of Bill staying out drinking and coming home drunk. She told her employer that on one occasion Bill had pulled a knife on her and tried to cut her throat. The employer saw the lacerations on Cathy's throat and forearm from the incident.

"How were you notified of Cathy's death?" the detectives inquired.

"I received a telephone call from a friend who said that she had just received a disturbing telephone call from Bill Hightower Jr. He told the neighbor and friend that he had killed Cathy and wanted the friend to come to his house. Her son didn't want her to go to the residence, so not knowing what to do, she called."

The co-owner said that Hightower appeared to be crazy about Cathy and that on one occasion he called while the couple was separated and told the employer he loved Cathy and would do anything for her.

Another employer of Cathy's was questioned. She said that on the night of the murder, she came to the lounge at 4:30 p.m. to clear the cash register for the evening shift. She said that Cathy told her that Bill was in the lounge and pointed him out to her. She asked the victim if he was giving her any trouble. Cathy told her that he had threatened to kill her. She then asked the victim why she didn't call the police and have him removed from the bar. She said that he told her he still loved her.

The co-owner changed the cash register, and Cathy gave her a white sealed envelope containing money. She asked how much was in the envelope and Cathy said that she thought there was about $100. She did not ask where the money came from but rather wrote Cathy's name on the envelope and placed it in the cash register under the money tray.

"Do you still have the envelope?" the officers questioned.

"Yes," she replied, walking to the cash register and opening the drawer. She pulled the envelope out and took it to the officers. The officer opened the white sealed envelope in the presents of the employer and found that the envelope contained $235. Detectives took the money into custody and gave the employer a receipt.

Continuing, she said that Cathy was supposed to go to a friend's house to help fix supper, and she asked Cathy if she wanted a ride.

Cathy asked her husband if he was going to take her to her friend's and he told her he would. She said that she talked with the Hightowers for about five minutes, and they seemed to get along fine.

She called back to the lounge about 5:00 p.m. to see if Cathy had left her friend's yet, and the barmaid told her the Hightowers were still there. The employer said there was no trouble, that they were just sitting there talking.

At approximately 6:15 p.m., Cathy called from the lounge and said that a friend wanted to talk to her. She asked Cathy if she was still going to the friend's and Cathy told her that she was leaving at that time. That was the last time she saw or heard from the victim.

Police then interrogated a barmaid who was working the night of November 21. She said that she had known the victim for about one month (the time that the victim had worked at the lounge). She said that when she arrived at work, Bill and Cathy were sitting at the north end of the bar. They seemed to be getting along. There was no visual indication of any arguments or disagreements taking place. She said that she did not serve a lot of drinks, possibly two or three at the most, and neither of them seemed to be intoxicated.

The couple remained at the lounge for about an hour and a half. She said she did not know the time when they left, but she did say that she was surprised that they left as early as they did. Bill's van was parked in front of the business, and when they left, they did so without saying a word to anyone.

"Did she make any telephone calls?" detectives asked.

"No, not that I saw."

"Did you see him give her any money?"

"No, I didn't. But I did hear him say that he had given her close to three hundred dollars. He made the comment when she paid for the drinks."

"What were they drinking?"

"Cathy was drinking vodka and grapefruit juice. Bill was drinking whiskey and coke."

"Is there anything else that we should know?"

"Well, yes, I gave Cathy a ride back to the motel one night. Cathy told me that she was tired of getting beat up, and that she was not going to live with anyone who would beat or stab her."

The probe continued with an interview of a close acquaintance of Bill Hightower's. She said that at about 7:00 p.m. on November 21, she received a telephone call from Hightower.

"I've shot Cathy!"

"Oh, Bill. No!"

"Have you called the police yet?"

"No. Will you come over?"

"Yes, but only to pacify you. That's all!"

She hung the phone up and told her son what Hightower had said. He didn't want her to go to the residence, and while they were talking, she received another call from Hightower.

"Have you notified the police yet?"

"No, but I have called my mother. You know I should do the same thing to myself that I did to Cathy."

"Now, Bill! You know better than that."

"Would you please come over?"

"Yes," she replied and hung the phone up.

The friend then called the police and reported the incident as an accident because she could not believe that Bill had really done it. She said that Hightower sounded frightened when he called, but didn't sound drunk. Detectives asked what she knew of the Hightower's relationship. She said the couple had a lot of problems but thought that most of the trouble was because of money. She said that she first met Cathy when she started working at the lounge, and also she was friends with other members of Cathy's family.

On the day of the murder, Cathy called twice. The first time was at noon. She wanted to know how her friend's arm was doing since she had injured it and told the friend that she would be off work at 4:30 p.m. and would come over and help her with dinner.

The second time was at 4:30 p.m. when she called to let the friend know that she was off work and would be there shortly. The friend asked if the victim wanted her to come and pick her up, and she said that Bill was at the lounge and told her that he would drive her. "That's the last time I talked with her."

States Attorney Chuck Garnati knew that he had probable cause to file murder charges on Billy G. Hightower Jr., although he still was waiting on the laboratory results of the physical evidence.

On December 6, 1985, the defendant appeared in the First Circuit Court in Williamson County, Illinois, and Judge David Nelson charged Hightower with three counts of murder. Hightower showed no signs of emotion during the hearing but pleaded not guilty to the charges.

On December 10, 1985, the Bureau of Forensic Science, Southern Illinois Forensic Laboratory, submitted the evidence to Barnes.

The discharged shotgun shell that had passed through the victim's head and embedded in the den of the residence was matched with the Browning 16-gauge shotgun found lying on the air conditioner at the crime scene. However, none of the latent prints found on the gun was suitable for comparison.

Blood standards and hair standards found on the slug, patio, and van matched the victim's.

The tape from the Cobra Telephone Answering System indicated that Bill Hightower Jr. made three calls: one to a family member, one to a friend, and one to his attorney. Each time the defendant indicated that he had shot his wife. In his own words, "I blew that bitch away, right through the side glass—I didn't miss this time."

In March 1986, Billy G. Hightower Jr. stood trial in the First Circuit Court in Williamson County, Illinois. The trial lasted for three days, and the twelve-person jury found the defendant guilty of three counts of murder. He was sentenced to forty years and is now serving that sentence in Menard State Prison in Chester, Illinois.

Case 6

Kinfolk Killers

John Hawkins
May 31, 1986

Johnson City, Illinois

Ryan Mocaby
May 23, 1987

Pittsburg, Illinois

W hen you ask someone whom they think of when you say, "Murderer," most often you get answers like, "John Wayne Gacy," or "Gary Gilmore," or "John List," or some other well-known criminal. That is the common myth, but the police officers know well the most sensational murders account for only a small percentage of the homicides that take place in the United States.

The common types of murder usually occur when parties are given and alcohol is involved. The arguments or altercations often involve matters relatively trivial to anyone but those involved. Quarrels over money, over girlfriends, and in bars are common. The FBI estimates 42% of murders follow this pattern.

Family homicides usually involve one spouse killing the other, but on occasion, children are the killers or victims.

While serving as sheriff of Williamson County, I had two such murders—senseless murders—that I will never forget.

The sheriff's office received a call at 2:50 a.m. on May 31, 1986. An ambulance had been dispatched to Parkview Drive in Johnson City, Illinois, in response to a call that someone had been stabbed. Deputies arrived a few minutes later to find a man lying in the front yard of the residence with a blood-soaked towel over his abdomen. As two relatives of the victim attempted to hold the wounded man still until the ambulance arrived, each wiggle of his body sent blood gushing from his left side.

Police were told that the victim, John Hawkins, had been stabbed by his brother, Mark Hawkins, whom the family wanted arrested. They believed that Mark was probably at a friend's house, a couple of houses down the street. Detectives found the suspect at the residence and took a statement from the neighbor. She told the police that Mark Hawkins arrived at her house about 3:00 a.m. He was carrying a six-pack of beer between his legs. He sat quietly for a few minutes, then said, "I just stabbed John."

"You did what?" the neighbor gasped.

"I just stabbed John."

About that time, the deputies knocked at the door. The officers placed Mark Hawkins under arrest and transported him to the police station.

Meanwhile, police returned to the crime scene to continue the investigation. They found three large spots of blood on the kitchen floor in front of the refrigerator and blood smeared on the back door on the west side of the kitchen. A piece of bologna was in the skillet, but police were not able to locate the knife. The area was photographed and blood samples were taken from the kitchen floor. The officers had just finished the crime scene process when they received a call from dispatch. John Hawkins had died while on the operating table.

Detectives continued their investigation with an interview of Mark's girlfriend. She told police that she and Mark had a party that started at approximately six thirty that evening and lasted until about midnight. Sometime after that, John came to the house. He was very intoxicated. She helped one of her friends carry some plates that they had borrowed back to her friend's house. She stayed for a few minutes, then returned home.

As she neared the house, she noticed Mark Hawkins walking away from the house. He seemed to be upset. She asked him what was wrong, and he told her that he would tell her later. She went inside and found some blood on the floor. She thought that John and Mark had gotten into a fistfight. She went to the backyard and found friends trying to help John. That's when she found out that John had been stabbed.

Mark Hawkins told police that John had arrived at his girlfriend's house at about 1:00 a.m. He was carrying a bottle of whiskey and half a six-pack of beer. He tried to pick a fight with several people, but they all ignored him. Then Mark went into the kitchen to make a bologna sandwich. While Mark was cooking the bologna, John came into the kitchen and grabbed his brother by the back of the neck. He shook Mark and said, "You're nothing but a punk."

Mark tried to push his brother away, but John came at him and struck him on the back of the head three times. It was then that Mark picked up the knife and John fell across him. Mark told police that the knife went into John's left side. John grabbed the wound. Mark saw some blood and ran out the back door. He then went to the friend's house where he was arrested.

The evidence and testimony enabled the police to get a murder conviction. Mark Hawkins was sentenced to twenty years at Menard Penitentiary.

The irony of this senseless murder was the attitude of the suspect. He told the police while they were en route to the county jail—before he knew of his brother's death—that he was going to escape and go back to Johnson City and kill his brother. The officer told him that if he tried to escape, the officer would have to do what ever was necessary to restrain him. Mark said, "That's okay! I won't try to escape. I'll wait till I get out of jail, then I'll kill him!"

The second case that comes to mind occurred after an argument over a fish on a holiday weekend family camp out.

Memorial Day weekend had been unusually quiet for the police until 3:22 p.m. on May 23, 1987. Marion Police received a call to report to the emergency room of the local hospital to investigate a stabbing that occurred that day.

A few minutes passed and Officer Steve Cannon walked into the hospital. The first thing the police officer noticed was two men standing outside of the emergency room talking. One man was dressed in blue jeans and was wearing no shirt. Both of his hands, his chest, and his jeans were covered with what appeared to be dried blood. The officer noticed that the man was wearing a leather belt with a stainless steel hunting knife and a black sheath strapped to his right hip.

When the man spotted the officer, he immediately walked over to him and introduced himself as Terelius Mocaby. A strong odor of alcohol smacked the officer in the face. The policeman noticed that Mocaby was having a difficult time maintaining his balance.

The officer reached for the knife and pulled it from the sheath. The blade of the knife contained dried blood. The suspect then stated without being questioned, "That's the knife! That's the knife that stabbed my boy! I did it! I didn't mean to stab my boy! How is he?"

The officer ordered Terelius Mocaby to put his hands on the wall. The officer did a pat-down search to see if the suspect had any other weapons on him. Officer Cannon then handcuffed the suspect. The policeman moved Mocaby into an unoccupied room so that he could be easily guarded.

A few minutes later, the Marion patrolman was joined by Deputy Sheriff Hank Banacky of the Williamson County Sheriff's Department. The officers learned that the incident had occurred north of Pittsburg, Illinois. Deputy Banacky read Terelius Mocaby his Miranda rights and asked the suspect if he understood them. The suspect indicated that he understood his rights and then stated, "Hey, I'm guilty! I did it!"

At approximately 3:38 p.m., the attending doctor reported that he was unable to revive the victim. The victim appeared to have been stabbed once in the heart. Officer Banacky then transported the suspect to the sheriff's department for further questioning.

According to Terelius Mocaby, he and his son Ryan had gone to a farm pond north of Pittsburgh, Illinois, on Friday, May 22, to spend the weekend fishing. Terelius and Ryan had arrived at approximately 6:00 p.m. Both were fishing and everything was fine. They spent the night alone and consumed quite a bit of beer. Father and son woke up around 9:00 a.m. on Saturday, May 23. The remainder of the family arrived at the farm around 10:00 a.m.

The suspect told police that Ryan had caught a large bass weighing possibly five pounds, put the fish on the stringer, and then put the stringer back in the water. Later in the day Ryan was bragging about his catch to family members. He went to the pond to get the fish so he could show it to everyone.

When Ryan pulled the stringer up, the fish was gone. Ryan went into a rage and begun accusing everyone of letting his fish go. This went on for some time. Then Ryan began pushing people.

The family was preparing to have a cookout around a campfire that had just been lit. Mocaby said that Ryan continued yelling at different members of the family. Mocaby said that he had had enough, so he drew his knife, ran over to Ryan, and stabbed him once. The suspect told police that he couldn't remember stabbing his son, but he did remember Ryan running down the hill toward the pond and collapsing.

Mocaby said that Ryan had consumed about a six-pack of beer, but he wasn't drunk because "Ryan could handle his beer!" He further stated that he himself had consumed about eight beers. "Nobody else stabbed him. I did it!"

Six other eyewitnesses were interviewed by Detective Robert Mc-Cluskey, and their statements coincided with the defendant's.

An autopsy was performed on May 23 at the local hospital. The autopsy revealed one stab wound to the victim's lower left chest area. The location wound was five centimeters down from the victim's left nipple and four centimeters to the left of the victim's sternum. The report indicated that it was a very deep wound. There were no other obvious wounds, either offensive or defensive, on the body.

The knife had gone through the chest cavity cartilage between the fifth and sixth ribs, cutting the inner cartilage and severing the sixth rib. The cardiac sac had been punctured and was full of blood. Further, the knife had entered the heart in the right ventricle area, had pierced the right ventricle area, had pierced the right ventricle chamber, and had gone through the heart puncturing the right side of the diaphragm. Death was from massive internal bleeding from the heart.

Terelius Mocaby was arraigned in the First Circuit Court in June 1987 and charged with the stabbing death of his son, Ryan Mocaby. Although the defendant had told police on several occasions that he had stabbed his son, and six eyewitnesses had confirmed the defendant's story, Mocaby pleaded not guilty and requested a trial by jury. On March 1, 1988, Terelius Mocaby, after seven hours of deliberation, was found guilty of murder.

The five-pound bass on that Memorial Day weekend led to Ryan Mocaby's death. It also led to twenty to forty years in prison for his father, Terelius Mocaby. The defendant is now serving his sentence at Menard Penitentiary in Chester, Illinois.

Case 7

Buried Beneath The Basement

Betsy Ann Morris
November 18, 1986

St. Charles, Missouri

St. Charles, Missouri, deputies were enjoying a quiet November 21, 1986, morning and until they received a call from Bruce Morris at 7:02 a.m. The frantic husband wanted to report that his wife, Betsy Ann Morris was missing. "She has been gone for three days now," Morris told the lawman. He described Betsy as thirty-years-old; five feet, five inches; 180 pounds; with brown hair and brown eyes. He added that her complexion was fair and she had a scar on her right ankle.

Bruce told the police that he and his wife had been married for twelve years and they had one daughter, age twelve. Bruce said he and his wife got along well, but he admitted that recently they had some trouble. Betsy had left the house after she had a discussion with her husband about some personal matters. However, he explained to the officers, nothing Betsy had said led him to believe that she had intentions of leaving him.

Bruce told the police that he and his wife went to bed around 10:30 p.m. on Tuesday, November 18. His twelve-year-old daughter was already asleep. At three o'clock on Wednesday morning, Bruce was awakened by the cat. His wife was not in bed, so he got up to check on her and learned she was gone. Bruce had no idea how long his wife had been gone or what mode of travel she had taken. "We only have one car," he informed detectives. "She is possibly carrying a brown suitcase. There is one missing from the house."

Detectives asked Bruce Morris why he'd waited so long before contacting the police. Bruce explained that at first he was not concerned for Betsy's safety. He thought that she had gone to a relative's or a friend's house. After a couple of days, when Betsy had not contacted him or his

103

daughter, he began to get worried that something might have happened to her. He then began to search on his own. Bruce contacted all the area hospitals and all his wife's friends and relatives. When no one had seen or heard from Betsy, Bruce decided to call the police.

Police asked Bruce if his wife had ever been suicidal. Bruce told them that she had never attempted suicide, but occasionally when she got mad at him she would say she was going to kill herself. "I never took her serious," Bruce said.

"Did she say anything about suicide when she spoke with you last?" police asked.

"No, but she been acting strange lately," Bruce stated.

Detectives filed a missing-person report in the National Crime Information Center (NCIC). Then, concerned that Betsy Morris might be a possible suicide victim, Detective Steve Roach ordered deputies from the St. Charles Sheriff's Department to search the neighborhood's ditches, ravines, and several open fields. Their search was fruitless.

After the search, Detective Steve Roach went back to the Morris residence. Roach asked Morris once again to explain the circumstances surrounding his wife's disappearance. Bruce Morris told Roach that on November 17, at approximately 6:30 p.m., he arrived home from work. He found his wife sitting at the kitchen table, writing a letter. He told police that he could not remember exactly what the letter said, but Betsy had told him in the letter that she didn't love him anymore and was going to leave him. "I tore the letter up and threw it away," Bruce told Detective Roach. Later that night, Bruce told Roach, his wife left the residence for a while, and when she returned she wouldn't tell him where she had gone. "As I said before, she has been acting strange lately," Morris stated.

Betsy was in charge of paying bills, and Bruce found out about a month earlier that she had not made a house payment since April 1986. He had to borrow $1,600 to pay the house loan, Morris said. Since then he had been getting calls every day from creditors wanting money for back payments on bills. "I have no idea where the money was spent," he added.

Morris admitted that Betsy was upset because Bruce was working out of town. One night after work, when he was out of town, Bruce stopped at a local bar with some of his co-workers. It was just a bunch of guys who got together to have a few drinks. Before he knew it, Bruce said, he was blasted. He got back to his hotel room late and missed a call in the early-morning hours from his wife.

Bruce said he tried to explain the whole thing to Betsy, but she did not believe him. From that point on, Betsy accused him of having an affair.

Bruce said that he didn't want to accept it, but the opposite was true. Betsy was the one who was having an affair with another man. Bruce said that Betsy never told him directly that she was having an affair, but she seemed very troubled and had once told him that she was an unfit mother.

"I've been married for twelve years and I have never had an affair. She left and didn't even say goodbye to our daughter," Bruce Morris said emotionally.

Detective Roach ordered a canvass of the Morris neighborhood. A neighbor of Betsy's revealed to lawmen that in a recent conversation with Betsy, Betsy told her that she was going to leave Bruce. The friend explained to the police that Betsy was a very family-oriented person. She and Bruce had begun to have trouble about four months earlier when he began to work out of town for the telephone company at Jefferson City. At the time, Betsy thought that Bruce was having an affair herself.

Three days later, at 9:00 a.m. on November 23, Detective Roach received a call from Bruce Morris, who informed him that he had received five returned check notices in the mail. His wife had written them all. The checks totaled $600, but Morris said that he had no idea whom they were written to.

At 4:00 p.m., November 23, Bruce contacted the detective again. He informed the detective that the checks he'd called about earlier had been written after his wife's disappearance. He said the bank was already closed, but he was going to contact bank personnel in the morning and find out where Betsy had cashed the checks so he could determine if Betsy was still in the area. One other thing Bruce mentioned was that there were two clothes baskets missing from the house. Bruce was sure the baskets had been there after Betsy had left.

Detective Roach was puzzled by the call from Bruce Morris. How could he know the amount of the checks and the date they were written without knowing where they were cashed, he wondered. He would have to have had the checks in hand to know the information. And if he had the checks in hand, he would also know where they were cashed.

Detective Roach continued the probe. Dina Carter, a relative of Betsy's told Roach that she last spoke with Betsy on November 17 at about midnight. They talked for almost three hours. At the time, Betsy told Dina that she thought Bruce was having an affair in Jefferson City, and if he was, she didn't want to live anymore. Their conversation ended around 3:00 a.m. on November 18. Dina told Betsy to call her when she got home because Dina was concerned about Betsy's welfare. Dina said that Betsy called her about 3:30 a.m. Dina asked her how things were going and she said Betsy replied, "No one ever knew I was gone." Dina further told police that she thought it was strange for Betsy to leave in the middle of the night because Betsy was afraid of the dark.

On November 19, at 2:00 a.m., Dina received a call from Bruce. He asked Dina if Betsy was there, and when Dina told him that she wasn't, he asked her what he should do. Dina advised him to check with the neighbors. At 4:30 a.m., Bruce arrived at Dina Carter's house. He told Dina that he had been to all of the local hospitals and then he showed her a photo of Betsy that he said he'd shown to hospital authorities. Bruce said that he had also checked out Highways 40 and 94. He then told Dina that he first noticed Betsy was gone at around midnight on November 18, when he was awakened by the cat.

Detective Roach returned to his office. He received a call from one of Betsy's relatives, who told him that Bruce Morris was a chronic liar and the relative suspected foul play in Betsy's disappearance. The relative could not be specific about the foul play, but the police themselves were beginning to get suspicious of Bruce Morris as he continued to make daily phone calls to them. First, he'd called to say the five checks were written before Betsy's disappearance. Then he called to let the police know that two clothes baskets were missing. But no one had seen Betsy, and the police had looked everywhere.

Meanwhile, police received a call from Dina Carter, who informed them that a woman had recently moved into the Morris residence. "Betsy has only been missing for two weeks!" Dina said.

Detective Roach immediately proceeded to the Morris residence. He knocked on the door. When a woman answered, Detective Roach identified himself and asked who the woman was. She informed him that she was a friend of Bruce Morris's. She said he had asked her to stay with him to take care of his daughter. Detective Roach asked the woman if she knew where Betsy Morris was. She told Roach that Bruce said his wife had been injured in a car accident and had sustained serious injuries to her head. Bruce had told the woman that Betsy was alive, but a vegetable.

Lawmen asked Bruce Morris to take a polygraph. He was upset with the idea, but said that he would take it. The polygraph was scheduled for

December 4, 1986, at 10:00 a.m.

On December 4, Bruce Morris arrived at the St. Charles Sheriff's Department for his polygraph examination. He was given the Miranda Rights and said that he understood them.

The polygraph examination began with Bruce Morris being asked, "Do you know what happened to Betsy?"

"No," he replied.

"Do you know for sure what happened to Betsy?"

"No," Morris replied once again.

"Are you deliberately withholding any information about what happened to Betsy?"

"No," he responded.

At the conclusion of the interrogation Bruce Morris was informed that he had not passed the polygraph exam. Detective Roach then told him that several statements he had made in the last couple of weeks were not believable and that he believed Betsy was dead. Further, Roach said he thought Bruce knew where she was.

Upon hearing this, Bruce began to cry. With his hands covering his face, Bruce Morris said, "She is in the basement."

"You need to be more specific," Detective Roach insisted.

"She has been after me to put a bathroom in the basement; she is there."

"Is she buried in the earth or under concrete?" Roach asked.

"Concrete!"

"Where in the basement?" Roach asked.

"It is where I roughed in the plumbing for the bathroom," he responded.

"Is it easily seen?" Roach asked.

"No, I covered it with some boxes, a table and chair," Morris replied.

"Tell us what happened that night," Roach urged.

Bruce Morris then told another story. He explained that on the night of November 18, he and his wife were preparing for bed when they got into an argument. Betsy ran out of the bedroom and down the hall toward the living room. She tripped over their pet cat and hit her head as she was falling. Bruce ran to her aid. She was unconscious and bleeding from the head. He felt for her pulse, but couldn't feel any. He then got a plastic bag and placed it over Betsy's head. He carried Betsy to the garage, wrapped her in a sheet, and placed her on some chair pillows.

At 2:00 a.m. on November 19, he called Dina Carter to ask if she had seen Betsy. She had not and she suggested that Bruce get his daughter up so the two of them could go look for her. He called relatives and friends to see if they had seen Betsy.

"Why did you do that knowing that Betsy was already dead in the garage?" Detective Roach asked.

"I was scared. I didn't want anyone to know what happened. I didn't think they would believe me," Morris replied.

Continuing his story, Bruce said that he then woke up his daughter. He told her that Betsy had left and that he wanted her to go with him to look for her. The two of them drove around on Highways 40 and 94 and then went to Dina Carter's house. After about thirty minutes, he left and returned home. The next day Bruce went to a local lumber company and bought some plastic. He went home, wrapped his wife in the plastic and then buried her in the basement.

Lieutenant Robert Boerding of the St. Charles Sheriff's Department felt he had probable cause and applied for a search warrant for the Morris residence, pending possible charges of second-degree murder against Morris.

Meanwhile, probers found out that Bruce Morris had rented a jackhammer from a local rental agency on November 25. He had paid cash for it and returned the jackhammer on November 26, between 7:30 and 8:00 p.m.

On the afternoon of December 4, 1986, Lieutenant Boerding was issued the search warrant for Bruce Morris's residence. The sleuths proceeded to the house and began their painstaking search. At 8:59 p.m., the sheriff and deputies entered the basement from the south stairwell leading off the kitchen. The basement was in the process of renovation. Two walls were partially covered with sheetrock, while the other two had no sheetrock at all. Electrical wires and water pipes crisscrossed like routes on a road map across the unfinished ceiling. The southeast corner was partially partitioned to provide what appeared to be an area for working with models. A model train display was found inside the partition with several model parts scattered over the floor. A desk and file cabinet were set against the north wall. The center west area was partitioned into an area nine feet by ten feet to provide a bathroom. Lawmen studied the diagram that Bruce Morris had given them and determined that the body would be located in the center west area. Officers moved a table, chairs, a saw, sheetrock, two cardboard boxes, and a television set. The cleared area had newly poured concrete seventy-seven inches by thiry inches with two PVC water pipes protruding from the floor.

Detectives used three-pound and eight-pound sledgehammers to break the concrete. Several chunks of concrete were removed, and the officers found that the PVC pipe was connected to the main basement drain. The officers removed the pipe and continued to dig. Detectives removed the remainder of the concrete and a couple of inches of dirt.

A body was discovered lying face up with the head pointing south. The victim was wrapped in duct tape and plastic with the legs slightly bent at the knees. Probers noticed a red substance oozing from the plastic as they measured the length of the body from head to toe. The depth of the grave varied, with the head lying twenty-one inches down and the feet thirty-one inches. A large amount of fluid had seeped from the body, leaving a puddle in the deepest part of the grave. Photographs were taken and the body was removed for transportation to the medical examiner's office in St. Charles, Missouri.

Officers collected two long-handled shovels, one three-pound short-handled sledgehammer, one eight-pound sledgehammer, two concrete finishing trolls, one bag of concrete mix, seventeen bloodstains from a chair, a blanket containing a large number of red stains, and a mop containing a large number of red stains, which was found in the bottom of the grave. A receipt from the local rental agency for one jackhammer was taken from the desk top.

Officers continued their search of the Morris home, checking the rugs in the living room and hallway. Then they went into the garage and found three empty bags of concrete mix lying on top of the trash can along with a quantity of plastic. Police discovered a hole that had been cut into the ceiling of the garage. Using a wooden stepladder the officers crawled into the attic space of the garage. From there, detectives recovered a brown suitcase and five plastic trash bags. The bags contained the clothing of Betsy Morris as well as her purse. The purse contained all of the victim's identification, including her driver's license.

Meanwhile, Detective Roach attended the autopsy on the victim, which began at 12:30 p.m. on December 5, 1986. The medical examiner began to unwrap an outer layer of gray duct tape around the body. Once the tape was removed, a second layer of yellow plastic was removed. Underneath the yellow plastic, the pathologist found that the body was wrapped in a flowered bed sheet secured with duct tape at the ankles, upper legs, waist, and neck. The bed sheet was removed. The victim had a green garbage bag over her head. She was dressed in white panties and a white T-shirt trimmed in blue. The victim's hands were palms down on her stomach.

The pathologist observed that the body was wearing a Timex wristwatch that had stopped at 9:40. The M.E. noted a laceration on the upper left side of the victim's head, a laceration that he believed was caused by a blunt instrument but which, he determined, was not the cause of the death. Officers determined that this was the injury Bruce Morris had said his wife sustained when she fell, the accidental blow that he claimed had killed her. The pathologist, however, found a laceration on the back of Betsy's head and determined that it was the cause of death.

St. Charles County Sheriff Edward E. Uebinger and Detective Roach immediately returned to the St. Charles County Jail to interrogate Bruce Morris once again. Officers asked him to show them where his wife had injured herself when she fell. Bruce Morris told officers that although he did not see Betsy fall, he knew she hit her head on a table in the hallway. "Right here," he said, pointing to the upper front side of his own head.

"We just came from the autopsy, Bruce. Your wife was killed as a result of an injury to the back of the head," officers told Morris.

"I don't know where she was hurt, there was so much blood," Bruce Morris responded.

"Did you have anything in your hand when she was hurt?" Sheriff Uebinger asked.

"Yes, I had a two-by-four in my hand," the suspect admitted.

"What did you do with the two-by-four?" lawmen asked.

"I had a two-by-four in my hand and she looked up at me and laughed and I hit her," Bruce Morris said, his face contorting with emotion.

"How many times?"

"I don't remember, I don't remember," Morris replied.

Sheriff Uebinger asked Morris to tell them the whole story of what happened that night. Morris told them that on November 18, he and Betsy were getting ready for bed. He asked her why she had not yet made the house payment, and this sparked an argument.

"I told her I had an affair while I was in Jefferson City. She ran out of the room and down the hall, stumbled over the table and fell. I went down the hall and asked her if she was alright. She looked up at me and started laughing."

Morris then quoted his wife as saying, "I had an affair, too, while you were in Jefferson City. He was better than you. You're only half a man."

Sheriff Uebinger then asked, "Is that when you hit her with the two-by-four?"

110

"I had a piece of two-by-four in my hand, and all I could see was her lying on the floor with blood all over her. I dropped the two-by-four and reached for her. I held her in my arms, but I couldn't stop the bleeding. She wouldn't wake up."

Morris said he then felt Betsy's wrist. There was no pulse. She was not breathing so Bruce put a plastic bag over Betsy's head and carried her body into the garage, placed her in some chair pillows, and covered her with a sheet. He put the two-by-four in the fireplace, then went into the kitchen and smoked a cigarette. "I kept washing my hands because I could not get the blood off of them," Morris told police.

Later, officers got a videotaped confession from Bruce Morris, and he was charged with first-degree murder.

Bruce Morris was arraigned in Circuit Court in St. Charles, where he was convicted of first-degree murder. Sentenced to forty years in prison, he is now serving that sentence in the Jefferson City State Penitentiary in Jefferson City, Missouri.

Case 8

The Anti-Freeze Murder

Charles T. Ellis
November 21, 1986

Shawneetown, Illinois

The chill of winter filled the air at Shawneetown, a historical river community with a population of twelve hundred, located along the banks of the Ohio River in Southern Illinois. Chief of Police Robert Patton sat in the Shawneetown Police Department completing a report.

It was November 21, 1986, 1:00 p.m., when the phone rang. The call was from a man in Phose County, Indiana. He called to report that a local resident, Charles T. Ellis, sixty-one years old, had died at approximately 10:00 a.m. that morning at St. Mary's Hospital in nearby Evansville, Indiana.

The coroner reported that because of the unusual circumstances of the victim's illness, doctors received permission from the family to perform an autopsy. The results of the autopsy were now complete and they indicated that Ellis had died as a result of acute renal failure due to ethylene glycol, a substance found in antifreeze, waxes, varnishes, lacquers, and shoe polish.

Chief Patton knew the dead man. The fact that he may have been poisoned came as a shock. Chief Patton sat for a few moments to collect his thoughts, then began to move quickly.

The chief, after conferring with Gallatin County Coroner Tony Cox, requested assistance from the Department of Criminal Investigation (DCI) to assist in an investigation of the incident.

State Policeman Detective L.S. Huggins was assigned to the case. He and Chief Patton began the investigation by first conducting interviews with physicians who had attended Charles T. Ellis.

Detectives first interviewed a local doctor who told police that family members brought the victim to his office on Thursday, November 6. The victim, according to the doctor, was very unbalanced, dizzy, and had

113

slurred speech. The doctor examined Ellis and found that he had no heart blockage. All the symptoms indicated a possible stroke. The doctor referred the victim to the attending physician at the nearby hospital where he was taken by ambulance.

Police interviewed the attending doctor at the local hospital. She said the first time she saw the victim was on November 6 when the victim was admitted to the hospital in Eldorado, Illinois. The physician said that Mr. Ellis told her he had awakened that day around 7:00 p.m. with "a funny taste."

The doctor confirmed that Mr. Ellis was very unbalanced, nauseous, and had slurred speech. These symptoms are typical of a possible stroke and, therefore, the doctor referred Mr. Ellis to the Deaconess Hospital in Evansville, Indiana. The victim seemed better the next day, and he was discharged from the hospital and sent home.

The physician said that a few days after the victim was discharged, the Ellis family called her. They reported that Charles's bowels and kidneys were not functioning properly and, as a result, he was re-admitted to a hospital in Evansville, Indiana, on November 14, 1986.

The detectives then spoke with the kidney specialist from Indiana hospital that treated Charles Ellis. The specialist said that he was suffering from a degeneration of the kidneys and was in an advanced stage of kidney failure. The injury to the victim's kidneys had been present for at least one week, the doctor added.

After Mr. Ellis died on November 21, the specialist obtained consent from relatives of the victim to perform an autopsy. The pathologist dissected sections of the kidneys and the doctor found substantial calcium oxalate crystals. The doctor explained that calcium oxalate crystals are a result of poisoning by ethylene glycol, which is found in antifreeze, waxes, varnishes, lacquers, and shoe polish; however, the doctor explained that ethylene glycol is most commonly related to antifreeze.

The doctor also indicated that ethylene glycol poisoning most commonly kills within twelve to thirty-six hours, but because the victim had been on kidney dialysis, he lived a little longer.

Chief Patton's hunch that he had a murder case on his hands was now something more than a hunch. Thus, he began questioning close relations.

One relative told police that she awoke at approximately 3:00 a.m. on November 6 and dressed for work. A relative working for the same employer came by her residence shortly after she got up and stayed until they both left for work at 4:15 a.m.

The relative said that there was a pitcher of tea in the refrigerator and that she had taken a swallow of the tea with her medicine. The tea tasted strong but the family member thought nothing of it, since she preferred brewed tea rather than the instant lemon tea, which was in the pitcher.

She told police that at the Ellis residence, there were two pitchers used to make tea. That morning the tea was in an orange pitcher with a handle. A yellow pitcher with the handle broken was no longer in use. To the best of her memory, the relative said, the orange pitcher was filled to approximately one and one-half inches from the top and contained no ice when she first took a sip that morning.

Continuing, she said that she did not know who made the tea but did know the pitcher was not in the refrigerator when she went to bed the previous evening. She also thought that Charles Ellis had already been in bed before the pitcher full was made.

Finally, she explained that Mr. Ellis and one other family member were avid tea drinkers and consumed as much as two or three jars of instant tea per week.

The detective asked, "Do you keep any antifreeze around the house?"

"Yes," the relative replied, "there was a container of antifreeze which had been setting inside the door of the residence near a desk for sometime."

"The antifreeze is gone now?" the detective asked.

"Yes!"

"Do you know what happened to it?"

"No, I didn't pay any attention," she replied.

Detectives continued the probe by interviewing another family member. He said that he arrived at the Ellis residence at approximately 3:30 to 4:00 a.m. to pick up a relative for work. He informed police that he drank a mouthful of tea from an orange pitcher in the refrigerator. The relative told detectives he spit the tea out because it tasted bad.

Police inquired if there was any antifreeze in the Ellis residence. The family member explained that Charles Ellis had purchased one case of antifreeze the previous year and that there were several gallons still located in the residence. He also said that Charles H. Ellis, Charles T. Ellis's son, had brought a half-gallon of antifreeze into his home around November 12 and said he purchased it to winterize his truck. The relative had no knowledge of how long Charles H. Ellis had had the antifreeze.

Next the detectives sought out and interviewed still another close relative who had accompanied the victim to the hospital. She said that on one occasion, Charles T. Ellis was hospitalized, that approximately $150 had come up missing, and that the money was hidden in the Ellis residence. Also, family members found out at that time that the victim's son had borrowed approximately $5000 from a local bank in Illinois.

After the victim died, family members confronted Charles H. Ellis about the debt. She said that he told the family that he had consolidated several notes at the bank and had signed his parents' names to the note along with his own, but he had been given permission from his father. She told police that Charles T. Ellis had never been willing to incur debt or co-sign notes for any of his children.

When the family confronted Charles Jr. about stealing the money hidden in the Ellis residence, he denied any knowledge of the money at all. The relative indicated, however, that within a day or two, Charles H. Ellis gave his mother approximately $120 and told her that he had sold a gun to procure the money.

Further, the relative explained that on November 8, she picked up the instant tea jar from the Ellis residence and took it with her to have it analyzed. However, she forgot to leave it with the hospital personnel and the tea was brought back home by other family members.

On November 10, when Charles T. Ellis returned home, she was told by Charles H. Ellis not to worry about the tea. He had taken it to the State's Attorney Tony Dhyrkopp and had the tea analyzed. The tea was okay! She asked Charles H. where the tea was now and he said that he had dumped it out.

The relative further told police that Charles H. Ellis had been adamantly opposed to an autopsy being performed on his father.

Chief Patton obtained copies of several loan notes taken out for trailer repairs by Charles H. Ellis at the local bank. The notes were numbered 120625 for $1500, 121158 for $500, 120686 for $600, and a consolidated note for $5,016.87. There were signatures on the notes from Charles H. Ellis, his father Charles T. Ellis, and other relatives.

Patton took the notes to the Ellis residence and presented them to family members. They stated that the signatures were not theirs and that the signatures for Charles T. Ellis was not his signature either.

At approximately 4:00 p.m. on Wednesday, November 26, detectives questioned Charles H. Ellis at his residence. The twenty-nine-year-old, 270-pound Ellis filled one side of the coach. Each forearm displayed seven or eight small cuts from what police later learned were cult rituals. Cutting the arms and "bleeding," as the ritual is called, then drinking the blood is common in devil worship. A friend informant indicated that both he and Ellis had been involved in the activities.

Ellis sat quietly observing Chief Patton, a fellow neighbor and former schoolmate. Patton began the probe. Charles H. told police that on the morning of November 6, relatives got up at approximately 2:30 or 3:00 a.m. to get ready for work, but that he did not get up until approximately 6:30 to 7:00 a.m. His father was already up and had his usual cup of coffee. Charles H. fixed himself a couple of eggs and stayed at the residence until approximately 8:30 a.m. He said that when he left, his father was sitting in his chair, watching TV and drinking lemon tea.

Charles H. said that he had made the tea the night before and had consumed about one quart of it. He then placed the remaining tea (approximately one-quart) back in the refrigerator before going to bed.

The son returned home at approximately 9:00 a.m. with the mail. He told police that his dad was washing dishes, complained of being dizzy, and finally had to lie down. Charles H. remained at the residence for about ten or fifteen minutes and then left. At approximately 1:30 p.m., a relative telephoned him at a friend's residence and said that his father was sick. Charles H. returned home where he found his father in bed and he departed the residence again.

Chief Patton asked him what had been done with the remaining instant tea. He said that a family member made a pitcher full, which tasted strong, and it was dumped out. However, Charles H. advised that he made several glasses of tea with the remainder of tea from the jar and it tasted okay. Further he said that he told the family that he intended to take the remaining tea to Gallatin County State's Attorney Tony Dhyrkopp for analysis, but was told by the rest of the family that they were going to take it to the Deaconess Hospital for the same purpose.

Chief Patton locked eyes with Charles H. and began to probe. "Have you ever used a pitcher as a container for antifreeze?"

"I used a broken handled pitcher and poured some antifreeze into it about one week before my dad got sick."

The detective then displayed a copy of a loan consolidation in the amount of $5,016.87 from the local bank in Shawneetown made out to Charles H. Ellis.

"Can you explain the circumstances of this loan?" he asked.

"Yes, I borrowed the money and had the other notes combined into one. I also signed my parents' name to the notes along with my own," Ellis explained.

"In fact, you forged your parents' names on the notes?"

"Yes, I did!"

"Do you work?" the detective asked.

"No! I'm on General Assistance. I get $140 a month," Ellis responded.

"Do you know of any reason why someone would want to hurt any members of your family?"

"Well, about four years ago, I was receiving threatening notes about my dogs running loose but I didn't want to get the police involved and I burned the notes. I only got one."

"Anything since then?"

"No!"

"Do you think your dad would intentionally take antifreeze?" the chief asked him.

"Well, he had real bad cataracts and about two years ago he said to more than one person that he would rather be dead."

"Who did he tell this to?"

"Well, I can't remember that, but I recall hearing him say it several times."

The chief ended the interview at 5:10 p.m. and returned to the police station. He knew he had his man, but there was no physical evidence to tie him to the crime. The detective's only hope was to get a confession. He called and asked the suspect if he would come to the police station for further questioning.

At approximately 6:30 p.m. later that day, detectives again questioned the suspect, this time at the Shawneetown Police Department. Both Chief of Police Patton and Gallatin County Coroner Tony Cox were present.

The suspect told police that he had used a pitcher with a handle to put antifreeze in his vehicle on several occasions between November 1 and November 5. He said it was an orange pitcher, the same one his father used to drink tea from. Charles H. said he used the pitcher to put antifreeze in both his Ford Courier pickup truck and the family's Ford Limited passenger car.

The suspect explained that on the evening of Wednesday, November 5, at about 8:00 p.m., he poured some all weather antifreeze from a pitcher into the Ford Courier pickup truck. He then added about a quart of water to the remaining antifreeze and poured about one-half of the contents into the pickup. At that point he took the pitcher back into the house and left it with the remaining solution of about an inch or so water and antifreeze sitting in the kitchen. He then took another pitcher, washed it out, and left that pitcher out for his father's use.

"Is the pitcher that you described as the one you mixed antifreeze in the same pitcher that you observed your father drinking from on the morning of November 6?" detectives asked.

"Yes!" the suspect replied.

"Did you tell your dad that he was drinking from the same pitcher that you used the night before to mix antifreeze?"

"No! I did not. I made the tea on the night of the fifth and placed the tea in the refrigerator."

The police interrupted the suspect.

"If you will remember our conversation earlier this evening, you told me that you drank about a quart of the tea prior to placing the reminder in the refrigerator."

"No sir. I did not drink any of the tea that I made on the evening of the fifth. I was referring to another time when I made the tea. I made the tea in the pitcher which contained antifreeze solution, but I didn't know that the antifreeze solution was in the pitcher when I made the tea."

Detectives had caught the suspect in several discrepancies. The police were now sure they had their man and decided to conduct a taped interview with him. On December 1 at 3:30 p.m., I. S. Huggins, Chief Robert Patton, and the Gallatin County Coroner met with Ellis at the Shawneetown Police Department and began the interview.

Once again, Ellis explained that on November 5, he returned home at about 5:00 p.m. At about 8:30 p.m. the suspect said that he went out and checked the oil and antifreeze in his vehicle and his parents' vehicle. He told police that both were a little low on antifreeze so he went into the residence and put antifreeze into his dad's orange tea pitcher. He said that both his parents were in bed reading at the time.

He took the antifreeze solution in the pitcher and poured part of the solution in both vehicles. He then returned to the residence and put approximately one quart of water in the antifreeze solution then finished filling both vehicles. Approximately one pint of solution was left in the pitcher when he returned to the residence and set the pitcher on the table.

A short time later, he made a quantity of lemon iced tea in an orange glass, which he poured into the orange pitcher. Ellis then told police that he put the filled pitcher of tea into the refrigerator so that the family would have some the following morning. He said that at the time that he placed the tea into the orange pitcher, there was another white pitcher sitting on the table. The suspect explained that he used the wrong pitcher by mistake.

Ellis told detectives that he had not drunk any of the tea as he had stated earlier. Rather, he had drunk a quart of tea on the night of the election on November 4.

He said that a relative came into his room at 4:00 a.m. on the sixth and asked if he had change. Also, the family member asked if he had made the tea, complaining that the tea tasted strong. At 7:00 a.m., he got up and observed his dad drinking tea from the pitcher. His dad asked him about the tea and Charles H. told him that he made the tea a little stronger. The suspect said that he had some breakfast and brewed him some tea, then left at about 8:30 a.m. He returned to the residence at about 10:30 a.m. with the mail and his dad complained that the tea tasted strong.

Detectives asked Ellis, "Are you willing to take a polygraph examination?"

"Yes sir, I don't have nothing to hide," Ellis responded.

The interview ended and Officer Roy Hall gave Ellis a ride back to his residence. A short time later, the officer returned to the police station. He told the detectives that while taking the suspect home, he asked Ellis if he had ever taken a polygraph examination. Ellis had not and told him, "They are very accurate!" Ellis sat quietly for a minute or so and then wanted to know if he could ask Hall a question off the record. Hall said Ellis could ask him anything he wanted to.

Ellis asked, "If I did this, what kind of time can the judge give me?"

Officer Hall told him he didn't know and the conversation ended.

On December 2, Charles H. Ellis was examined at the Southern Illinois Forensic Science Laboratory in Carbondale, Illinois.

Charles H. Ellis was asked, "On November 5, 1986, did you mix antifreeze with iced tea on purpose?"

"No."

"Did you intentionally poison your father with antifreeze?"

"No."

"When you placed that pitcher of iced tea in the refrigerator, did you know then that it contained antifreeze?"

"No."

When the suspect was advised that the results of his polygraph examination indicated that he had intentionally caused his father's death, the suspect immediately confessed. He said that in early October he had purchased antifreeze, a radiator hose, and filters at a local automotive store. On the night of November 5, the suspect said, he had gone outside his residence to check the radiator levels in both vehicles. After finding the levels low he returned into the house and got an orange container which was normally used for iced tea.

He said the container was about six inches in diameter and a little over a foot tall. He poured the antifreeze into the container. Then he added water till it was full. He used the mixture to fill the vehicles then returned to the residence, setting the pitcher on the kitchen table. He told police the container had about a quart of the mixture left in it.

The suspect then went in and began watching television. Suddenly, he decided to mix tea in the container and place it back in the refrigerator, knowing that his father would drink it and die.

When he was asked why he did it, he said that subconsciously he was thinking about the $2000 insurance money and getting caught up on credit.

"I lost all will power. It was like I didn't have any control and somebody or something came over me and caused me to do it."

Ellis was transported back to the Shawneetown Police Department. At approximately 7:00 p.m. on Tuesday, December 2, 1986, Gallatin County State's Attorney Dyhekopp advised Chief Patton to charge Charles H. Ellis with murder. At 7:20 p.m. Chief Patton advised Ellis of his Constitutional rights as guaranteed by Miranda.

Chief Patton asked Ellis if there was anything he would like to tell him about the case.

Charles said he did not know why he did it but it wasn't for the $2000. He just wanted his father to get sick because of the disability credit life insurance on the loans at the bank.

The chief asked if there was any other reason that he could think of for murdering his father. The only thing that stuck in the suspect's mind was remembering that his father got him by the throat two or three years ago.

"Even though you don't know why you did it, didn't you put the tea in the antifreeze intentionally, knowing it would kill your dad?"

Ellis replied, "I know it now."

In January of 1987, in the First Circuit Court in Gallatin County, Charles H. Ellis pleaded guilty to the murder of his father, Charles T. Ellis. He was sentenced to twenty to forty years and is now serving his sentence in Menard State Penitentiary in Chester, Illinois.

Case 9

The Execution Murder

Stanley R. Mayo
April 29, 1987

Mt. Vernon, Illinois

Wednesday, April 29, 1987, was a warm spring day. Two Illinois Department of Transportation workers were enjoying the sunny weather as they drove along Interstate 64, west of Mt. Vernon, Illinois. Suddenly the passenger of the maintenance truck sat up straight in his seat. "Hey, I think that was a body back there!" he explained.

"We better turn around and take a look!" the driver said.

Moments later, any hopes of a mistake were gone when they pulled to a stop at mile marker 70 on westbound I-64. A white male was lying on the grassy shoulder approximately sixteen feet from the edge of the pavement. The excited state employees called on their radio for the state police. It was 12:40 p.m.

Illinois State Trooper Carl Dorich arrived at the scene twelve minutes later. The transportation workers were waiting for the trooper and pointed him in the direction of the body. The lawman found a white male who appeared to be in his twenties or thirties. The victim was dressed in a light-blue shirt, a black or dark-blue pair of pants, a dark-blue tie, a pair of black shoes, and black belt with a set of keys clipped to the left side of his belt. He was lying face up and appeared to have some kind of head wound.

The body was cold and stiff. The trooper immediately notified headquarters and requested that a crime scene technician from the Department of Criminal Investigation be sent to the crime scene.

Crime Scene Technician (CST) Jerry Barnes arrived at the scene at 1:30 p.m. Detective Mike Anthis of the Jefferson County Sheriff's Department, who assisted Barnes in the crime scene procedures, met him.

Barnes scanned the body and the immediate area around it before approaching the body.

The victim's head was pointing west. His left arm rested along his side, while his right arm was pointing to the south. He had what appeared to be multiple gunshot wounds to the back of the neck and one gunshot wound to the back of the head. On the left side of the victim's belt was a key ring with numerous keys attached to it. There was blood on the grass and on the white rock on the shoulder of the highway. A razor-blade-type box opener lay on the paved portion of the shoulder. It appeared that the blade should have been an extra one carried by the victim to insert into the box opener.

A blue checkbook bearing the name Stanley R. Mayo and his account number at a bank in Mt. Vernon, Illinois, was in the victim's rear pocket. Many coins were found in the victim's front pocket, along with some additional keys and a one-dollar bill lay in the grass near his head. CST Barnes photographed and processed the crime scene and collected, packaged, and marked, in addition to those items, six federal .22-caliber discharged cartridge cases, a white rock marked with blood, a razor-blade box, and a razor with blood on it.

The detectives then did a walk-through search in the immediate vicinity with a metal detector, but they found no other physical evidence.

At approximately 2:40 p.m., the victim was removed by ambulance and transported to a local hospital where, at 5:40 p.m., an autopsy was performed. The pathologist found six wounds on the victim. The first one was a slit-like wound located on the left posterior neck, the second, a slit-like wound on the right posterior neck, and the others were wounds to the head. None of the wounds had powder, tattooing, or stripping. The pathologist found no other evidence of trauma other than the bullet wounds to the neck and head. The pathologist further indicated that the victim was in full rigor mortis at the time of the autopsy. The report indicated that Stanley Mayo had died before 9:00 a.m. on April 29.

At the conclusion of the autopsy, CST Barnes collected additional physical evidence from the victim, including inked fingerprints and palm prints, clothing, head hair standards, and six fired bullets. Barnes then submitted for processing all the evidence from the victim and the crime scene to the Southern Illinois Forensic Science Laboratory at Carbondale, Illinois.

Meanwhile, police had found out that Mayo worked at a local business in Mt. Vernon and they began their canvass with an interview of his employers. The employers said Mayo had worked the night before. According to his routine, he should have made a night deposit, and the employers indicated that there would be no problem with the night deposit because the bank would have called first thing in the morning. They told police that the victim would have closed up at midnight, and when they came into the store, everything appeared to be in order.

The victim was described by his employers as a good worker and well-liked by fellow employees and the customers. They said that he had recently purchased a new dark-blue Mercury Topaz that he was very proud of. When the detectives asked them if Mayo had any enemies, they indicated that he did not. However, there had been a night manager who had been fired recently and he and the victim had not gotten along. The employer did say that they had never seen the two of them get into a confrontation.

Detectives continued their probe by interviewing an employee of an all night store. He indicated that at about 1:15 a.m. on April 29, Stanley Mayo had come into the store to purchase some fast-food items. Mayo did not have enough money to pay for them and decided to put the soda back so he would have enough money for the rest of the items. The employee said that he told the victim to go ahead and take all the items and he could pay later.

The victim had two dollars in cash, which would leave a balance owed of $1.88. He told the store clerk that he would go home, get the money, and return to pay him. Mayo left the store and the store clerk never saw him again.

The police then interviewed a family member who said that he had not seen the victim since about three o'clock on the afternoon of April 28. At that time, Mayo was getting ready for work. The relative said that the reason he had not missed Mayo was because [the relative] had spent the night with his girlfriend. He told police that the victim had purchased a new car about two weeks ago. He knew of no one who disliked Mayo.

The canvass continued with an interview of the ex-night manager, who had not gotten along with Mayo. The former employee said that there were problems between him and Mayo, but they were over management philosophies and confined to the store. Mayo had believed him to be too slack, but the former night manager said he'd had difficulty with a couple of female employees who were not doing their jobs. Mayo thought they were doing their jobs.

The former employee indicated that he had spent the night of April 28 and all day April 29 with his family. He told police that he thought that Mayo had a lot to do with his losing his job but that he did not hate Stanley Mayo.

Two days went by and the police began to worry. So far, they had a dead man with no enemies who'd been shot in the neck and head six times and a missing car and not another lead to turn to.

Then, on May 1, Detective Mike Anthis got a break when he received a call from Detective Sergeant Mullins of the Sheriff's Department in Hillsboro, Missouri. According to Mullins, a Hillsboro police officer received an anonymous phone call from a woman who said that she had overheard a conversation describing a murder in Mt. Vernon, Illinois. The woman said that the victim's car was parked within a six-block area of the suspect's residence.

The Hillsboro police traced the call to a residence on Magnolia Street in St. Louis, Missouri. They found out that William Phillips and a girl-friend were living with a couple in a house to which the telephone call had been traced. Officer Mullins, in fact, had personally stopped William Phillips and another man, Victor Burkart, recently for suspicious activity. The detective suspected both men in several burglaries that had occurred in the Hillsboro area.

The Hillsboro detective confirmed that a homicide had occurred in Mt. Vernon, and that he had obtained the license plate number of Stanley Mayo's vehicle, then hurried to the residence on Magnolia Street. There the officers arranged to meet at headquarters with a woman who claimed to be a girlfriend of one of the men. She admitted to making the call. She said she wanted to talk to the police, but she was afraid that Phillips would come home while the police were there. She agreed to go to the police station for an interview. After waiving her Miranda rights, she told the police that Phillips had come to her residence at approximately 6:20 a.m. on April 29. Later he'd handed her a small silver gun that belonged to her.

"Here's your gun," she said Phillips had told her. "I took it for protection. Get rid of the gun," Phillips said.

"Why?"

"Cause somebody has been shot with it."

"With my gun?"

"With your gun! He was shot four or five times!"

"Where at? What happened?"

She said that Phillips seemed tense as she relayed what she said he'd told her. Burkhart and he had been involved in a shooting; the victim was the owner of a car they were trying to steal. The shots had been fired when the car owner said, "I'll remember you...."

"Is there anything else you can remember?" police asked.

The girlfriend then signed a Consent to Search and Seize form and the police escorted her to the residence on Magnolia Street. She took the investigators to a bedroom in the northeast corner of the residence, lifted the mattress and retrieved a .22-caliber automatic pistol wrapped in a white tube sock. The officers immediately packaged and marked the Jennings .22-caliber automatic pistol. Detectives then took inked fingerprints and palm prints from the girlfriend and submitted the evidence to the Forensic Science Laboratory at Carbondale, Illinois.

Sergeant Mullins contacted Detective Anthis and the two detectives began to move quickly. It emerged that on April 28, Phillips went to see his relative in Mt. Vernon, accompanied by Victor Burkhart.

When Phillips returned, she said that he was very tired, white as a sheet, and scared to death. He lay down with his clothes on and fell asleep for a few hours and then got up the next morning and took her to work. He was quiet and in the afternoon, he finally started talking to her. He said that they had gone to see Phillips's relative at the hospital. After the visit, he and Victor Burkhart went to a local tavern. Phillips said that Burkhart decided that he was going to rob this guy and take his car. Things went sour and the guy ended up getting shot in the head. He said that they had driven the victim's car back to the St. Louis area.

The investigators' next step was to pick up and interrogate Victor Burkhart. Burkhart was cooperative and gave a voluntary statement to the police after waiving his Miranda rights. He told Detective Anthis that the last time he had been in Illinois was on May 1, when he went to his place of work in Cahokia, Illinois. He told the police that he knew William Phillips and used to be tight with him. He said that William Phillips asked him to take a trip to Mt. Vernon to see a relative who was in the hospital, but he did not go.

Burkhart said that he had been in Mt. Vernon with Phillips in 1986 and had gone to a relative's house with Phillips at the time. Then he said he had seen Phillips's car about a week ago. He explained that on Monday, April 27, he had gone to work at about 5:30 a.m. He returned home about 2:30 p.m. the same day, rented a couple of movies, and stayed home until Wednesday morning, April 29.

The suspect then said that on April 29, he went to work about 5:30 a.m. and got home at about 7:00 p.m. On April 30, he went to work about 6:30 a.m. and returned about 2:00 p.m. He did not leave home that evening.

Detective Anthis left the interview room for a few minutes to talk with the woman he'd previously interviewed. Shortly, he returned and informed Burkhart of the information he had received from his informant.

The detective admonished the suspect that this was the time to tell the truth. Further, he informed him that he was going to be arrested for the murder of Stanley Mayo.

"Phillips isn't going to help you. The only person that can help you is yourself!" Anthis told him.

Burkhart began to cry. "Man, I can't do no more prison time. Man, I didn't kill that guy. I thought he was going to tie him up. I'll cooperate. I'll tell you everything."

Then Burkhart regained his composure and went on. Phillips asked Burkhart to go to Mt. Vernon with him to see a relative. Burkhart agreed and they left April 28. After visiting the relative at the hospital, he and Phillips went to a local bar for a couple of beers. They went driving around for a while and Phillips decided that he wanted to steal a car. They didn't have any tools, so Burkhart suggested they forget it and go home. "He says, 'No, I'll just steal one from somebody.'" Then Phillips spots this guy on the square in Mt. Vernon and says, "I'll steal that one! Follow that car!" Burkhart said he followed this car to a store. "Phillips says, 'Let me out and wait until the car leaves. Then follow the car,'" Burkhart paused for breath.

Burkhart said he drove around the back of the store and let Phillips out. He waited for a short time until the car left. Burkhart wasn't sure if Phillips was in the car, so he followed it. He could see a passenger every so often "as we went by streetlights but didn't know which one was Bill." Burkhart followed him around. Phillips made a bunch of turns down back roads, came back by the store, around the square, and then headed out toward St. Louis on I-64. They drove for a while and Bill pulled over to the emergency lane. Burkhart pulled up behind him and stopped. Phillips got out of the driver's side and walked around to the back of the car to the passenger door. He opened the door and pulled the man out and put him on the ground.

Burkhart began to cry. "Man, I thought he was going to tie the guy up and just leave him there. I didn't know he was going to kill him." Burkhart sat quiet for a few minutes and then continued. Just a few seconds after he laid the man down on the ground, Burkhart heard five or six shots. He told police that he panicked, backed the car up and took off.

A short time later, Phillips caught up with him and pulled around in front of him. Burkhart followed Phillips for a few miles and Phillips pulled over again. Phillips came back to the car and said, "Well, man, it's done." He didn't say what he had done or why.

Burkhart agreed to take a polygraph examination. The exam was conducted on May 7. Part of the question-and-answer session follows:

"On April 29, 1987, did you shoot Stanley Mayo?"

"No!"

"Did William Phillips shoot Stanley Mayo?"

"Yes!"

"Were you in Sherry Young's car when Stanley Mayo was shot?"

"Yes!"

Polygraph Examiner Dennis Smith met with Detective Anthis after the exam was complete. He indicated that Victor Burkhart was telling the truth to the question that he did not shoot Mayo and that Phillips had, but he was not telling the truth about being in the car.

Detective Anthis confronted Burkhart and he began to cry. He said that he would give another statement. He told the police that when he and Phillips pulled to the side of the road, he got out of the car and walked around the front of his vehicle and stopped at the back of the passenger side of the victim's car. The victim was lying on the ground with his head pointing toward the front of the vehicle. William Phillips stepped across the victim bent down and placed the gun close to the victim's head. Burkhart said he heard five or six shots. He ran to his car and drove off.

Meanwhile, the Hillsboro police had obtained a Diagnostic Center Report on William Phillips. William Phillips had been sentenced to ten years in the state of Missouri on a charge of murder in the second degree. On August 8, 1981, he'd shot and killed a relative's boyfriend after the boyfriend who was visiting his relative at her St. Louis apartment threatened him. He claimed that the victim had attempted to get a knife out of Phillips's pocket, at which time he shot the victim.

In the Mayo homicide, the police were sure they had their man. From Phillips's girlfriend, they established that he was holding up in a relative's house in Mt. Vernon. On May 1, 1987, at 7:50 p.m., a surveillance vehicle checked the residence and radioed the police station that the relative's vehicle was not at the residence.

An hour passed. At 8:50 p.m., the surveillance radioed the police and informed them that the relative's car had returned and that two men and a woman exited the vehicle and went into the residence. One of the men fit the description of William Phillips.

Police surrounded the residence on Harrison Street in Mt. Vernon. One officer went to the front door and knocked. The relative answered the door and was brought out of the doorway. The officer glanced into the house and saw the girl at the top of the stairs. She was ordered to come out.

After the girl came out of the house, police asked the relative if William Phillips was in the residence. He indicated that he was. Just then, the suspect appeared at the top of the stairs. He was ordered to put his hands up and slowly walk to the entrance. He did as the police told him and was taken into custody for the murder of Stanley Mayo.

Police entered the residence after the relative gave consent for them to search it. Inside was a small arsenal. The police seized a loaded Remington found standing next to the stairway entrance, a loaded Titan .25-caliber automatic pistol on the bookshelf, a glass ashtray on the bookshelf in the living room containing forty-nine live .22-caliber shells, and a loaded Glenfield .22-caliber semiautomatic rifle in the corner of the living room.

William "Bill" Phillips was read his Miranda Rights at 9:22 p.m. on May 1. He refused to waive his rights and refused to cooperate with the police in any manner. He was incarcerated in the Jefferson County Jail.

In the meantime, the relative whom the suspect had been staying with waived his Miranda rights. He told police that William Phillips and a friend named Vic came to see him at the hospital on April 2. Both of the men appeared to be intoxicated. The relative was out of cigarettes and Vic went to get some for him.

While he was gone, the relative asked Phillips what he was doing in Mt. Vernon and he said that he and Vic had come to lift a car. Vic was going to steal it and drive back to St. Louis; Phillips was going to drive the car they came in. The relative told him that it was stupid to steal a car.

Vic returned about that time and the two men left. He said that Phillips had called him at a friend's house on April 29 and wanted the relative to call him. The relative said that he got busy with other things and didn't return Phillips's call until April 30 in the afternoon. William told the relative that he and his girlfriend were fighting and that he had troubles. He wanted the relative to pick him up and take him back to Mt. Vernon as soon as possible.

At 7:30 p.m. on April 30, the relative went to St. Louis and picked Phillips up. He asked the relative to go to a local truck stop, so he could talk with his girlfriend. Before leaving the truck stop, Phillips placed a rifle and small brown bag in the trunk of the car. They then returned to Mt. Vernon.

The police located the victim's car on Halliday Street in St. Louis. Crime Scene Technician Alva W. Busch of the St. Louis City Police Department, Third District headquarters, processed the vehicle. He photographed the Blue 1986 mercury Topaz, bearing Illinois license plate KYV259. All the doors were locked.

A locksmith from Collinsville, Illinois unlocked the vehicle for Busch. Busch found one spent .22-caliber shell casing located on the center section of the rear seat, hair collected from the right front seat area and left front seat area, one latent print from the front door window of the vehicle on the inside, and projectile fragments collected from the roof of the vehicle. The vehicle was then turned over to the Department of Criminal Investigation and returned to Illinois.

The results from the Forensic Service Lab in Carbondale indicated that the projectiles taken from the victim's neck and head were discharged from the Jennings .22-caliber automatic pistol, serial number 126421.

On July 10, 1987, Victor Burkhart, twenty-three, of St. Louis, Missouri pleaded guilty to aiding and abetting William Phillips in the murder of Stanley Mayo on April 29, 1987. He received twenty-five years in the Department of Corrections in the state of Illinois.

On July 10, 1987, William Phillips, twenty-six, of St. Louis, Missouri, pleaded guilty to the actual shooting of Stanley Mayo. On September 23, 1987, Chief Judge Terrence Hopkins sentenced Phillips to spend the rest of his natural life in prison. Both defendants are presently serving their sentences in Menard State Prison in Chester, Illinois.

Author's Note

Sherry Young is not the real name of the person so named in the foregoing story. A fictitious name had been used because there is no reason for public interest in the identity of this person.

Case 10

Murder By Armed Robbery

Jason Jackson
October 14, 1989

Carbondale, Illinois

On October 14, 1989, Patrolman Jim Wilson of Illinois' Carbondale Police Department was in the 100 block of Washington Street looking for a suspect involved in a burglary. The weather was unusually warm for the time of year—sixty degrees. The officer had his car window rolled down as he crept down the street scanning the area.

Suddenly a series of popping sounds broke through the quiet of the night. Pop! Pop! Pop! Pop!

Those were gunshots Patrolman Wilson heard. At the same time, he tried to figure out which direction they were coming from. Wilson sped up and, in the 200 block of Washington Street, he saw an employee of a nearby restaurant looking in all directions. Officer Wilson reached the intersection of Washington and Jackson Streets when he saw three people running north across the 200 block of East Jackson Street.

"We have been robbed. They shot Jason!" the trio said, all yelling at the same time.

The officer approached and saw a man lying on the grass between the street and the sidewalk. The victim was lying on his left side in a semi-fetal position. Patrolman Wilson called dispatch for an ambulance. Then he exited the squad car and ran to assist the victim. Dressed in a white tuxedo shirt and black pants, the victim had a gunshot wound to the left side of his chest. He was in shock and unable to talk. Shortly thereafter, the ambulance arrived and the victim was taken to a local hospital. It was 2:45 a.m.

Meanwhile, Wilson called dispatch and gave a description of the armed robber as being five feet, eleven inches to fix feet tall. He weighed about 160 to 170 pounds and was wearing a large, dark-green hooded sweatshirt. He left the scene on foot heading north across a vacant lot on Jackson Street, witnesses told Wilson.

The officer then scanned the crime scene and found one bank deposit bag and a shoe belonging to the victim lying on the grass near the location where the victim was found.

Shortly thereafter, Sergeant Don Strom spotted a man standing in an alley a few blocks away from the crime scene. The sergeant immediately considered the man a possible suspect and took him to the crime scene for identification.

The three victims of the robbery told police that this was not the robber. The robber was much taller and was wearing different clothing, they said. As a result, the man was released.

Sergeant Strom then secured the crime scene, directed several squad cars to make a patrol search of the area, and then reported to the hospital. The sergeant was informed that Jason Jackson had died. It was now 3:07 a.m.

Patrolman Wilson continued the investigation with an interview of the female victim of the armed robbery. She explained that she and three male employees were taking the deposit receipts from the restaurant to the night deposit at a nearly local bank. Suddenly, a man came running from the north side of Jackson Street, across the parking lot, and confronted them from about twelve feet away. He displayed a blue or black revolver.

"Drop the bags and nobody gets hurt!" the man ordered.

The witness said she then threw the three night deposit bags down on the parking lot in front of her. The robber knelt down, picked up the bags, and then fired a shot into the ground. He then fled across the parking lot a short distance, stopped turned, and fired two shots in the direction of the four victims. As he turned, Jason said, "That was a cap pistol!" and pursued the suspect.

Crossing Jackson Street, the victim tackled the suspect. There was a short struggle and then gunshots rang out. The robber jumped up and fled north across a vacant parking lot.

Detective Paul Echols arrived at the crime scene and scanned the area. He determined that there were two crime scene areas: the parking lot behind the bank where the robbery had occurred and the murder scene where Jason Jackson had been shot dead. Echols questioned one of the robbery victims, who directed the detective to the northwest corner of the parking lot, the location of the robbery. The victim stated that when the suspect knelt down to pick up the moneybags, he fired his gun toward the southwest, but the witness was not sure of the angle.

Officers conducted a search of the asphalt, the alley, and the rear wall of the bank to locate a bullet or bullet impact. Their search was futile.

The witness told police that the suspect fled in a northeasterly direction, and Jason Jackson chased him. The suspect stumbled when he crossed Jackson Street and fell. When Jason got near the suspect, the robber fired his gun three or four times. The victim told the police that he might have fallen off the suspect when he was shot. The suspect then regained his composer and fled across the vacant lot.

Detective Echols approached the scene of the murder. Immediately, the crime scene was photographed. Police then collected a black bow tie, one shoe belonging to the victim, and a brown canvas moneybag dropped by the suspect. In addition, sleuths collected blood from the grass, from the leaves, and from the sidewalk. A metal detector was then used at both crime scene areas to locate either bullets or brass casings, but the search was futile.

The following morning, at 7:00 a.m., Lieutenant Larry Hill distributed to the media a profile of the suspect as a black male, approximately twenty to twenty-five years old, 160 to 170 pounds, slender build, erect posture, thin face, high forehead, thin eyebrows, long nose, brown eyes, smooth skin, a haircut to a quarter-inch off his head, high cheekbones, and puffy lips. The division commander then organized the homicide investigation. They included Detective Randy Corey, Detective Michael Osificer, Detective Jim Temple, Officer Lynn Trella, Detective Mark Dedtrick, Detective Don Barrit, and Detective Echols. For hours the officers tirelessly conducted an inch-by-inch grid-square search of the crime scene. Then detectives searched every dumpster and trash can in the area. Still they came up empty-handed.

Meanwhile, an autopsy was performed on the victim. Their were four wounds on the left arm, two wounds on his left side, two wounds on his abdomen, and one wound on his back. Some of the wounds were slotted. The pathologist determined after examining X-rays that only one projectile, intact, remained in the body and was located on the left side of the chest. After doctors examined the body more closely, they determined that there were three bullet wounds. The highest wound appeared about three inches above the bend of the victim's left arm. The slug perforated the muscle, exited about five inches above the elbow, and reentered the body about four inches below the armpit. It then went through the heart and lodged in the chest. This was determined to be the fatal wound to the victim. The second wound was located on the left arm about two inches below the elbow, perforating the muscle and exiting at the bend of the arm. The third wound was located on the abdomen about four inches to the left and about two inches below the navel. The projectile's path was just below the skin and did not penetrate any body organs. All three of the projectiles were at slightly upward angles. The examiners placed the victim's arm at a forty-five-degree angle and found that the bullet wounds in his arm matched those in his chest.

Detectives then collected the victim's clothes, hair samples, blood samples, inked fingerprints, fingernail scrapings, and the sheet underneath the victim's body.

Detectives re-interviewed the three victims of the armed robbery. They gave the same story about the robbery as they had the night before. However, one witness did indicate that as they left the restaurant, she saw several people in the area. According to the witness, she and the other three employees gathered the money and left the restaurant through the front door. As they were walking across the parking lot, she noticed a black male with a dog on a leash, talking to someone in a car. She indicated that she and the other employees had a discussion about the kind of dog the man had. The employee indicated that she thought the dog was a Doberman but Jason Jackson indicated that it was a Rottweiler. The next thing the employee knew, the robber appeared.

Another victim, the assistant manager of the restaurant, told detectives that one of the two bank-deposit bags recovered at the scene contained $1,858.56, the other $2,297.73 The bag the robber got away with had $1,551.64 in it. The assistant manager then gave the police a list of the restaurant's employees.

At 4:00 p.m., Lieutenant Hill received a call from a man who told him that he had some information about the Jackson robbery and murder. The caller did not want to give his name, but asked Lieutenant Hill to meet him near a local business in town.

Hill drove to the area. A middle-aged man got into the squad car with the detective. He did not identify himself, but said that several friends knew what happened and that police should go to the restaurant and talk with the cooks. They had information that would help police.

Detective Randy Corey interviewed a cook at 5:17 p.m. The employee told the prober that about two or three weeks earlier, he was standing in his front yard when Dennis Harris and Harris's girlfriend approached him and asked questions about the night bank deposits. He wanted to know how often the deposits were made. He asked weather they were made at the same time every night and which of the bags had the most amount of money in them. What route did the employees take to make the deposit? Harris also asked. Harris then told the employee that he had a plan to successfully rob the restaurant employees. Harris would get a BB gun, station himself on the route of the employees took to make the night deposit, and act as if he were drunk. He would then ask the employees for help. When they approached him, he would pull out his BB gun and tell them to give him the money.

The employee told the detective that he did not mention the conversation to anyone because he thought that Harris was just joking around.

The probe continued, but now the focus was on finding Dennis Harris. At 8:35 p.m., Detective Osificer and Dedrick went to the residence of the prime suspect and interviewed a relative of Dennis Harris.

She said Dennis had left on October 13 and did not return that night. She acknowledged that he could have slipped in during the night and left early the next morning, but she didn't believe so. The relative added that Harris had come by during the afternoon for a short time, then left again. She told the detectives that Harris did not own a hooded sweatshirt or a gun. She said that Dennis was probably at his girlfriend's house in Carbondale. The police asked the woman for permission to search the residence. The relative told the police they could not because the house was too messy.

Police next went to the residence of Harris's girlfriend. They were warned that if Harris was in the mobile home, his girlfriend might not tell them. So detective Jim Temple and Patrol Officer LouAnn Brown went to the door and pretended to be doing a canvass of the area. When Harris's girlfriend came to the door, Temple questioned her for a few minutes. At the same time, he looked and listened for signs of someone else being inside. Temple questioned Harris's girlfriend for a few minutes, then heard someone else moving around in the trailer. The officers asked to come inside. When they stepped into the mobile home, a man popped around the corner from the hallway. Patrol Officer Brown asked the man to identify himself and he refused. Detective Temple recognized the man as Dennis Harris. He was asked to identify himself once again, but refused. The officers were concerned that Harris's girlfriend might be in danger from being forced to hide the suspect, so they asked her to step outside.

Detective Corey took her to the car while the other officers stayed with Harris inside. Detective Corey told Harris's girlfriend that Harris was a prime suspect in a robbery and murder case and that it might be dangerous to allow him to stay at her residence.

The girlfriend seemed frightened but said she did not think that Harris had anything to do with the crime. She told the officer that she had never heard Dennis speak of a robbery, that she had never seem him with a gun, that she had never seen him with any large amounts of money, and that to her knowledge he did not own a hooded sweatshirt.

Corey asked her to wait in the car and went back inside the mobile home. Dennis Harris identified himself and told the police that he would talk to them only if his parole officer were present. The parole officer was contacted and asked to meet them at the police station, where Harris and his girlfriend were then taken.

Detective Corey interviewed Harris's girlfriend. She stated that she first met Dennis Harris a couple of months earlier when she was living in a college dorm. He lived with her for a while at the dorm, then they moved in with his relatives. She said there was trouble between them because he would come in and beat her. She went to a shelter for a while for protection, then moved into her present apartment. He had been staying with her off and on for the last couple of weeks.

On the night of October 13, at about 7:30 p.m., she left town with another friend whom she had met while both were working at a local grocery store. They went to Karnak, Illinois, to visit some of his friends, then went on to Paducah, Kentucky. Afterward they went to a local club and left Paducah about 12:40 a.m. on October 14. The friend drove back through Marion, Illinois, and stopped at another friend's house. He dropped her off at her home at about 2:30 a.m., and she went right to sleep.

Dennis Harris woke her up the next morning, banging on the door. He was wearing a pair of sweat pants and a blue Southern Illinois University T-shirt with white letters—the same clothes he had been wearing the day before. He told his girlfriend he had come by around 1:00 a.m., but couldn't get in because he didn't have a key, so he stayed the night with a friend. She said she didn't ask Dennis who the friend was and he didn't volunteer any names. He didn't have anything with him when he came to her residence, not even cigarettes. The girlfriend added that Dennis did not take drugs and that she only drank wine.

Police then asked her if she knew any employees of the local restaurant that had been robbed. She indicated that she did and named the witness who had informed police about Dennis Harris. She said that the employee was a neighbor.

She further testified that the next day at about 12:30 p.m., she and Dennis went for a walk in the neighborhood and heard a lot of stories about the Jackson murder. She asked Dennis if he was in town the night before and he said that he was. She returned to her residence and started cooking supper. She said the police came to the door and when they knocked, Dennis hid behind the door in the hallway and told her not to tell them he was there. She told the police that she thought there was something strange going on when the police arrived and wanted to talk to her about Harris.

Police then asked the woman if they could search her residence. She voluntarily signed a permission-to-search form. The police asked her if she had any money hidden in her apartment. She said that she had approximately $150 to $200 tucked in her yearbook. She said it was her rent money and added that Dennis did not know about the hiding place. Harris's girlfriend said she changed her hiding place all the time so that Dennis couldn't steal her money.

Officers went to the residence with the girlfriend and conducted a complete search. They found a rubber surgical glove underneath the bed, but the woman told the police she had stolen the glove while at the hospital. The search was fruitless.

While this was going on, lawmen were interrogating Harris at the police station.

They read him his Miranda rights. He indicated that he understood his rights and agreed to continue talking with the police.

The suspect told detectives that a family member informed him the police asking about Harris's whereabouts had questioned her. The family member further told him that a man had robbed a local restaurant and had shot one of the employees several times.

Harris told the police that he had nothing to do with the crime. He said that he had spent the night with a female friend in Carbondale. He didn't know her last name, but did give the detectives her address on Birch Street. The Carbondale friend wanted to get some money together to make a dinner for a sorority group she belonged to. Harris had borrowed four dollars from a family member during the day and took the money to this friend in Carbondale so she could buy the food for the dinner. Harris didn't give specific times to the police.

Harris said that about 4:00 or 4:30 p.m., the girlfriend he lived with dropped by the residence on Birch Street and stayed for a few minutes, then left. Shortly after that, he returned to the mobile home. About 6:00 p.m., Dennis's girlfriend left with another friend and went to Paducah, Kentucky. He said he stayed at her apartment by himself until 11:00 p.m. Then he wrote a note to his girlfriend letting her know he was going out to get some cigarettes. He walked over to a friend's house on Birch Street and they drove to a local lounge, arriving there about midnight. Harris said he had several shots and some beer. He became very drunk because he had not had anything to eat during the day. About 12:30 a.m., his friend wanted to leave because she was not dressed properly. She drove him to his girlfriend's house. His girlfriend still had not returned. Harris did not have a key, so his friend said he could stay with her.

When he got to her apartment, he lay down on the waterbed and was feeling pretty sick. He went to sleep, and around eight o'clock the next morning, October 14, his friend woke him up and drove him to the mobile home.

Detectives asked Harris what he was wearing when he went into town. He said he wore a blue Southern Illinois University T-shirt, white jogging pants with Salukis written down the side, and black high-top tennis shoes.

Detectives asked Harris if he knew any of the employees who worked at the restaurant. He named three people, including the witness and neighbor who had told police that Harris had talked about a plan to rob the restaurant.

Lawmen told Harris they had heard he was a cocaine user. Harris admitted to the police that he did use cocaine on occasion.

Officers then asked him if he had talked with an employee of the restaurant about robbing the restaurant. He said that he had not. At that time, police informed Harris that they had learned he had approached a friend, also an employee of the restaurant, with a plan to rob the place. Harris said the employee was lying, that he was just trying to set Harris up because he wanted to move in with Harris's girlfriend.

Detectives decided to take a ten-minute break from the grilling. They left the room and conferred. They had a hunch that Dennis Harris was lying. His girlfriend's story and his were conflicting. The reason for the employee making up the story was weak at best. So detectives decided to start from the beginning.

Ten minutes passed. The detectives returned to the interview room and asked the suspect to go over his activities once again, starting from 4:00 p.m. on October 14. Harris reiterated his story that he went with his friend to a store to get some groceries, then returned to the apartment on Birch Street around 5:00 p.m. His girlfriend and another acquaintance arrived at the Birch Street apartment around 5:30 p.m. She told Dennis she was going to Paducah for the evening. He said he asked her for the keys to the mobile home. She gave them to him and left. Shortly thereafter he returned to the mobile home. He was there alone until about 8:00 p.m. when his friend called and asked him to come over for brownies. He walked over to the apartment and had brownies with his friends. She received a phone call and said that she had something she had to do, so they went back to his girlfriend's residence. He said that he got there about 9:30 p.m. At about midnight he needed some cigarettes, so he walked back to his friend's house on Birch Street. He went inside and she had someone with her, so he left and walked to a local lounge. He stood outside and bummed a few cigarettes and about 12:30 a.m., his friend from Birch Street pulled up. They went into the lounge and she bought him some cigarettes and several drinks. They left the lounge in her car about 1:30 a.m., and went to her apartment. Harris fell asleep right after they went into the apartment and slept until the next morning when his friend woke him up.

Police asked Harris if he owned a hooded sweatshirt. He told them that he did not own a hooded sweatshirt or a gun and had nothing to do with the Jackson murder.

Officers asked Harris if they could take a photograph of him. He said they could. They then asked if he would stand in a lineup for possible identification as the robbery suspect. He said, "Sure I will, cause I ain't done nothing!" He then told the police that he was getting very tired and wanted to go home.

The police took a photograph of Harris and asked him if he would wait for a few minutes while they showed the photograph to one of the robbery victims. He agreed, and the police took Harris's photograph along with four other photos of people with similar characteristics. Probers showed the photographs to the victim, who immediately made a positive identification of Dennis Harris as the person who had robbed them and shot Jason Jackson.

The detectives returned to the interview room and informed Dennis Harris that the robbery victim had positively identified him as the robber.

The police then informed Harris that he was under arrest for murder and armed robbery. Harris again denied having anything to do with the crime and said the person who identified him just wanted the reward money.

Detectives then asked Harris to show the front and back of his hands. They detected a small cut on the inside of the suspect's right hand. Detectives then asked him to raise his shirt. The suspect had two bandages on his back from fresh cuts. Police photographed the cuts located on the small of Harris's back and then transported him to the Jackson County Jail.

Detectives knew they had their man, but they also knew they had to get more evidence to get a conviction. They went to interrogate the friend who had been with the suspect on the night of the murder.

She told police that Dennis Harris first came to her house about 3:00 p.m. She had left her purse at a sorority house and Dennis went with her to pick it up. Upon returning to her residence, they ran into a relative of Dennis's and took her and Dennis to his relative's house. They sat on the front porch and talked for a while. About 5:00 p.m., Dennis's girlfriend came by the house and took a key from Dennis and left. A short time later, she dropped Dennis off at the mobile home and then went to the grocery store. She returned home, and, at about 6:00 p.m., a friend came over to her house and stayed for about thirty minutes. After he left she made brownies. At about 8:00 p.m., Harris came over. According to the friend, he stayed until about 9:30 p.m. He returned about midnight, whereupon she and Dennis went to a local lounge. She said he told her he had been there drinking earlier in the evening. She said while there with her, Harris drank heavily. They left the lounge at 1:30 a.m. They drove by his girlfriend's mobile home, but he couldn't get in because he didn't have a key. She told him he could stay at her house for the night so they drove there. She told police that Harris went inside and went to sleep right away. She left her apartment to go to another friend's house for awhile. There were no lights on at her friend's house, so she drove around for a while. She spotted a friend in the 200 block of Jackson Street. She talked with him for a few minutes, then returned to the apartment at 2:30 a.m. Dennis was asleep and she went to bed.

Detectives told the woman about the inconsistencies in the suspect's story. They informed her that Dennis Harris had been positively identified in a photo lineup by one of the victims as being the armed robber. The woman began to shake. Officers left her in the interview room.

Lieutenant Hill knew the woman was involved and that he needed her testimony to make a case. He called the state's attorney and asked whether

142

he could offer the witness immunity if she revealed the whole story of the crime. The state's attorney agreed, and Lieutenant Hill returned to the interview room. He made the offer to the witness who nervously agreed to cooperate. They started from the beginning once again.

The witness stated that in September 1989, Dennis Harris came to her apartment along with another man by the name of Stan Algee, a former employee of the restaurant. They told the witness they planned to rob the restaurant and wanted her to help them. She said she didn't want to, but at the time she did not tell Dennis she wouldn't be involved.

The last week in September, Dennis, Stan, and a third man named Rick came to her apartment to plan a robbery of the restaurant that night. Rick was to be the robber. They planned five getaway points. The witness was to be at point A, then something went wrong and they didn't show. She went to point B, then to point C, and so on. The robbery did not go down because Rick would not do it. The robbery was planned for the next night, and again he did not do it. The robbery was planned for the next night, and again it did not go down because Rick, at the last minute, refused to go through with it.

Dennis and Stan decided that just the three of them would commit the robbery. On October 11, Stan Algee came up with a master plan to rob the restaurant. Dennis Harris was to purchase a gun and hide in some nearby bushes until the employees approached. Stan would be walking his dog down the street and if any of the victims gave Harris any trouble, Stan would turn the dog on them. Again, five getaway points were established.

On the night of the robbery, the witness dropped Dennis Harris off in an alleyway just north of East Jackson Street. She then proceeded to a parking lot and parked in a meter stall on the East Side of Jackson Street. Stan was not there, but should have been. The witness sat there for about ten minutes and then saw Stan walking down Jackson Street with a dog. He came up to the car, crawled in, and started talking to her.

At 2:45 p.m., four people came walking out of the restaurant carrying bank bags. The witness hit her brake lights to signal Harris that the employees were coming out of the restaurant. Then, when they started walking across the parking lot, she hit her brake lights twice. Stan said goodbye loud enough so that the employees would hear him, then got out of the car. The witness then drove to getaway point A, which was North Marion Street at the intersection of the alley that runs parallel with Jackson Street.

The witness heard two gunshots. She panicked because she thought that they shot him. She then drove to point B on Oak Street and sat in her car in the middle of the road with her lights on and her foot on the brake. She was scared because Dennis said that the gun would not be loaded.

Then she heard what sounded like two more faint shots. She drove to point C on North Gum Street. Dennis came running up to the car and got in. He was out of breath and talking very fast. He began swearing and yelling that he had shot and killed someone. He had a smirk on his face, was pumped up, and acted as if he had just made a touchdown.

The witness asked him how many bags he got. He said he only got one because he dropped two during the struggle. He said that he threw the gun into the yard of an abandoned house as he passed by.

He started yelling at the witness because she had been sitting in the middle of the street with the car's lights on.

As they drove off, Dennis Harris complained about getting his back hurt and was concerned that his blood might have gotten on the victim.

They drove down one of the streets and Dennis saw a car that he thought was the police. He opened the car door and dropped the money-bag in the street. When he saw that it was not a police car, he had his friend back up and retrieved the bag.

He opened the bag and started swearing because the bag had mostly receipts and not very much money in it. They drove north on Route 127 through Pinckneyville. On the north side of Pinckneyville, Harris changed clothes and rolled down his window. Then, he began throwing receipts out the window.

They arrived at Fairview Heights at about 3:30 a.m. and pulled into a service station off I-64. Harris discarded in a dumpster the sweatshirt and blue shirt he had worn during the robbery. They then drove around the St. Louis area until the next day, when they returned to Carbondale.

Detectives called the Belleville Police Department in Illinois and asked them to check the dumpster at the location provided by the witness. A short time later, they called Carbondale police back to say they had recovered a hooded sweatshirt and blue shirt.

Detectives searched the area north of Pinckneyville for the receipts thrown out the car window by Harris and the abandoned house for the gun thrown in that area by Harris. No evidence was recovered.

Stan Algee was arrested on October 16 and charged with murder. Although he originally denied being involved in the crime, he finally confessed to his participation. He pleaded guilty to murder and was sentenced to forty years. He is now serving his sentence in Menard State Penitentiary.

Dennis Harris received a trial by jury in the First Circuit Court of Jackson County, Illinois, in May 1990. He was convicted and sentenced to life in prison. He too is at Menard State Penitentiary.

Author's Note

Rick is not the real name of the person so named in the foregoing story. A fictitious name has been used because there is no reason for public interest in the identity of this person.

Case 11

Homicidal Hitchhikers

Keith D. Young
Ford J. Parker
April 29, 1990

St. Charles, Missouri

Deputy Sheriff M. O. Neill was cruising toward Missouri's St. Charles County Sheriff's Department with three things in mind—in five more minutes, he would have another shift under his belt, he would be hefting a cold beer, and he would be lying on a soft bed. It was 7:55 a.m. Monday, April 30, 1990. Neill was only two blocks from headquarters when those thoughts were interrupted by a radio call from dispatch instructing him to respond to Silvers Road in St. Charles, Missouri. Someone had reported that two men were lying in a ditch in that area. The person, who made the report said, "They looked dead!"

At 7:59 a.m., Deputy Neill arrived at the scene. He got out of his car and realized one thing right away: the victims not only looked dead—they *were* dead. Neill radioed dispatch and requested assistance from the shift supervisor, Sergeant W. Schwab, and the criminal investigation and identification divisions. Minutes later, the requested officers were on the scene.

The detectives carefully stepped into the sixteen-foot-wide ditch and began to inspect the crime scene. The first body, a white male in his thirties, was lying face up. The victim's head was positioned to the east with his legs to the west and was located approximately eleven feet, six inches south of the gravel roadway.

The blue-eyed victim's reddish brown hair was matted with a crust of congealed blood near his right ear. His face was frozen from the rigor mortis in a winking position, his left eye was glaring toward the key, his right eye tightly closed. Thin streaks of blood criss-crossed his face from

147

the nostrils and the corners of his mouth. His arms were bent at the elbows with his hands resting on his upper chest. The man's left leg was extended straight from the hip and the right leg was bent slightly at the knee.

Dried mud caked both knees of the victim's blue jeans, the palm of his right hand, the fingernails of both hands, and the tan thong shoes he wore.

Approximately fifty-eight feet west of the first body lay another white male, this one in his forties, with his head in a west direction parallel to the roadway. His stiff body was lying face up and he had streaks of blood crisscrossing his face from his eyes, nose, and mouth. The man's hair and beard were matted with a mass of congealed blood. His body was positioned slightly to the left side, with his right arm bent at the elbow and his forearm and hand resting on his left shoulder. The victim's left arm, bent at the elbow, rested on the lower portion of the right arm next to a blue baseball cap he had apparently been wearing. His right leg was extended straight from the hip and his left leg was slightly bent at the knee, like the other man's leg.

The investigators began processing the crime scene by photographing, measuring, searching, and seizing twenty-four pieces of evidence, recording inked fingerprint impressions of the two victims, and performing gunshot residue tests on both. Then the okay was given for the St. Louis County Medical Examiner's team to remove the bodies from the crime scene and transport them to the local hospital.

As she began to examine the corpses, Dr. Mary Case, a pathologist with the St. Charles County Medical Examiner's Office, found a driver's license on the first victim which identified him as thirty-eight-year-old Keith D. Young and showed an R.F.D. address in Desoto, Missouri. Dr. Case discovered an entry gunshot wound and an exit wound to the right forearm, with the entry being in the back and the exit being toward the front, an entry gunshot wound to the left shoulder area with the projectile lodged in the spine, and a gunshot wound to the right temple area. A small-caliber gun caused all the wounds. In addition, there was trauma to the center chest area, possibly caused by blows or kicks delivered by his assailant.

A vial of blood, fragments of the projectiles from the spine and brain, and hair samples were removed from the victim. Tests determined that Keith Young had a significant condition of acute ethanol intoxication, with a blood ethanol level of .206. The cause of death was the gunshot wound to the head.

Dr. Case also found a driver's license on forty-eight-year-old Ford J. Parker of a San Juan address in St. Charles, Missouri. Parker had a gunshot wound to the right side of his forehead and another wound just below his right eye. A small-caliber weapon caused both wounds. He had trauma to the abdomen area, possibly caused by his having been hit or kicked. In addition, a burr hole in the left rear of the skull was discovered. This type of hole, which is made surgically to relieve pressure in the skull, was done some time ago for an injury to the skull.

A vial of blood, five metal fragments, and a partial bullet were removed from Parker's body.

Parker, too, had acute ethanol intoxication, with a blood alcohol level of .116. The cause of death was two gunshot wounds to the head.

So far, the detectives had only bits and pieces to go on. They knew from the wounds that at least one of the shots in each of the victims was received while each man was facing away or fleeing from the perpetrator—probably fleeing, the detectives surmised, since snake-like tracks were found on the bank and gravel road at the crime scene. The only other information they had were the names and phone numbers found on the victims.

The investigators' next move was a door-to-door canvass of the homes near the crime scene. One resident said that at approximately 10:00 p.m. on Sunday, April 29, she heard what sounded like two gunshots about fifteen seconds apart come from the area where the bodies were found. No other local residences had seen or heard anything unusual.

Then the police received a tip from a local citizen who'd read about the murders in the newspaper. The woman said that she'd passed by Silvers Road at approximately 9:30 p.m. on April 29 and had seen a car parked along the road where the bodies were found. The investigators questioned the witness under hypnosis in an attempt to develop her recall of the vehicle. She said that the car was red. Its license plate was black with white letters—"MD 726 or MD 792." Further questioning revealed that the vehicle had Blackwall tires with gray circular hubcaps. It was a four-door and had rusty chrome running the full length. There were two men in the car. The passenger was a white male and had short hair. The witness was unable to describe the driver.

Teams of probers also canvassed the neighborhoods where the two victims lived. Their neighbors knew little about the victims' activities. Several did say that when they met either of the victims on the street, both Parker and Young were polite and mannerly.

149

Meanwhile, investigators also searched the residences of both victims. One of the items they found was a piece of notebook paper with the name Lisa Pulley and an address on Arnold Way in St. Charles, Missouri. The detectives immediately contacted Lisa Pulley.

Pulley told the police that she had known Ford Jerry Parker and Keith Dennis Young for six years. She and Parker were going to be married on her birthday, May 11, and Young was going to be their best man. She said that Jerry and Dennis came by her residence on April 29 at about 8:30 p.m. Dennis talked about putting a new stereo in his car and had cashed two checks for more than $200 to pay for the stereo. He had the money on him that night. About a half-hour later, the three went to the local VFW and picked up some beer, rented a movie, then returned to her residence. Pulley told the police that the victims were not intoxicated when they left. Her eyes welling up with tears, she said, "I don't know why anyone would want to kill them."

The detectives were stumped. Their investigation was leading nowhere.

The break in the case came on the evening of April 30. At 9:15 p.m., a man from Kansas City called and asked Sheriff Edward J. Uebinger if he was investigating the death of two people in the St. Peters area.

"Yes, we are," the sheriff replied. "Why?"

"I think I might have some information on who did it!" the caller said. He identified himself as a relative of an individual named Robert Shafer. The caller said that Shafer had telephoned another relative and told her that he had shot two people. The woman checked to see if the gun they kept in the house was still there.

"When she found that the gun was gone, she became very upset and called me," the man on the phone explained. He told the sheriff that Shafer was living on Marina Drive in St. Charles and worked at a nearby fast-food restaurant. The caller said that Shafer was driving a green nova. Shafer had indicated that he was going to turn himself in to the sheriff's department after he went to visit another relative who lived in Texas.

"Do you know where Shafer is right now?" Sheriff Uebinger asked.

"About an hour ago he was at his residence," the caller replied. He went on to say that Shafer had once been arrested in Kansas for beating up some girl. "He can't control his actions," the caller said. "He needs to be stopped!"

Sheriff Uebinger and several detectives immediately drove to the residence on Marina Drive in St. Charles. They did not find Shafer at home, but they did speak with other relatives of his at their home.

One of the relatives told the investigators that Robert Shafer had come to their apartment a couple of hours earlier and said, "I did something out of the ordinary—illegal." Then, suddenly, Shafer left his relative's apartment.

At that time, the relative said, he called another family member who immediately asked him, "Did Robert kill two people?" The relative's stomach tightened into knots as he realized that the story of the killing must be true.

That same day, Robert Shafer and another man, David Steinmeyer, turned themselves in to the police. Detectives read them their Miranda rights before questioning them. Steinmeyer refused to make a statement, but Shafer told the police that he wanted to talk. He began by declaring that he didn't feel he was guilty of murder. Shafer said that he and Steinmeyer had been hitchhiking along North Highway 94 when a car bearing the two victims, Ford Parker and Keith Young, approached them. The hitchhikers told Parker and Young that they were headed for Shafer's girlfriend's house in St. Peters. According to Shafer, a strong odor of alcohol came from the car, indicating that both victims were intoxicated.

Shafer and Steinmeyer climbed into the backseat. Young was driving and Parker was on the passenger side in the front. Shafer said he gave Young five dollars for gas, and Young quickly handed the money to Parker.

Young headed toward the river access areas on North River Road in St. Charles. Shafer said that he asked Young why he wasn't heading toward St. Peters as he had asked. Young replied that he and Parker were just out drinking and having fun. They would eventually take Shafer and Steinmeyer to St. Peters.

Young then took I-70 westbound and headed for St. Peters. Shafer said that he told Steinmeyer he thought that Parker and Young were gay. Steinmeyer expressed agreement with Shafer.

"Why did you think they were gay?" one of the detectives asked.

Shafer sat for a moment, shuffling his feet and looking down at the floor. "They just acted funny," he finally muttered.

As the interrogation continued, Shafer said that Parker asked him if he smoked pot. Shafer said that he did and Parker told him that if he would go with them to a residence on Fifth Street in St. Charles, he could supply some pot—"Maybe even free."

Parker then told Young that he had to use the bathroom. Young took the Mid Rivers Mall's exit, went west through Old St. Peters, proceeded across a set of railroad tracks and made a left onto Salt River Road, and then turned north on Silvers Road. They drove for about two or three miles before stopping in the middle of the road.

Shafer said Parker got out of the vehicle and Steinmeyer followed him. Then Young got out and shifted the seat forward so that Shafer could climb out.

Shafer said that as he climbed out he heard a commotion on the passenger side of the car. He looked over and saw Parker running for the ditch. Steinmeyer yelled, "They're faggots!"

Shafer said he turned and saw Young coming at him from the rear. Shafer began punching Young, and Young fell to the ground near the front of the vehicle. As Young attempted to get up, Shafer kicked him in the groin and the face. Young fell into the nearby ditch and appeared to be unconscious.

Parker, who was also in the ditch, began running away from the car, with Steinmeyer chasing him. They ran for about thirty or forty feet when Shafer said he saw Steinmeyer shoot Parker two or three times. Steinmeyer was standing and told him that the gun had been in Parker's belt and that Parker had made several sexual advances toward him, thus causing the fight. Steinmeyer placed the gun on the hood of the car and told Shafer to watch out behind him.

Shafer turned around and saw Young coming toward him, yelling that he knew karate and that he was going to "beat him up."

Shafer said he punched Young in the stomach and face, and then picked the gun up off the hood of the car. Young ran and Shafer began pulling the trigger. The gun clicked a couple of times, then began to fire. Shafer said that he shot Young two or three times.

Shafer and Steinmeyer jumped into the vehicle and drove for a short distance, then turned around and drove back past the bodies. "If they are not dead," Steinmeyer said, "let's take them to the hospital."

Shafer, declaring that he did not want to have anything to do with the bodies, told his pal, "I am getting sick to my stomach."

Shafer said he drove the vehicle back to St. Charles using the South Service Road to South Fifth Street, where he drove to the old St. Charles Bridge. He drove onto the bridge heading east into St. Louis County. He stopped on the bridge and threw the gun into the river.

The suspects then drove to the end of the bridge, turned around, and went back into St. Charles. They drove north on Highway 94, back to the food store near his relative's home and parked the car in the food store parking lot near the loading dock.

The suspects went to Steinmeyer's apartment, where Steinmeyer changed his clothes. Shafer said that he then went home and threw the keys to the vehicle in the woods behind his house.

Shafer sat for a moment, staring at the floor. Then he went on to tell the investigators that when he was about ten years old, he'd had a bad sexual experience with a friend of one of his relatives. Shafer said that the friend performed oral sex on him and Shafer swore that he would never let that happen again. "I just lost it!" he said. "The whole incident was out of control."

"Did you know either Ford Parker or Keith Young before you got a ride with them?" one of the detectives asked.

"No!" Shafer responded.

"Did you take any money from them?"

"No!"

The detectives were sure that the suspects had done the shooting, but the declared motive for the murders was still suspicious. The police weren't buying the claim that Shafer and Steinmeyer had shot down two people simply because they were gay. After all, they had already learned that Parker was getting married. There was also the matter of $200 that was missing—the money that had been in Young's possession.

The probers found the victim's car, a 1976 Honda, at the food store parking lot. They had it photographed and checked for prints, and then they collected all the items present inside the car.

Meanwhile, another lawman went to Steinmeyer's residence and recovered a blue steel Thunder Chief .22-caliber pistol, serial number A111687, and a Colt Combat Commander, 9mm, blue steel, serial number 70DS81137.

Lieutenant Peggy Neer searched Robert Shafer's 1968 Chevrolet. After photographs were taken, Lieutenant Neer recovered a long-sleeved shirt and a pair of stone-washed blue jeans that the suspect claimed he wore the night of the murders.

The detectives followed up by collecting supportive information to support their hunch that Shafer's story was suspicious. First, a family member told them that Shafer did not seem to have any remorse or conscience when he did something wrong and even described Shafer as a habitual liar.

During the probe, four different friends of Shafer and Steinmeyer informed the investigators that the suspects were actually friends with Parker and Young, and that they had seen all of them together on many previous occasions before the night of the murders.

Another bit of information from several longtime friends of Parker and Young affirmed that neither of the victims was gay.

On Saturday, May 5, the detectives received yet another vital piece of information with a call from a woman named Lisa Morgan. She told the police that her fifteen-year-old daughter, Judy, had some information about the murder. Judy wanted to talk with the police.

The detectives interviewed Judy that same day. She told them that she and her boyfriend, Greg Little, were friends with David Steinmeyer. She said that they saw David after school on Monday, April 30. They were in the car talking, and all at once, David said, "I never have seen so much blood in all my life. The first one took off running. I shot him in the back. The other one fell down, yelling, "Please don't kill me, I don't want to die." David said he responded, "Too bad, man—you've already seen my face!" Then he said he put the gun to the man's face and shot him.

When the detectives interviewed Greg Little, he confirmed Judy's story. He added that the suspect said, "It is really cool, man, to kill someone. I got my gun, shot him in the back, and ran up to him. He begged for his life, I smiled at him and said, 'sorry, dude, you have already seen my face,' and shot them in the head."

Now the police returned to interrogate Robert Shafer further. They told him that they wanted to clear up some points.

"You told us that you didn't know the victims—is that correct?" one of the detectives asked.

"That is correct," Shafer responded. "I've never seen them before."

"Was there a struggle inside the car?" the police asked.

"No! No!" the suspect replied.

"Why was the gear shift broken? Why was is so dirty inside the car?"

"I don't know! Uh, Young was having problems shifting the car before we shot him. I don't know why the car…"

"Did you take anything from the victims?"

"No. We had some beer when Parker offered it, but that's all."

"Whose gun was it?"

"Parker's, I guess. It came from his side of the car."

The investigators told Shafer they had learned that the victims were not gay, that Shafer and Steinmeyer had known the victims before the murders, and that the police believed the gun belonged to Steinmeyer.

Shafer told the probers that he did not want to talk to them any longer. He clammed up.

Robert Shafer and David Steinmeyer were charged with two counts each of first-degree murder, armed criminal action, and tampering.

The ballistics tests from the crime lab revealed that the gun seized at Steinmeyer's residence matched the bullets taken from the bodies of the victims.

Several months later, David Steinmeyer turned state's evidence and admitted that the motive for the murders was robbery. He pled guilty to second-degree murder and on October 21, 1992, he was sentenced to twelve-and-a-half years in prison. He is now serving his sentence in Missouri's Jefferson City Penitentiary.

Robert Shafer pled guilty to two counts of first-degree murder and two counts of armed criminal action. On January 4, 1993, he was sentenced to death by lethal injection. He is currently on death row at the Jefferson City Penitentiary, awaiting his appointment with ultimate justice.

Author's Note
Greg Little, Lisa Morgan, and Judy Morgan are not the real names of the persons so named in the foregoing story. Fictitious names have been used because there is no reason for public interest in the identities of these persons.

Case 12

The Attempted Cover-up

Bruce Scott
February 16, 1991

Carbondale, Illinois

Saturday morning, February 16, 1991, was a busy day for Illinois's Carbondale Police and Fire Departments. It began with a call to the police at 11:45 a.m.

"We need the police, somebody has been stabbed!" an excited voice bellowed through the phone.

Lawmen hurried down to East Green Street where the caller claimed the stabbing took place.

Upon entering the residence, lawmen rushed across the room to a man who was lying on the floor. He was holding his chest and gasping for air. Police opened the man's shirt and noticed what appeared to be a knife wound in his upper chest near the heart.

"What happened?" the officer asked.

The victim just looked at the officer blankly and gasped for air.

About that time, another man who was lying on a nearby couch sat up slowly, rubbing his eye. "What's going on?" he asked.

"We thought you might tell us," the officer responded.

"I was asleep I don't know," he said staring at the officers with bloodshot eyes.

Suddenly, emergency medical technicians (EMTs) rushed through the door and to the victim. Police stood back as the EMTs went to work. They attached a portable oxygen mask over the victim's nose and mouth, placed him on a stretcher, carried him to the ambulance, and hurried to the hospital.

Lieutenant Larry Hill, Detective Don Barrett, and Detective Randy Corey from the Carbondale Police Department began to search the house.

They detected a strong smell of alcohol as they moved from room to room. They found several empty wine bottles strewn about on the floor. But aside from that, there were no signs of violence in the house.

Police then questioned the man who had been lying on the couch. He identified himself as Willie Rosemand and said the victim was Bruce Scott. Rosemand told police that he and Scott lived together. He said they had been drinking wine all morning. Pablo Kenner and Genetta Smith, both friends of Scott, stopped by with a couple of people Rosemand didn't know. Shortly after they arrived, Rosemand said he laid down on the couch and passed out. When he woke up, the officers were in the room. At 12:55 p.m., lawmen at the crime scene were contacted by radio and informed that forty-one-year-old Bruce Scott was dead on arrival at the hospital. Doctors confirmed that the victim had died for a single knife wound to the chest.

At 1:30 p.m. that same day, crime scene technicians from the Illinois State Crime Lab arrived to process the scene. They photographed the scene, then dusted for fingerprints. Police discovered a paring knife in the kitchen that was consistent in size with the wound of the slain victim. Although the knife had no visible bloodstains on it, the police sent it to the crime lab anyway to be tested just in case.

They soon received the results of the tests on the knife, as well as the blood and fingerprint tests. The lab didn't find any blood on the knife. And the fingerprints weren't discernible.

Next, the probers began a door-to-door canvass of Green Street. The narrow, two-way street was a hodgepodge of rundown one-story houses, vacant lots, and mobile homes. The investigators were hoping to find a witness who might have seen or heard something that would give police a clue in the case. One by one, however, the neighbors told the detectives that they did not know where either Pablo Kenner or Genetta Smith was, nor had they seen or heard anything that aroused suspicions.

At eight o'clock that evening, forensic pathologist John Heidings-felder performed an autopsy on Bruce Scott. The test revealed Scott's blood-alcohol level at 2.204 The pathologist said that the single knife wound was in the upper chest, but the wound angled downward and had slightly pierced the edge of the heart. The doctor determined that the wound would have caused the victim to drop immediately. The victim had died of internal bleeding.

Shortly after Detective Barrett returned to the police station, he received a call from dispatch. "You better come down here," the dispatcher said. "Genetta Smith just walked in, and she wants to talk to someone."

Police took Smith to the squad room and began an interview. She told the police that she had been with Pablo Kenner at the house on East Green Street where the stabbing took place. According to the witness, Kenner was her boyfriend and they, along with two of Kenner's friends John Wood and Leroy Jenkins, had stopped by to see Bruce Scott. They were all drinking Thunderbird wine and, at about ten o'clock in the morning, the supply ran out. Kenner gave Scott $10 and asked him to buy some more wine. Scott returned shortly from the liquor store. Between the group, they drank a gallon of wine.

A short time later, Kenner and Scott got into an argument. Genetta Smith said that she didn't pay much attention to them because it was typical of their relationship.

After about twenty or thirty minutes of name calling, Scott went into the bedroom to rest for a while. Kenner went into the kitchen, returned to the living room, then walked into the bedroom where Scott lay on the bed. The duo starting yelling at each other again. Smith said she didn't actually see Kenner stab Bruce Scott, but suddenly, the yelling stopped. Everything was quiet for a moment. Then Scott stumbled backward through the door and fell to the floor holding his chest and gasping for air.

Genetta Smith ran to a neighbor's house and called the police. She told police that she got scared and left the area with Kenner and their other two friends.

Just as police were wrapping up the interview with Genetta Smith, another witness, John Wood, showed up at the police station. He confirmed what Smith had told police with the exception of one thing. He told probers that he saw Pablo Kenner stab Bruce Scott.

Having completed the interrogation of Genetta Smith and John Wood, the Carbondale police obtained an arrest warrant for forty-six-year-old Pablo Kenner, who lived on Elm Street in Carbondale. In short order, Kenner was arrested without incident and taken in handcuffs to the police department.

Investigators read Kenner his Miranda rights and asked him if he would talk with them. Kenner claimed he was innocent of any wrongdoing but refused to talk with the police about his involvement in the crime. Police booked him for the murder of Bruce Scott based on the information they had received from the two witnesses.

The murder investigation was in its eleventh hour when the Carbondale Fire Department responded to a call at the same address on East Green Street. Firefighters rushed to the scene and found the house engulfed in flames. The heat from the fire was so intense that the paint blistered and storm windows exploded on the home next door. Firefighters fought furiously against high winds and extreme heat to bring the fire under control. Four hours later, the scene was nothing but smoldering ashes bordered by the partially-burned frame of the house.

An arson investigator from the Illinois State crime Lab arrived shortly after the fire was extinguished and began processing the scene. Floodlights were used to light the area, and within a few minutes, police discovered another shocking surprise: two charred corpses lay in the rubble.

The arson investigator determined that the bodies were in the living room, where, he believed, the fire had started.

Detectives Randy Corey and Don Barrett once again returned to the crime scene. They, along with the other members of the investigative team, worked to protect the scene by cordoning it off with yellow crime scene tape and holding back the curious onlookers. Other probers took photos, dusted for prints, and bagged evidence. Police discovered the water faucets had been turned on in the kitchen and fingerprints were found on them. But it wasn't likely to do much good until they had a suspect.

The bodies were removed from the scene and taken to the local hospital. The coroner ordered that autopsies be performed on the bodies to identify them and determine the cause of death.

Questions demanding immediate answers jumped into the minds of the detectives concerning the connection between the stabbing earlier in the day and the fire. Who were the two victims found in the house? Were they murdered? Police were baffled.

A break came when one of the police officers patrolling the area of the house fire spotted seventeen-year-old Dallas Keller. The officer recognized Dallas as a suspect who had been wanted for questioning in a battery incident that took place the day before. The officer stopped Keller and asked him where he was going. He answered that he was returning to a relative's home. The lawman then asked Keller where he had been, and he said he had been at a friend's house.

Police checked this story out. Later, they told Keller that his friend said he hadn't seen Keller in two days.

Keller said that he didn't know what he was thinking about when he told police that he had given them the name of the wrong friend. The detectives checked his story once again and found out that he had not been at that location at that time, either.

A patrol officer took Dallas Keller to the police station for further questioning. Police asked if he was involved with the fire in any way. He told police that he didn't know anything about the fire.

Records at the police station revealed that Dallas Keller was a relative of Pablo Kenner's girlfriend. Police discussed the relationship and the possibility of a connection between the fire and the earlier stabbing of Bruce Scott.

Detectives asked Keller if he knew Pablo Kenner. He said he did, but he still didn't know anything about the fire.

"Why did you lie to us about where you were during the fire?" detectives asked.

"I didn't want to get in trouble for breaking curfew. I'm on probation," Keller responded.

Police told Keller that they knew he was in the house because they had found his fingerprints on the water faucets. They asked Keller if he would voluntarily take a polygraph examination. Keller agreed.

On Sunday morning, the day after the fire, officers were once again on the scene doing a door-to-door canvass. Neighbors said they had seen nothing unusual the night before, but they did tell police that two other men besides Bruce Scott lived in the home. Neighbors identified them as sixty-nine-year-old Hersley W. Scott and fifty-nine-year-old Willie L. Rosemand. According to the neighbors, all three men were nice people and none of them ever caused a problem.

At 10:00 a.m., forensic pathologist John Heidingsfelder performed autopsies on the two victims. The pathologist determined that both victims had died from smoke inhalation. From further testing, the doctor concluded that the bodies had no bruises or injuries that would indicate a physical assault on the victims. Finally, with the use of dental records, the doctor confirmed the identification of the two victims as Hersley W. Scott and Willie L. Rosemand.

Later that same day, Keller was scheduled to take the polygraph examination. The lawmen read Keller his Miranda rights and Keller told them that he wanted to talk. He began his statement by confessing to the police that he had set the fire. He said he went to the house to visit. Hersley Scott and Willie Rosemand were both intoxicated. After a while, they went to sleep and Keller said that he got bored. He got a book of matches and started flipping lighted matches on pieces of cardboard and paper that were in the living room. When the fire started, Keller said he couldn't put it out, so he tried to wake the victims up. He shook and shook them, but he couldn't get them to wake up. He went into the kitchen, turned on the water faucets, and left the house.

When Keller finished his story, police arrested him on two counts of murder and one count of felony arson. He was incarcerated in the Jackson County Courthouse, a stone building centered in Murphysboro, Illinois.

The state's case, as argued by prosecutor Chuck Grace, rested on two key witnesses: Genetia Smith and John Wood. They confirmed to the police on February 16.

The defense's case rested on the testimony of the defendant who continuously claimed he had nothing to do with the crime. Defense Attorney Brocton Lockwood contended that the state had no physical evidence in the case.

Closing arguments began on March 13. Lockwood argued that there were too many pieces of the puzzle missing. There were no fingerprints, no hair, no blood, or other trace evidence belonging to Pablo Kenner. Further, the police had never produced a murder weapon. The defense attorney stressed that it was the responsibility of the state to prove the defendant guilty beyond a reasonable doubt. The state's case rested solely on circumstantial evidence, the defense maintained. Lockwood suggested other ways the murder could have occurred.

The defense counsel then directed the awesome responsibility of deciding the guilt or innocence of his client upon the jury. Did the state present evidence that gave proof beyond a reasonable doubt or were there other plausible possibilities, he asked. If so, then the jury had to find the defendant not guilty.

In closing, Prosecutor Grace told jurors not to let questions draw them away from the evidence presented. He compared it to a puzzle. Sometimes all the pieces may not be there, but when the border pieces and many in the center are available, you get the general picture. Pablo Kenner was the man who stabbed and killed Bruce Scott, the prosecutor stated.

The jury came back with their verdict before noon. They found Pablo Kenner guilty of first-degree murder.

Next, in the First Circuit Court in Jackson County, Judge David W. Watt Jr. set sentence for Kenner. After weighing Kenner's previous record and the circumstances of the case, the judge sentenced him to forty-five years in prison for the murder of Bruce Scott. Kenner was transported to Menard Prison in Chester, Illinois to serve his sentence.

On May 21, about a month after Pablo Kenner's sentence, a hearing was conducted to determine if Dallas Keller was fit to stand trial for the murder and felony arson. The court was informed that Keller was in the eleventh grade, but only had a second-grade reading level and the mental age of a ten-year-old.

On May 22, the six-person jury took about one hour to deliberate. Dallas Keller was found fit to stand trial.

A short time later, the state was ready for trial. Their case began to shake, however, when the defense attorney asked Keller's confession be suppressed from the trial. The attorney argued that the only records available to him of Keller's confession were the transcripts, which might be inaccurate. Police had not provided a tape of the confession, although they had one.

The defense attorney said the police had told Keller that his prints were on the water faucets in the house in order to get him to talk. This was false information and a coercive method to get the defendant to confess to the crime, the lawyer argued.

The defense also argued that Keller only had the mental ability of a ten-year-old and said he did not believe that his client could understand the Miranda rights given by the police before his confession.

In rebuttal, the state informed the court that they had heard the tape of the defendant's confession and the transcripts presented to the court were accurate.

The state contended that the police told Keller his prints were on the faucets to get him to admit that he was in the house. This was an investigative tool used by police that had been upheld by a previous Supreme Court decision.

The state argued that the defendant had been given a hearing in which a six-person jury had found the defendant fit to stand trial.

On October 17, 1992, Judge Watt suppressed Keller's confession, stating that the Miranda warning was improper. The court felt that because Keller was limited in mental ability, there was reasonable doubt to believe that the defendant did not fully understand his constitutional rights.

The state's attorney appealed the case to the Illinois State Appellate Court.

As he awaited the decision of the appellate court, Keller was released on bond.

Finally, the appellate court returned a decision that denied the state's appeal. The confessions would remain suppressed.

On January 30, 1993, the state's attorney at a news conference explained that without Keller's confession, the state did not have enough evidence to convict Keller for murder and arson. Therefore, all charges against the defendant were dropped.

Author's Note

Genetta Smith, John Wood, Leroy Jenkins, and Dallas Keller are not the real names of the persons so named in the foregoing story. Fictitious names have been used because there is no reason for public interest in the identities of these persons.

Case 13

The Stolen Gun Scam

Earl Gulley
November 25, 1991

Carrier Mills, Illinois

Illinois's Saline County Sheriff's Major Ed Miller and Captain Jim Wheatcroft were starting a typical week of reviewing weekend incident and arrest reports until they received a disquieting call at headquarters about 8:10 a.m. on Monday, November 25, 1991. "There has been a shooting at the Earl Gulley residence in Carrier Mills," a frantic voice spouted over the line. "You need to get someone out here!"

After hanging up, both officers rushed to the Gulley residence located on Pankeyville Blacktop Road about 4.3 miles southeast of Carrier Mills. A relative of Earl Gulley's who told them that he'd found Earl lying on the kitchen floor met them. He said that the victim was dead and appeared to have been shot.

Upon entering the residence, the officers moved cautiously from room to room until they reached the kitchen. There they saw a white male lying on his back on the floor. His head was beside a hutch at the south wall. The victim's right arm was extended out from the body and his left arm was bent back at the elbow, with his chest. He was wearing jeans, a short-sleeved shirt, cowboy boots, and eyeglasses. Blood covered the victim's face, clothing, the kitchen wall, and the floor. He had a severe wound to the lower right neck and upper right chest, which the detectives believed to be a gunshot wound. On the kitchen floor near the body lay a shotgun shell casing.

The lawmen secured the crime scene and put in a call requesting the assistance of a crime scene lab technician from the Illinois State Police Department of Criminal Investigation (DCI). Then they searched the outside area around the residence, but they found nothing of help to the investigation.

Meanwhile, crime scene technician Frank Cooper arrived and began processing the crime scene. He found numerous long guns and handguns in the south bedroom. In the north bedroom, he found a galvanized water bucket completely full of coins, positioned in plain sight next to the bed.

After photographs and measurements of the crime scene were taken, Cooper began to collect, package, and mark the physical evidence. He collected a 12-gauge, Federal brand, three-inch Magnum 4 Buckshot shell casing on the floor, miscellaneous papers with possible bloodstains, footwear impressions from the kitchen floor, a partially full pack of Doral cigarettes and a Marlboro Lights cigarette package from the kitchen table, a single head hair from the kitchen table, a button from the kitchen floor, and hair from the west side of the hutch.

That same day, the corpse was transported to a local hospital morgue, where a forensic pathologist, Dr. John A. Heidingsfelder, performed the autopsy on Earl Gulley's body. The pathologist determined that the forty-eight-year-old victim had sustained a shotgun wound to the right upper chest and right base of the neck region. The wound to the neck was seven centimeters in diameter, with plastic wadding and cardboard wadding in the base of the wound. The pellet tracts were in the direction from left to right, with pellets lodged in the victim's left lung, right lateral and posterior lateral chest wall, and the right side of the rib cage. Based on the clinical evidence provided by the crime scene technician, the victim might have been sitting in a chair when he was shot. The assailant was probably in a standing position, at least four to six feet from the victim, when he fired. The right carotid and subclavian arteries and right jugular veins were severely damaged. The damage to these blood vessels caused extreme exsanguination—that is, bleeding—resulting in rapid death.

The officers continued the probe by canvassing the neighborhood. They were hoping to find a witness who might have seen a stranger or a strange vehicle near Gulley's residence or someone who might have heard a gunshot. One neighbor told the police that she saw something while she was driving home from work about 10:30 p.m. on Sunday, November 24, where she always took a short cutoff road next to Gulley's residence. When she turned onto the road, she saw a gold, older-model sports car parked in the driveway. The engine was running, the headlights were on, and the driver's side door was open. The neighbor said she was able to see a man sitting at the kitchen table by the window. He was wearing a green hat. She did not see anyone else. No one else in the area had seen anything unusual or heard anything that aroused suspicions.

Next, the police questioned Betty Smith, an acquaintance of Gulley's. They found out that Earl Gulley had called Betty on Sunday, November 24, around 8:30 p.m. She told the probers that Earl asked her to dinner later that evening. She told him she was in for the evening and did not want to go out. Earl told her that he had company coming around 9:30 p.m. and would be by her place after they left. She stayed up till 1:00 a.m., but Earl never showed up, so she assumed that he had lain down and fallen asleep, since he mentioned that he did not feel well because of a cold. Earl never did tell her who would be visiting him.

Meanwhile, Deputy Jim Dunn arrived at the crime scene and informed the investigators that he had been working with Earl Gulley to recover several stolen guns that had been taken from Gulley's residence during a burglary a week earlier—Monday, November 18. The burglar had entered Gulley's residence through the west window of the living room. The deputy learned from Gulley during the burglary investigation that twelve long guns and a gold ring were stolen. The lawman had processed the crime scene, but he'd been unable to turn up any clear fingerprints or other evidence to help solve that case.

Dunn had questioned Gulley about possible suspects. Gulley told the deputy that Lester Wilkes, a relative of his, would be the first person he would suspect. Gulley's reason for his suspicion was the past dealings with Wilkes. Gulley wanted to offer a $500 reward for the recovery of the twelve guns.

Deputy Dunn said that two days later, on November 20, Gulley contacted him. Gulley told the lawman that a fellow named Quentin Holmes had called him to say that he had bought five of the long guns. He thought that those firearms had been stolen from Gulley's residence. Holmes said that some guy named Jim from Eldorado had the guns, and Holmes bought them from Jim for $300. Holmes was at his girlfriend's house and had the guns there.

Gulley hurried to the residence. Upon being admitted, he found the guns lying on the bed in the south bedroom. They were wrapped in a wet quilt. Gulley checked the guns to make sure they were his and then paid Quentin $400 in cash—$300 for the guns and $100 for recovering them.

On November 22, Earl Gulley contacted Deputy Dunn a second time and told him that he had just paid Quentin Holmes $700 for six long guns and two pistols, which he had not known, was missing. Holmes told Gulley that he recovered these guns from a guy named John from Raleigh, Illinois. He drew a rough map for Gulley showing the location to Jim's residence in Eldorado, but made no indication where John lived in Raleigh. Gulley gave the map to Deputy Dunn.

On Saturday, November 23, Gulley contacted Deputy Dunn once again and relayed several bits of information he had received that day. First, Quentin Holmes had called and was going to bring Gulley's last missing gun to him on Sunday morning, November 24, and then show Gulley where John lived. A short time later, Lester Wilkes, the relative Gulley had suspected of pulling the burglary, stopped by and told Gulley that he had just seen a gold Camero parked at a wooden bridge about three-quarters of a mile from Gulley's residence. Holmes and another man with long brown hair were in the car. A short time later, Holmes telephoned Gulley and told him that he found a man who'd witnessed the burglary. Holmes was going to bring the guy out to Gulley's place the next morning.

On Sunday morning, November 24, Holmes showed up with a man who told Gulley that he'd been hunting behind Gulley's residence on Monday, November 18, and witnessed the burglary. He said he saw Lester Wilkes and another large man with long hair carrying items from Gulley's residence. After telling the story, Holmes told Gulley that he would be back around 9:30 p.m. with the last of the missing guns.

About 10:30 p.m. that same day, Deputy Dunn called Gulley to find out if he had recovered the gun. Gulley's responses sounded vague and hesitant. Dunn asked if someone was there. Gulley told him yes, so the lawman hung up. About thirty minutes later Dunn called again, but he found out that someone was still there, so he told Gulley that he would contact him the next morning. That was the last time the lawman talked with the victim.

Deputy Dunn told the investigators that he had one other thing to mention, "The trunk between the television and the couch had a scarf and three pictures sitting on it. Somebody has moved that scarf and knocked over two of the family photos." Dunn said that it looked as though someone had been sitting on that trunk. He figured that more than one person might have been at Gulley's residence.

Major Miller contacted Sheriff George Henley and briefed him about the burglary investigation. Although the police were not sure if the burglary and the murder were related, Sheriff Henley decided that the detectives should interview Quentin Holmes as soon as possible.

A short time later, Sheriff Henley and Deputy Mike Jones paid a visit to Holmes at his residence on Railroad Street in Carrier Mills. After, Holmes invited the lawmen inside and Sheriff Henley informed Holmes that he needed to talk with him. The lawmen asked Holmes if he would come to the police headquarters for in interview.

"I'll have to change clothes," said Holmes's girlfriend, who was also present.

"What's this all about, George?" Holmes asked the sheriff.

"Let's wait until we get to the county to talk about it," Sheriff Henley responded.

"I think I know what it's about," Holmes went on. "My mother called me earlier and told me that Earl Gulley was killed."

The sheriff told Holmes that he needed to get back to the crime scene. If Holmes didn't mind, the sheriff would give Holmes a ride to headquarters, while Deputy Jones waited for his girlfriend.

Holmes agreed, and a few minutes later, he and the sheriff were en route to headquarters. Upon arriving, Sheriff Henley asked Holmes to wait there until Henley returned. Holmes agreed to do so, and then he said, "George, I can help you solve this thing. I can probably give you the guy that done the shooting, but you've got to help me first."

"Don't make any statements now—wait until I return," Sheriff Henley instructed Holmes.

After finishing the crime scene processing, Sheriff Henley, Major Miller, Captain Wheatcroft, and State Police Detective David Elwood returned to the sheriff's headquarters to begin interviewing witnesses.

Under questioning, Holmes's girlfriend said that Holmes told her that on the night of November 24, he'd gone to Eldorado to look for a guy named Jim. He wanted to see him about the stolen guns that belonged to Earl Gulley. Holmes could not find Jim, however, so he returned to Harrisburg and went to Lester Wilkes's house. Holmes told his girlfriend that Wilkes wanted to go to Gulley's house to talk with Gulley about the stolen guns. Shortly after they arrived there, Holmes said Gulley accused Wilkes of stealing his guns. An argument erupted and Wilkes shot Gulley. Holmes did not provide any details as to how the shooting actually took place, but he said that when Wilkes got into the car after the shooting, he pulled a gun on Holmes and said, "If you involved me in this in any way—I had no part in it—I'll kill you! You just saw me kill a man! If I can't get to you, I'll get to your old lady and those kids!"

In continuing her story to the police, Holmes's girlfriend said Holmes told her that Wilkes made him drive to the town reservoir, where Wilkes got out of the car and threatened Holmes again. However, Holmes didn't go into detail about what Wilkes did at the reservoir. After the stop at the reservoir, Holmes took Wilkes back to Harrisburg.

Meanwhile, Detective Elwood was interrogating Quentin Holmes in another room at the sheriff's headquarters. The lawman read Holmes the Miranda warning. Holmes waived his right to an attorney and said that he wanted to give a voluntary statement.

Holmes told the police that Lester Wilkes contacted him at his girlfriend's house on Wednesday, November 20, and told him that some guns had been stolen from Earl Gulley. Wilkes just wanted to know if Holmes knew anything about it. Wilkes told Holmes that there was a $500 reward to get the guns back. Holmes said that since he had been in trouble before, Gulley probably thought he stole the guns, so he called him. He told Gulley that Wilkes had contacted him about the stolen guns and wanted to help. Then Gulley gave Holmes the serial numbers to all the stolen guns.

Continuing his account, Holmes confirmed what the police had already learned from the interview with Deputy Dunn—the $400 gun transaction with Jim Owens, the $700 gun transaction with John from Raleigh, and the meeting plan for the evening of November 24 to return the last missing gun, a .30-caliber rifle. In addition, Holmes told the investigators that during the transactions, Gulley declared that he didn't trust Wilkes. "I got my suspicions about the boy," Gulley told Holmes. "I don't want to blame him, but I am halfway convinced he took my shit!"

In the meantime, Holmes had been talking to some people in Carrier Mills who told him that a guy named Tim Anderson had some information about the burglary at Gulley's residence. Holmes said he spoke with Anderson, who said that he'd been hunting behind Gulley's residence and saw Wilkes carrying guns from there.

On Sunday morning, November 24, Holmes and Anderson went to Gulley's home and told him the story. Holmes said that he and Anderson left there around 11:00 a.m.

Holmes said that later the same day, he called Gulley and told him he couldn't find the guy to get his gun. Gulley told him to come over anyway that night.

About 9:30 p.m., Holmes said, he returned to Gulley's residence. He parked his car out back behind the barn because Earl did not want anyone to know he was there. Holmes said they were sitting in the kitchen talking when Wilkes pulled into the driveway. Earl told Holmes to go out the back door. Holmes said that as he was walking toward his car, he heard Gulley and Wilkes yelling at each other. Then he heard what sounded like a shotgun blast. Holmes got into his car, drove slowly by the barn, and eased onto the road. He said he did not turn his lights on until he was at least half a mile away, because he didn't want Wilkes to know he'd been there.

As Detective Elwood listened to Holmes's story, he came to suspect that something was not quite right with it. He stopped the interview for a moment and sat silently looking at Holmes. Then he picked up the interrogation again with a series of quick questions.

"Did you kill Earl Gulley that night?" Elwood asked Holmes out right.

"No, sir. No, I did not," Holmes replied.

"Did you see anybody kill him?" the detective inquired.

"No!" Holmes answered.

"What kind of cigarettes do you smoke?"

"Doral Lights."

"Did you leave any Doral Lights out at Earl's?"

"Yes, I did."

"Why?" the prober asked.

"Well, I was in a hurry–I mean I seen that truck pull up and I was gone," Holmes replied.

"Did you see any money or jewelry sitting around?"

"No!"

"Did you see any shotguns?"

"No."

"Where was Earl sitting?" Detective Elwood asked.

"He was sitting at the table with his back to the wall," Holmes responded.

"How many packs of cigarettes did you leave there?"

"Well, I left a pack of Marlboro the first time and the Doral Lights the second time. The Marlboros I just forgot, and the Doral Lights because I was trying to get the hell out of there."

"Where were you sitting?"

"I was sitting to the left of Earl at the kitchen table."

"He had his back to the wall?" the lawman asked.

"Yes." Holmes replied.

Detective Elwood concluded the interview at 9:04 p.m.

The investigators were dubious about Holmes's protestations of innocence. They asked permission to search his residence as well as his girlfriend's dwelling. The police told Holmes that they wanted to check his clothing for blood spatters. If his clothing were not spattered, it would bolster his statement that he was not at Gulley's residence when the victim was murdered. Holmes and his girlfriend agreed to the search and signed consent-to-search forms waiving their constitutional rights and allowing the police to search their homes.

The probers searched both homes, but they were unable to turn up any evidence pertinent to the case.

The police arranged to drop off Holmes at his girlfriend's residence and asked him to return to the sheriff's department to have his statement taped.

Meanwhile, Major Miller and Deputy David McLearin found Lester Wilkes. During a thirty-minute interview, they learned that Wilkes had a solid alibi for November 24, the night of the murder.

The police continued the probe with an interrogation of Jim Owens and a voluntarily permitted search of his residence. The search proved to be fruitless and after intensely questioning him, the police were convinced that Owens had nothing to do with the burglary or the murder.

At half past eleven that same night, the detectives read Quentin Holmes his Miranda warning. Holmes waived his constitutional rights and, once again, he underwent an interrogation. The police informed Holmes that Wilkes had a solid alibi and that they did not believe Holmes himself was telling the whole truth. If he had shot Earl Gulley in self-defense, the probers assured him that they would pass on the information to the state's attorney.

Holmes sat silently for a moment, and then he dropped his head. Finally, he began speaking. He told the lawmen that he was at Earl Gulley's residence and they were at the table talking when Gully accused him of committing the burglary and trying to sell the guns back to him. Holmes said he thought that the victim was going to grab a gun on the table, so Holmes himself picked up a shotgun off the kitchen counter and fired at the victim.

Now Holmes told the police that he wanted an attorney. The police stopped the interview and assured him that he did indeed have a right to an attorney.

About thirty seconds later, however, Holmes told the police that he wanted to continue his statement. The police reminded him that the interview was terminated because he had asked for an attorney. Nevertheless, Holmes told them that he wanted to continue talking without an attorney.

At 12:18 a.m. on Tuesday, November 26, the investigators again read Quentin Holmes his Miranda warning. Once more, he waived his rights and again told the police that he'd shot Earl Gulley in self-defense.

Holmes said that he took a ring and two watches from the victim's home to make it appear that a robbery had taken place. He also took the shotgun he'd used in the shooting and threw it in the Carrier Mill Reservoir.

Five minutes past one that same morning, the detectives drove Holmes to the reservoir. He pointed to an area on the northwest end where he said he'd thrown the shotgun. Holmes also pointed out a place on a gravel road about one-fourth of a mile from Gulley's residence where he thought he'd thrown the ring.

At 2:30 a.m., Quentin Holmes was returned to the sheriff's department and charged with three counts of first-degree murder, one count of unlawful possession of a weapon by a felon, and one count of theft over $300.

Two days later, at about 10:00 a.m. on Wednesday, November 27, the Underwater Rescue-Recovery Team and the Saline County lawmen returned to Carrier Mills Reservoir to search for the evidence of the crime. At 10:35 a.m., scuba divers recovered a semiautomatic shotgun bearing the serial number M711506M from the water approximately twenty-three feet from the west bank and forty feet from the north bank. The shotgun was submerged in nine feet of water with its stock protruding toward the surface.

The police searched along the road where Holmes said he'd thrown the ring, but they were unable to find it.

For the next couple of months, the police prepared their case for court. They had a solid case, but during all this time, Captain Wheatcroft had been mulling over the theory. He figured that the scarf and the family photos which had been on the trunk in Earl Gulley's home must have been moved by another person who was present when Earl Gulley was shot. Wheatcroft hadn't told anyone yet, but he suspected Tim Anderson. The first time the police had interrogated Anderson, there had been nothing in his statements that would indicate his involvement in the crime. Still, Wheatcroft had a gut feeling.

Shortly before noon on March 27, the probers questioned Anderson one more time. First he told the police that he knew nothing about the murder. Then he changed his story and said that he'd been at Earl Gulley's residence, but that he had not been inside the house when the shooting occurred. Then, twenty minutes into the interrogation, Anderson finally broke down and told the police what he said was the whole story.

In this account, Anderson said that he was riding with Quentin Holmes on the night of Sunday, November 24, when Holmes pulled into Earl Gulley's driveway. Holmes told him he had to run in and talk to Earl for a few minutes. "He'd be right back out and left the car running and the door open. I set there for about ten or fifteen minutes, and then went into Earl Gulley's home." Anderson said.

Inside Anderson said he noticed several guns on the table and a shotgun lying on the kitchen counter. After a while, Anderson and Gulley began talking. Meanwhile, Holmes rose from the table, picked up the shotgun, turned from Gulley, and started walking away.

"I thought he was going to put the gun up," Anderson told the police. "It happened so fast. I saw blood fly and him [Gulley], his back hit up against the wall and he fell out of the chair. He was not making any motion towards his gun or nothing. Quentin wasn't even in the conversation. It was a shock. When I was a little boy I found dead bodies before in Chicago, but nothing this horrifying."

Anderson told the lawmen that in the early morning hours on Monday, November 25, he and Holmes disposed of several knives, three handguns, two watches, two rings, and two briefcases they had taken from the Gulleys' residence after the shooting. They hid the items in two creeks that run parallel to the Carrier Mills Reservoir.

At 12:13 p.m. on March 27, the police conducted a search of the two creeks. They recovered a .38-caliber pistol, a brown 501 buck knife, two briefcases, and a billfold containing papers belonging to Earl Gulley.

Two months later, on May 21, 1992, a pretrial hearing was held in the Saline County Court. Holmes's defense attorney made a motion requesting that the court suppress Holmes's arrest, his confession, and resulting evidence. The lawyer argued that his client was not informed that he was not under arrest and that he was free to leave the sheriff's department at any time. He also argued that his client did not knowingly and intelligently waive his rights as to counsel.

In his turn, State's Attorney Ron Wolf maintained that the police acted appropriately with their authority during the investigation. Just before every interview, the police had read Quentin Holmes his Miranda Rights, informed him he was entitled to an attorney, and at one point had dropped him off at his girlfriend's home and asked him to drive his own car back to the police headquarters so they would not have to drive him home after he made his voluntary statement on tape.

After hearing both arguments, the judge ruled in favor of the defense. The judge declared that although the testimony of the police officers, along with the facts, times, and places were all believable, nonetheless, Holmes's previous experience as a felon with the police could have led him to believe he was in custody. The facts suggested that officers collectively did take the defendant into custody for questioning without a warrant and without probable cause. Also, the court concluded that Holmes did not knowingly and intelligently waive his rights to council. Therefore, the court suppressed the arrest, confession, and all the evidence collected as a result.

State's Attorney Wolf appealed the local court's ruling to the Illinois Fifth Appellate Court in Mt. Vernon, Illinois, arguing that the police had acted within the defendant's constitutional rights.

It took the Fifth Appellate Court fourteen months to render a decision. In January 1994, the appellate court in Mt. Vernon, Illinois, overruled the circuit court decision to suppress the evidence in the case. The appellate court stated that the police had investigated the case within Quentin Holmes's constitutional rights and his confession and the other evidence collected by the police could be used in a jury trial.

On September 26, 1994, Holmes's trial got under way as the jurors listened intently to Prosecutor Wolf presenting the state's evidence. Over a seven-day period, the jury heard Quentin Holmes's previous statements to the police, Tim Anderson's testimony, and the physical evidence recovered as a result of the testimony, leading to a culmination of facts that all pointed to Holmes's guilt.

Defense Attorney David Hauptmann argued on the technicalities of the investigation. Then he asserted that his client had acted in self-defense.

After closing arguments were heard, the six-man, six-woman, jury deliberated for two and a half hours before returning with their verdict. They found Quentin Holmes guilty of first-degree murder.

On Wednesday, November 11, 1994, in the First Circuit Court in Harrisburg, Illinois, Quentin Holmes was sentenced to 105 years in prison for the first-degree murder of Earl Gulley. He is now serving his sentence in Menard Prison in Chester, Illinois.

Case 14

Murderer on Death Row

Kathy Woodhouse
January 18, 1992

Herrin, Illinois

On Saturday, January 18, 1992, Dispatcher Bruce Graul of Illinois's Herrin Police department was enjoying a quiet morning when the phone rang.

"Nine-one-one, emergency," Dispatcher Graul said into his mouthpiece.

"Yes, ah, there's been a rape and murder at Herrin, on the–uh, dry–in the–at the dry cleaning place," the caller muttered.

"A rape and murder?" Graul asked.

"Yeah," the caller replied.

"Uh-huh. Whereabouts, sir?"

"I don't–I don't know the–the, uh–the address or nothing to it."

"Okay. Is it at a residence or…?"

"It's–it's in Herrin."

"Okay. Can you tell me where the body and everything's at?" Dispatcher Graul asked.

"Uh…it's in the back of the place," the caller said. "You go in there. You go through a door. Seen this, you know. It freaked me out. It looked like she was, you know, she was stripped down. But there's blood everywhere. Looked like somebody bumped her."

"It's in a gas station?"

"No. It's in the dry cleaning place. It's right next to it."

"Okay. It's in the dry cleaning place."

"Yeah," the caller replied.

"It's inside the building?" Graul asked.

"Yes," the caller replied.

"What is your name, sir?"

"I can't tell you. This is 911. I don't want to get–"

"I've got to have your name, sir."

"I'm sorry, buddy–it's real! Go check on it!" the caller shot back impatiently just before he slammed the receiver down.

Officer Graul immediately put a trace on the call.

Sergeant Frank Vigiano and Detective Mark Brown were both in the dispatch office when the call came in. They hurried out to the dry cleaner on Park Avenue to check out the possible murder and rape.

As the lawmen pulled into the parking lot, they spotted a gold Dodge parked in front of the bay doors of what had once been a gas station, but was now converted into a dry cleaners. They quickly got out of their vehicle. Detective Brown looked through the front windows of the building while Sergeant Vigiano checked the two doors on the south side. Both doors were locked.

Vigiano continued around the building to check for other open windows or doors. When he got to the southwest corner of the building, he noticed a nylon stocking lying on the ground. He continued around the building until he met Detective Brown at the front door.

"There's a woman's stocking on the ground at the back of the building," Sergeant Vigiano informed his colleague.

Both officers cautiously entered the building. The front lobby was empty. The officers moved to a door at the north side of the room. Slowly, they opened it. On the floor a few feet inside the room beyond, they saw a black purse lying there with its contents scattered all over.

The officers moved through the door, but saw no one in the bay area of the building. Suddenly, however, both detectives' stomachs tightened with knots as what had been only the possibility of a prank call now turned into the reality of murder and rape.

Near the furnace at the back of the chamber lay a body of a white female, face down. The victim was nude except for a bra. Her head was turned slightly to her left. Her arms were underneath her chest. A mass of congealed blood matted her hair and covered the left side of her face. Next to the body lay a pair of pantyhose and a pair of panties. A pale-yellow plastic garbage bag was beneath the victim's legs.

Detective Brown walked over to the body, bent down, and felt her neck. There was no pulse.

"She's dead," Detective Brown said. "Let's secure the crime scene and call dispatch." His partner nodded.

Sergeant Vigiano secured the store while Detective Brown called the dispatcher. He asked that the crime scene technician from the Illinois Department of Criminal Investigation be sent to the scene. Just as the sergeant finished his request, Dispatcher Graul informed him that the 911 call had been traced to a pay phone on the corner of Cypress and Park Avenue, four blocks south of the crime scene. Brown immediately went to the phone booth and secured it.

At 9:30 a.m., crime scene technician Gary Otey from the Department of Criminal Investigation of the Illinois State Police (ISP) arrived at the crime scene. The dry cleaner's building consisted of a small sales room directly inside the front door. Upon entering, Otey noticed a small counter, a small table, and three racks for hanging clothes. On the counter top, Otey found a personal check made out to the cleaners and signed by a Milly Mason. On the table sat a partially-eaten pop-tart and a half-filled cup of coffee.

Otey discovered a purse, apparently the victim's, which had been dumped in the bay area of the building. Then he moved to the south end of the bay and behind the furnace, where the nude body was lying.

Technician Otey photographed the corpse and the scene. Then he collected more than one hundred pieces of evidence from the scene, including blood, hair, fingerprints, palm prints, clothing, a pair of eyeglasses, a plastic garbage bag, and a mop wringer.

After the crime scene had been processed, the corner's assistants transported the body to a local hospital for an autopsy.

Technician Otey drove to the phone booth from which the 911 call had been made and processed it, too. He lifted two latent fingerprints off the telephone receiver.

Meanwhile, Chief of Police Tom Cundiff initiated a canvass of the four block area around the murder scene.

A gas station attendant told officers that he'd seen a white male with short brown hair, wearing a white hat or cap, white coat, and blue jeans, talking on the phone at the booth to which the 911 call had been traced. The attendant did not see the man leave the phone booth.

A woman in the four-block area said that she saw a man running down Park Avenue around 9:00 a.m. The only thing she could remember about him was that he'd been wearing blue jeans.

Technician Otey contacted Chief Cundiff and informed him about the personal check found at the crime scene, apparently written by a Milly Mason of Herrin. The chief and Captain Tom Horn immediately obtained the address and went to the Herrin residence of Milly Mason.

Mason told the lawman that on Saturday, January 18, between 8:00 and 8:15 a.m., she'd gone to the dry cleaners to pick up some laundry. No one was behind the counter or in the room, so she wrote the check, picked up her clothes, and then walked to the back of the store, looking for the employee. There she encountered a brown-haired white male who was between thirty and thirty-five years old; six feet, two inches tall; weighing 230 pounds. He was wearing a blue sock hat, blue work shirt and pants, red plaid insulated vest, and brown lace-up boots. The man was walking towards Milly from the back of the building.

"I told him I laid a check on the counter for my clothes," she said, "and then I left. I thought he was an employee."

Chief Cundiff quickly realized that Milly Mason must have come face to face with the killer. He immediately contacted technician Otey and asked him to do a composite drawing of the suspect based on Mason's description. Copies of the composite were immediately distributed to businesses throughout the area.

In the meantime, the police found out through the owner's registration of the vehicle at the crime scene and from the manager of the dry cleaning business that the murder victim was Kathy Anne Woodhouse, a forty-year-old mother of two children.

About 10:30 p.m. that same day, forensic pathologist John Heidingsfelder performed an autopsy on Woodhouse's body. The pathologist concluded that the victim was sexually assaulted, based on her nude condition, the bruising of her private area, and the presence of dried semen stains on her skin. The doctor determined that at some point during the assault, the victim was placed on her abdomen and received a blunt-force blow to the left side of her head, just above the ear, resulting in extensive skull fractures. The pathologist concluded that the cause of death was a result of cerebral disruption and brain-stem compression, along with compound skull, orbital, maxillary, facial, and mandible fractures due to the blunt-force injury to the head.

The doctor also examined the mop wringer found at the crime scene. The wringer was bent and covered with blood. The doctor told the sleuths that the wringer was heavy enough to have been the blunt instrument that caused the victim's injuries.

The detectives continued the probe by interviewing Tammy Edwards, who also worked at the dry cleaners. Tammy told them that she and Kathy took turns working the Saturday morning eight-to-noon shift and that this Saturday had been Kathy's turn to work. Tammy had last seen Kathy on Friday, January 17, at 6:00 p.m., when she'd relieved Kathy at work. At that time, Kathy told her she had received a disturbing call in the afternoon. A person with a gruff male voice had asked Kathy what color toenail polish she wore.

Tammy said that the only other unusual incident Kathy told her about had occurred about three weeks earlier. That was when a white male, about six feet tall, weighing 200 pounds, with a large build and brown hair, came into the cleaners and asked to use the phone. It was raining outside and he led Tammy to believe that he needed to make an emergency call. After he dialed and began talking on the phone, Tammy realized that the call was personal. A few days later, the same man came in again to use the phone. Tammy told him that she was expecting a call, so he could not use the phone. He left and never returned. For the past several days at about noon, Tammy saw the same man walk by the store. However, she did not see him on Friday, January 17.

A relative of the victim's told the police that Kathy had not appeared to be apprehensive about anyone. The relative said that when Kathy was living in Marion, Illinois, there were three or four occasions when she came home and heard someone leaving from the rear of the house. She never saw anyone and never found anything missing. Kathy's relative had contacted the police on two of those occasions and then the incidents stopped.

Meanwhile, Herrin officers rounded up six people who fit the description of the suspect given by Milly Mason. The police asked the suspects to stand in a lineup. All agreed.

On January 19, a Sunday evening, Milly Mason attended that lineup and attempted to identify one of the men as a suspect. One of them looked similar to the man she'd seen in the dry cleaners, she told police, but she wasn't sure.

The police were quickly frustrated and worried. They had investigated the case continuously for three weeks. Every day they checked out leads called in by citizens. Yet they weren't any closer to a suspect than they'd been on the day of the murder.

On Tuesday, February 4, the detectives received an anonymous call that gave them their first real lead to a suspect. The caller told them to check out Paul E. Taylor, a parolee from Louisiana who was currently living with relatives on South 16th Street in Herrin. Taylor had been released from prison around Christmas. He had been serving time for aggravated attempted sexual assault.

Detective Mark Brown and John Allen of the Southern Illinois University Police drove to the residence on South Sixteenth Street. A relative of Taylor's told the lawmen that on Saturday, January 18, when she'd left for work about 6:30 a.m., Paul had still been in bed. When she returned, about 9:30 a.m., she'd found Paul in the living room watching television or playing Nintendo.

The lawmen had found out that Paul Taylor worked at a local fast-food restaurant, so they asked the relative when the best time would be to talk with Paul. She said she was going to pick up Paul at a friend's house around 6:30 p.m. She promised the detectives that she herself would bring Paul to the police station.

At 7:15 p.m., Detective Brown and Allen met with Paul Taylor at the Herrin Police Department. They informed him that he was not under arrest.

"This is a voluntary interview," Detective Brown explained. "You can leave at any time."

The police told Taylor that they were working on a homicide that had occurred on January 18 and Paul's name was one of many brought up, so they were simply checking out all the names.

"Paul, we would like to run a number of tests on you. Would you consent to being fingerprinted and photographed?" Detective Brown asked.

"Sure," Taylor responded.

"We would like to get blood, saliva, head and pubic hair samples, as well," detective Allen added.

"Okay," Taylor responded once again. The he signed consent forms, and the lawmen took him to the local hospital for the tests. After the tests they all returned to the police station. There, the police began to question Taylor.

"Paul, do you know why we asked to talk to you?" Detective Brown asked.

"Yes. Because you are investigating the murder of Kathy Woodhouse," Taylor answered.

"Did you kill Kathy Woodhouse?" Brown asked.

"No!" Taylor snapped back.

"Do you have any idea who might have killed her?"

"No. I don't know anyone around here."

The police asked Taylor why he thought someone would name him as a suspect. He said he didn't know, unless it was because of his height. Taylor also told the detectives that it did not bother him that he was being questioned about the murder, but he did hope that there were other people being questioned, too.

"Why would someone want to kill Kathy Woodhouse?" one of the detectives asked Taylor.

"Because they are sick!" Taylor answered curtly.

"Paul did you ever think about doing something like this, even though you didn't go through with it?"

"No, because it is wrong and I wouldn't have the nerve," Taylor replied.

"What do you think should happen to the person that did this?" Allen asked.

"Fry him!" Taylor shot back.

"What did you do on the morning of the murder?"

Taylor said that he was home until approximately 8:45 a.m. Then he left the house, went to a local grocery store to buy a pack of cigarettes, and returned home about 9:15 a.m.

"Is there any reason you would have for killing Kathy?" one of the lawmen asked.

"No," Taylor replied.

"Have you ever been in the dry cleaner where the murder took place?"

"No."

"Have you ever been questioned about doing something like this before?"

"No!" Taylor fired back.

"Would you be willing to take a polygraph examination?"

"Yes," Taylor responded.

With that, the police ended their interview with Taylor. They were suspicious of him and felt sure that he had lied about his past sexual offenses.

The next morning, the investigators went to the dry cleaner to review customer receipts. They discovered that someone from the restaurant where Taylor worked had recently taken some shirts to the dry cleaner. The police called the restaurant and asked if Taylor had been the person who'd delivered those shirts. The manager told them that Taylor had worked for the eatery for about three weeks, that he had indeed taken the shirts to the dry cleaner, and that he had just turned in his resignation, saying he was going back to Louisiana.

In the meantime, the police heard from the crime lab, which had conducted tests on the saliva standard taken from Taylor. The results showed that Taylor was a non-secretor. Interestingly, the person who'd raped and murdered Kathy Woodhouse was also a non-secretor. However, the lab did not have enough head and pubic hair standards for testing. The police would therefore have to bring Taylor back for additional samples.

Detectives Allen and Brown went to the Sixteenth Street residence and asked Taylor's relative if they could talk with Taylor. Then Taylor himself came to the back door. The detectives told him that the crime lab had requested more head and pubic hair samples from him to carry out the proper testing.

"I don't know, maybe I should talk to an attorney," Taylor said.

The relative urged Taylor to cooperate with the police, but Taylor stood silently staring at the detectives.

"Do you plan on leaving town?" one of the detectives asked him.

"No. I just got off work," Taylor replied.

"No, you didn't, Paul. You just quit your job and told the boss you were moving to Louisiana," Detective Allen told him pointedly.

"What's going on?" the relative asked Taylor.

At that point, the detectives asked the suspect's relative if she would give them permission to search the house. She agreed. Then the police asked Taylor if he would grant them permission to search his room. He also agreed.

After Taylor and his relative signed permission-to-search forms, the police went to Taylor's room. There they found a pair of stone-washed blue jeans lying on Taylor's bed. The blue jeans appeared to have some small bloodstains on them. Taylor said that those were the jeans he'd been wearing on January 18. In the closet, the police also discovered a white-and-black sweatshirt that Taylor had worn on the morning of the murder. When Detective Brown lifted the end of the mattress at the foot of the bed, he found a pair of pantyhose with one leg missing lying on top of two porno magazines. The police found another pair of bloodstained blue jeans in a dresser. They found no other evidence in Taylor's bedroom.

The probers continued to search the rest of the house and, while doing so, they asked Taylor's relative if Taylor had a hat. She said that he did and went to another bedroom where she pulled a blue hat from the dresser drawer. Handing it to the police, she said Taylor did not like to wear the hat.

With the search ended and no other evidence found, the lawmen asked Taylor if he would go to the hospital and give them more hair samples. He agreed.

At the hospital while the samples were being taken, Detective Eric Frattini of the Williamson County Sheriff's Department came into the examining room and asked Taylor if he would come down to the police department for further questioning. Taylor told the detective that he preferred to go home because he was going to a rock concert and wanted to get cleaned up.

Taylor was free to leave the hospital and Detective Allen gave him a ride back to the Sixteenth Street residence.

Meanwhile, the police put a surveillance team on Taylor, even as other lawmen took the evidence to the crime lab for analysis.

Taylor left the residence and went to the Southern Illinois University area for the concert. The surveillance team followed.

On Wednesday evening, February 5, Detective Frattini contacted the crime lab. Serologist Grace Johanson told the detective that Paul Taylor's blood standards showed a P.G.M. of (1+). (P.G.M. refers to phosphoglu-comutase, a protein that serves as a "genetic marker" and is useful on a more detailed level of blood-typing.) Johnson explained that these results, coupled with the earlier results showing Taylor to be a non-secretor, increased the chance of his being Kathy Woodhouse's murderer.

Detective Frattini then spoke with Glenn Schubert from the microscopy section. Schubert told the police that the stocking taken from Taylor's bedroom was similar not only in color, but also in fabric, to the one found near the crime scene. Schubert had also compared pubic hairs from the scene with those taken from Taylor. The hairs were similar.

When Frattini spoke with latent fingerprint technician Mike Pittman, he learned that the fingerprints found on the telephone matched Taylor's.

The case investigators immediately contacted Williamson County State's Attorney Chuck Garnati to make sure they had enough evidence to show probable cause for an arrest. Garnati advised them to wait until Taylor was back within Williamson County jurisdiction, and then make the arrest.

That same evening, Illinois State Trooper Daren Lindsay and Sergeant Bob McCluskey drove to the Williamson County line and waited for the suspect. Taylor left the rock concert and crossed the county line at 10:30 p.m. Trooper Lindsey and Sergeant McCluskey pulled Taylor's vehicle over and arrested him for the rape-murder of Kathy Woodhouse.

At 11:54 p.m., the detectives read Taylor his Miranda rights. Taylor waived them and agreed to talk with the police. He told the investigators that on Saturday, January 18, at about 8:00 a.m., he walked from his home to the dry cleaner. When he got there, he walked in and told the attendant, Kathy Woodhouse, that he was going to rob her. Then he took her to the bay area of the building. At the rear of the chamber, he picked up a mop wringer, hit Kathy twice in the head, and then left.

"When did you take Kathy's clothes off?' Detective Frattini asked.

"She was fully clothed when I left," Taylor replied.

Now the police told Taylor about the physical evidence found at the scene. Taylor looked down at the floor for a few seconds, then he looked up directly at the detective. "I raped her," he said.

"Okay, Paul, now tell me exactly what happened," Frattini prompted.

Taylor said that after walking the victim to the rear of the building, he ordered her to take off her clothes and lie down on the floor. Kathy lay down on her back. Then, Taylor said, he pulled his pants halfway down, got on top of the victim, and had sexual intercourse with her. He said that he told the victim he was having an orgasm.

Then, he said, Kathy asked him, "Did you hear that car pull up?"

Taylor told her that he didn't hear anything. He got up and told Kathy to get on her stomach. Then he walked toward the front of the store, where he saw a woman standing at the counter. She told him that she was there to pick her laundry and left a check in payment.

"Fine!" Taylor told her curtly.

The customer then walked out.

Taylor said he walked back to the rear of the building and picked up a mop wringer on the way. He hit the victim twice over the head with it. Then he went to the front of the bay, took $4 from the victim's purse, and dumped the rest of its contents on the floor.

After that, Taylor said, he walked down Main Street south of the cleaners. He found a pay phone and called 911 to report that there had been a murder and rape at the cleaners. Taylor said that the officer on the line sounded as though he didn't believe him, so Taylor told him, "It's real! Go check it out!" Taylor then hung up the phone and went home.

On Friday, April 10, 1992, Paul Taylor pled guilty to the murder and rape of Kathy Anne Woodhouse. On Thursday, October 15, 1992, a twelve-person jury sentenced him to death. Taylor is now sitting on death row.

Update

Paul Taylor's death sentence was commuted in a blanket commutation on January 10, 2003, by Governor George Ryan. He is now serving a life sentence in Statesville Correctional Center in Illinois.

Author's Note

Milly Mason and Tammy Edwards are not the real names of the persons so named in the foregoing story. Fictitious names have been used because there is no reason for public interest in the identities of these persons.

Case 15

The Candy Lady

Mildred Smith
March 11, 1992

Cairo, Illinois

The town of Cairo, Illinois, located at the southern tip of Illinois, is dominated by the confluence of the Mississippi and Ohio Rivers, and thousands of miles of navigable waterways. A person with sensitivity and imagination can revisit the nineteenth century and pick up the echoes of the Civil War that linger in the streets of the town. At Fort Defiance, the tramp of marching feet and the moans of wounded soldiers from the past can almost be heard. Along Washington Avenue, stately Italianate mansions speak in the hushed, cultured tones of the wealthy elite who once inhabited them. The windowless storefronts by the river yet ring with the echoes of honky-tonk pianos and crowds of river boat gamblers amid a medley of gentility and violence.

On Wednesday, March 11, 1992, Kawanda Moore didn't need her imagination to know that violence is still a very real part of life in Cairo today.

When Kawanda's neighbor, sixty-three-year-old Mildred Smith, didn't answer her door to several customers, Kawanda wasn't concerned. Mildred operated a candy store out of her apartment, and on occasion she would open later in the morning. But when the clock in Kawanda's living room showed that it was 12:30 p.m., her fears began to mount. She became worried that perhaps Mildred was sick or had fallen and injured herself.

Prompted by her concern, Kawanda telephoned Mildred. There was no answer. Then she walked over to Mildred's apartment, where she knocked on the door several times and called out to Mildred, but still received no answer. Out of curiosity, Kawanda tried the door and, to her surprise, she found it to be unlocked. She opened the door and called out again, but still

189

got no response. Kawanda slowly walked through the door into the small apartment and when she reached the kitchen, she received a shock. Mildred was lying motionless on the kitchen floor.

"Oh my God!" Kawanda screamed. She whirled about and out the door to her own apartment, where she called police. It was now 12:59 p.m.

Cairo city police officers arrived at the apartment minutes later. At first they thought that Mildred Smith had died of a heart attack or of natural causes. When they entered the residence, however, they immediately realized how wrong they were. Mildred was lying face down in front of the refrigerator on the kitchen floor. A large pool of blood covered much of the floor around and underneath her body. The victim was in full rigor mortis. A mass of congealed blood covered the upper part of her body and several stab wounds were discernible in her upper back.

The lawmen secured the crime scene and put in a call requesting the assistance of a crime lab technician from the Illinois State Police Department of Criminal Investigation (DCI). Meanwhile, Alexander County Coroner David Barkett arrived at the crime scene and pronounced the victim dead at 1:06 p.m.

About twenty minutes later, crime scene technicians arrived. First they scanned the crime scene, then they photographed it and dusted for fingerprints. Two detectives discovered and collected blood on the refrigerator door and on the entrance door of the apartment.

Next, the investigators began the task of measuring the exact location of the body. Thirty minutes later, they had Mildred Smith's body loaded into the ambulance and en route to the morgue.

The detectives were concerned that the murder might be gang-related. Just two days before the murder, the local authorities had requested state police patrols in the city because of a dramatic increase in violent crime in recent months. However, as the investigators continued to process the crime scene, they learned from Kawanda Moore that money, cigarettes, and a police scanner were missing from the apartment. They therefore concluded that the motive for the crime must have been robbery.

Officers moved to the outside area of the residence and conducted a search around the yard, but that search proved fruitless.

At about 6:30 p.m. that same day, a forensic pathologist performed the autopsy on Mildred Smith's body. The pathologist concluded that the victim had sustained in excess of twenty stab wounds to the upper back and chest area. One thrust in the upper chest had angled downward, piercing the edge of the heart. The pathologist concluded that the victim died of internal bleeding.

Continuing the probe, the police began canvassing the neighborhood. They were hoping to find a witness who might provide a clue in the case. One neighbor told the probers that she had seen several customers knock at Mildred's door before noon. None of them went inside, however, and Mildred never answered the door. Other than that, the neighbor hadn't heard or seen anything unusual.

The investigators continued to question the neighbors, but one by one, the neighbors said that they had not seen or heard anything suspicious.

Meanwhile, the police received the results of the test on the blood and the check on the fingerprints collected at the crime scene. The blood was from the victim. The fingerprints weren't discernible.

Several days into the probe of the robbery murder, the police had exhausted their remaining leads. None of them had borne fruit.

The investigators' next move was an appeal to the public, asking that anyone who might have information about the murder and robbery on March 11 call them. The police gave assurance that the callers could remain anonymous if they chose.

The appeal paid off on Monday, March 23, 1992, when the Cairo police received an anonymous phone call. The caller told the officers that a man named Isaac Davis and his brother, Danny Davis, had been spending a large amount of money and bragging about being involved in a robbery.

The lawman who took the call immediately alerted the other detectives and a team rushed to the Davis brothers' residence. They found only eighteen-year-old Isaac Davis at home. He told them that he did not know his brother Danny's whereabouts. Meanwhile, the police requested that Davis come to the police station for questioning. One of the detectives read Davis his Miranda rights and then asked him if he was willing to talk to the police. Isaac Davis told the detectives that he would talk because he had nothing to hide.

The detective began the interrogation by asking Davis if he knew anything about the murder and robbery of Mildred Smith. Davis told the officer that he knew only that she had been murdered, but that was all.

More to the point, the detective asked the subject where he'd been on the night of the murders. Isaac Davis said that he'd been home all evening with his brother Danny and a couple of friends.

Now the investigator asked when Isaac and his brother got all the money they had been spending lately. Isaac quickly looked at the floor in silence. Soon, his hands begin to shake. "I wasn't involved in the murder," he said finally. "Danny was, though."

About that time, the interrogation was interrupted when another detective came into the room with the information that he had found Danny Davis and had brought him to the police station.

The investigators read twenty-year-old Danny Davis his Miranda rights and asked him if he would talk with the police. Danny said that he would, but he declared that he had nothing to do with the murder and robbery of Mildred Smith. One of the lawmen told Danny that he had already interrogated his brother Isaac who told the police that Danny had been involved in the crime. Danny's head dropped as he began to cry. He sat silently weeping for a moment, then said that he would tell the police everything.

Danny Davis began by saying that a couple of days before the robbery, his brother Isaac, Curtis Cornell, and Danny himself were talking about how they could get some money. Curtis said they should hit "Miss Mildred," as they called the victim. They decided that they would wait until closing time, which was around 9:00 p.m.

On Wednesday, March 11, the trio met at Danny's house. Danny said that he and Curtis both had knives, but Isaac was unarmed. On the way to Mildred's apartment, Curtis told Danny that if Miss Mildred resisted, he was going to kill her. Danny said he thought that Curtis was just blowing off.

When the trio got to Mildred Smith's apartment, Mildred was just getting ready to close. The youths told her that they wanted to buy some soda and cigarettes. When Mildred turned to open the refrigerator, Curtis quickly stepped up behind her, pulled his knife, and started stabbing her. Danny said he ran up and he, too, started stabbing her. She didn't make a noise, but she did rise up and try to turn around. Then she fell to the floor. At that point, Danny dropped the knife and Isaac picked it up.

"He may have nicked her with it during the struggle," Danny said. "But he didn't take part in killing her. After she fell to the floor, we took the money she had on her, some cigarettes, and a police scanner. Then we ran out and back to my house. Later that night, we threw the knives in the river." Danny stopped for a moment and wiped tears from his eyes. "I was real scared. I asked Curtis why he stabbed her. Curtis said, 'I just wanted to see what it was like to watch someone die.'"

At the end of the interrogation, the detectives got directions to Curtis Cornell's residence and hurried there. They asked Cornell to accompany them to police headquarters for questioning about the murder and robbery of Mildred Smith. Cornell agreed to go with them but declared that he knew nothing about the murder.

Upon arrival at police headquarters, the detective read twenty-two-year-old Curtis Cornell his Miranda rights. He signed a waiver form stating that he understood his rights. Then the detectives questioned him for about one hour. He stuck to his story, however. He insisted he knew nothing about the crime.

That same evening, the police detectives searched each of the residences. They found the stolen police scanner and several cartons of cigarettes at the Davis brothers' dwelling. At Cornell's home, they turned up a pair of blue jeans that appeared to have small blood spatters on the pant legs.

The investigators returned to the police station after the searches and arrested Curtis Cornell, Danny Davis, and Isaac Davis, each on one count of first-degree murder and one count of armed robbery.

Then the detectives took the suspects through the booking process, taking fingerprints and mugshots and filling out the arrest reports. Following all that, they submitted the evidence collected at the murder scene to the crime lab.

Over the next several months, a series of motions were filed in Circuit Court in Alexander County by the defendant's attorney. In the first hearing, held on Tuesday, June 23, 1992, Judge Terry Foster denied a request by the defense attorney to consider the Illinois death penalty unconstitutional.

In a second motion, filed on August 14, the defense asked the court to suppress the statements made to the police on March 23 by the Davis brothers. Danny Davis told the judge that the police chief physically abused and threatened him after he was arrested.

He asserted that while he and the lawman were alone in the police interrogation room, the chief slammed his hand on the table and said that if Danny didn't talk, he was going to fry.

"I talked because I knew I couldn't whip him," Davis declared.

The youth also maintained that he had not signed any forms to indicate he was voluntarily waiving his rights under the Miranda Warning.

On his part, Isaac Davis asserted that he did not know he was under arrest when the police took him to the station. He also declared that he had not signed the Miranda consent forms.

State's Attorney Mark Clarke cross-examined Danny Davis and during that time produced the Miranda rights consent forms bearing Davis's signature.

Clarke followed up by calling Detective Don Rushing to the stand. Rushing testified that the Davis brothers did not appear to feel threatened or scared and that their statements appeared to him to be voluntary.

Rushing said he told Isaac Davis that the investigators would like to talk with him when they accompanied him to the Cairo Police Department. The detective testified that he assumed that Isaac knew he could leave at any time. "We read him his Miranda rights before we interrogated him," the lawman told the court.

After hearing the testimony of the defendants and the police, the judge ruled that the statements made by the defendant would be allowed as evidence in the trial.

In a third motion filed on August 15, 1992, the judge granted the defense attorney's request to have a separate trial for Curtis Cornell, because the Davis brothers had made statements about Cornell's involvement in the court. The brothers' trial was to be held first.

In early September 1992, just before the trial was to start, a plea-bargain agreement was struck between the state and the defense. The Davis brothers agreed to plead guilty to first-degree murder and armed robbery in exchange for the state's agreeing not to seek the death penalty.

Meanwhile, Curtis Cornell waived his constitutional rights to a jury trial and asked the judge to hear his case. The bench trial began before Judge Terry Foster on Monday, September 28, 1992.

The state's case, as presented by Prosecutor Clarke in his opening statement, rested on two eyewitnesses—Danny Davis and Isaac Davis—who had both already pled guilty to the crime and would testify regarding the defendant's involvement. In addition, physical evidence would be presented to support the testimony.

The defense case rested on the testimony of the defendant himself, who continually declared that he had nothing to do with the crime, on the testimony of one witness who would testify that Isaac Davis told him that Curtis Cornell was not involved in the killing, and on defense attorney Kim Noffke's contention that the state had no physical evidence in the case.

The state presented its case by calling Danny Davis to the stand. Danny testified that Curtis, Isaac, and Danny himself planned the robbery together. After giving the intimate details of his involvement in the crime, Danny finished his testimony by saying that Cornell said he did it because he wanted to see what it was like for someone to die.

The second witness for the state, Isaac Davis, testified for about one hour, supporting his brother's story.

The state's forensic evidence was of limited value. A forensic expert for the Illinois crime lab testified that the blood found on Curtis Cornell's blue jeans was the same blood type as the victim's. However, the blood type could also belong to thirty percent of the population. There was not enough blood in the sample for the DNA test to be done.

The state's case suffered a setback when the defense attorney began his cross-examination. He questioned Danny Davis for five hours and Isaac Davis for nine hours over the next two days. The defendants stuck to their story about Cornell's involvement, but the times, places, and events were in contradiction with their previous testimony.

Then the defense attorney put Curtis Cornell himself on the stand. Cornell told the court that he had been in the housing project on the night of the murder, but he was nowhere around Mildred Smith's apartment when the crime took place. The defendant said that he had known Mildred Smith since he was a small child and that Mildred was like a family member to him. There was no way he would harm "Miss Mildred," he declared. In addition, Cornell testified that the blue jeans taken from his home as evidence did not belong to him.

The turning point in the case came when the defense called a final witness. This witness testified that he had been in the Williamson County Jail with Isaac Davis a short time after the murder took place. He testified that Isaac Davis had told him that Curtis Cornell wasn't present when Mildred Smith was murdered.

The five-day trial ended on October 3, 1992, with the state's attorney and the defense attorney making their closing arguments before Judge Foster. The defense maintained that too many pieces of the puzzle were missing. There were no fingerprints, no hair, no blood, nor any other physical evidence linking Curtis Cornell to the crime. Furthermore, the police had never produced a murder weapon. The defense stressed that it is the responsibility of the state to prove beyond a reasonable doubt. The state's case rested solely on the testimony of two admitted murderers who had a "bad blood" relationship with Curtis Cornell.

"They say that my client was involved in the murder in court," the defense attorney observed, "yet one of the witnesses tells a fellow inmate that Curtis Cornell wasn't involved."

The defense then rested. Deciding the defendant's guilt or innocence now rested with the judge. Did the state present evidence that gave proof beyond a reasonable doubt, the defense lawyer asked, or were there other plausible possibilities? If the latter was true, then the judge had to find the defendant not guilty.

In closing, Prosecutor Clarke urged the judge not to let such questions draw him away from the evidence presented. Sometimes, all the pieces to the puzzle may not be there, but when the "border" pieces and many in the center are available, it is still possible to get the general picture. According to that picture, the prosecutor said, Curtis Cornell was one of the men who stabbed Mildred Smith.

After several hours deliberating, the judge returned to the court with a verdict. "As much of a travesty as it is to let a guilty person go," he said, "it is just as much of a travesty to send an innocent person away." He found Curtis Cornell not guilty of the charges.

On Friday, November 6, 1992, a sentencing hearing was held for Danny and Isaac Davis. State's Attorney Clarke argued that what was in the best interest of the Davis brothers had ended. "What is in the best interest of the little old ladies like Mildred Smith?" Clarke demanded. "The best interest of the community is to never see these horrible men again." Clarke then recommended that the defendants be sentenced to life in prison without parole.

The defense called a psychologist who testified about the brothers' troubled childhood, which included learning problems, being sent to foster homes, and participation in alcohol and drug treatment programs.

Then Danny Davis was called to the stand. "I feel we should be given a break," he said. "We did not kill her. I am not a violent person. I have a heart for everybody on this earth."

Danny then apologized to the Smith family and said, "I know how you feel," adding that he, too, had once lost a family member.

Then Isaac Davis told the court, "I am an accomplice, not a murderer. I don't have the heart to kill someone in cold blood like that."

The defense concluded by recommending that the court give the brothers a minimum sentence so that they could benefit from rehabilitation programs.

The judge considered the arguments and then made his decision. He declared that the defendants' behavior was brutal and that "nothing was done but stabbing and leaving a woman to die." He said he believed that Isaac Davis was more of a follower in the slaying than his brother Danny. The judge based his decision on his review of the pre-sentencing and psychological reports, the trial testimony, and the judge's own observation of the Davis brothers in court. He said he believed that Danny Davis had much more involvement in the slaying.

Judge Foster sentenced Danny Davis to life in prison without parole and Isaac Davis to a term of thirty-five years in prison. Both defendants are now serving their sentences in the Menard Penitentiary in Chester, Illinois.

Author's Note

Kawanda Moore and Curtis Cornell are not the real names of the persons so named in the foregoing story. Fictitious names have been used because there is no reason for public interest in the identities of these persons.

Case 16

Trio Slaughtered For Drugs

Sherry Scheper
Randy Scheper
Curtis Scheper
August 9, 1992

Cape Girardeau, Missouri

About 7:30 a.m. on Sunday, August 9, 1992, the quiet summer morning was disrupted with a disturbing call to Missouri's Cape Girardeau Police Department.

"There's a man lying on my front porch and my neighbor just called me and she thinks he's dead," a frantic female voice told the dispatcher who took the call.

"What's the address?" the dispatcher asked calmly.

"North Henderson," the woman replied.

"North Henderson?" the dispatcher repeated.

"Yes," the woman said.

"White male or black male?"

"I don't know, I haven't looked."

"What's your name and phone number?"

"Marshall," the caller replied, and gave a telephone number.

"Ma–?"

"Marshall," the caller's shaky voice interrupted the dispatcher.

"All right, what is your first name?"

"This is the Marshall residence and my neighbor just now called and I haven't looked out!" the woman blurted out.

"Okay! Okay! We will be there right away, ma'am," the dispatcher said. "You go to your front door."

Patrol Officer Roger Fields sped down the streets of Cape Girardeau and pulled up his cruiser at the residence on North Henderson Street minutes later. From the street, the lawman could see a man dressed in cutoff blue jeans lying on his right side on the front porch of the dwelling. His back was covered with congealed blood.

The officer approached the porch and discovered that the victim, who was lying in a large pool of blood, had three distinct stab wounds in the middle of his back. Closer examination of the body revealed that rigor mortis and lividity had begun to set in.

As Officer Fields began to inspect the scene, he found bloodstains on the front storm door of the residence. Then he observed that the bottom window of the storm door was broken. From what he saw, the lawman concluded that the victim had been knocking on the door to get help.

About that time, Patrolman Ricky Price also arrived at the scene. As the two officers looked around, they spotted a trail of blood and determined that it led to the residence next door. They followed the trail to the neighboring house and found the door standing open. Cautiously, they stepped inside the dwelling. On the floor in the dining room they were startled to see a woman lying face down in a large pool of blood. She was dressed in a bloodstained blue-and-white-striped shirt and a pair of blue shorts. She was obviously dead. Her appearance indicated that she had been beaten and stabbed several times.

Surveying the room, the lawmen noticed numerous bloodstains on the furniture and floor in the immediate area. A trail of blood led from the front door to the woman's body, then to the hallway, where the lawmen found more blood stains on the wall, a large pool of vomit on the floor, and a trail of blood continuing into another room.

Stepping carefully to avoid disturbing any possible evidence, the officers pressed on in their search of the house and came upon another male victim in the rear west bedroom. He was lying in a large pool of blood and appeared to have suffered a massive gunshot wound on the left side of his head.

The lawmen now had ample reason to suspect that the trail of blood was left by the man they found on the front porch next door. They figured that he probably went to check on both victims in the house before going next door to get help.

The officers went from room to room, but they found no other bodies or any weapons that might have been used in the murders. After checking all the doors and windows, they determined that there was no forced entry.

One of the officers secured the house while the other conducted a preliminary search of the outside premises. The lawman discovered that the telephone wires had been cut from the telephone box on the north wall of the house. Then he observed that a wooden fence which surrounded the backyard had an opening into an adjacent alley. The officer discovered tire impressions in the grass indicating that a vehicle had driven into the backyard, parked there, and left again.

In the driveway, the officers found a 1987 four-door Mazda bearing license plate number GHJ458. A vehicle registration check revealed that the owner was Sherry Scheper of that very Henderson Street address in Cape Girardeau.

Officer Fields went back to the house next door to interview the occupants who had reported the grisly find. He talked with Robert Marshall, whose wife Gail had called the police earlier. The agitated neighbor told the lawmen that he was awakened before dawn by someone pounding on the back door. When he went to the back door and looked out, he could see no one there, so he headed back to the bedroom. On his way, he passed through the living room and glanced at the clock. It was 5:00 a.m. After he got back into bed, it occurred to him that maybe the knocking had come from the front door, but since it had stopped, he didn't bother to get up to check that door.

As the officers questioned the Marshalls further, Gail said that she'd received a call from a neighbor who told her that there was someone lying on her front porch. "He is Curtis Scheper," she said. "He lives next door."

Upon leaving the neighbors' home, the officers secured the outside area of the crime scene and radioed a request for the detective unit to come to the North Henderson Street address.

Sergeant J. F. Keathley of the Missouri Highway Patrol arrived a short time later and began the crime scene processing. Other investigators arrived as he began to photograph the scene, dust for fingerprints, and collect physical evidence. The processing lasted throughout the day. Approximately 150 pieces of evidence were recovered, including fingerprints, hair fibers, blood samples, gunshot residue, fingernail scrapings from the victims, some marijuana, one .38-caliber Smith & Wesson revolver bearing serial number 77001, and an expended lead bullet from the south wall in the dining room.

The probers also instituted a door-to-door canvass of the neighborhood. The area was a crisscross of narrow two-way streets and a hodgepodge of single-story and two-story brick homes. The investigators were hoping to find a witness who might have seen or heard something that would provide a crucial lead in the case. Larry Woolard, one of the neighbors, told police that the Scheper family had lived in the neighborhood for about five years. He said that the Schepers had only a distant relationship with the neighbors. Shortly after the Schepers moved into their home, Woolard noticed an unusual amount of vehicle traffic there, often lasting into the early hours of the morning. The neighbor said he suspected that drug activity was taking place and kept a distance.

Another neighbor interviewed by the investigator said that she was sitting on her front porch until about half past nine o'clock on Saturday evening, August 8, when she saw a white four-door Lincoln with a dealer's license plates idling in the driveway at the Scheper's residence. The driver was white, had curly black hair, and was wearing a dirty blue ball cap and blue shirt. He kept the engine running and stared straight ahead as he sat there. The woman did not see anyone get in or out of the car during that time. After about fifteen minutes, the Lincoln pulled out of the driveway and headed off.

The investigators learned from another neighbor that a black man driving an old-model car had stopped at the Scheper residence at about 7:30 p.m. on August 8. He parked in the driveway, went inside the house through the front door, and a few minutes later returned to his car. Then he drove off, heading south on Henderson Street.

The probers also questioned the neighbor who had discovered the body on the front porch of the Marshall residence. She said that she'd looked out of her window about 7:00 a.m. and noticed the body there. She called up the Marshalls because the thought that it was Robert Marshall lying there and wanted to see if Gail needed help. The neighbor was unable to give the police any further information.

As the canvassing continued, one by one the remaining neighbors who were interviewed told the detectives that they did not know the Scheper family and had not seen or heard anything that aroused suspicions.

At 9:30 a.m. on Monday, August 10, 1992, Dr. Michael D. Jaricor began performing the autopsies on the bodies of the victims. The first victim, who had been found in the bedroom of the home, was identified as seventeen-year-old Randy Scheper. The pathologist found a single gunshot wound to the left side of the victim's head along with multiple skull fractures. Closer examination revealed that the left side of the brain had under gone massive damage from the gunshot, and the pathologist determined that the cause of death was from that wound. He removed the bullet from the brain and turned it over to the police.

Dr. Jaricor began the second autopsy, on twenty-two-year-old Curtis Scheper, at 1:30 p.m. The examination revealed that this victim had three stab wounds in his back. The pathologist discovered a wound which was 3 cm in width in the right middle of the back. The entry was at a forty-five-degree angle and 3.7 cm deep. The next stab wound was also located in the middle of the left back. The entry was at fory-five-degree angle and 3.7 cm deep. The last stab wound was also located in the middle of the left back. It was 54 cm in width and the entry was at forty-five-degree angle and 2.8 cm deep. Both lungs were punctured by these stabs. The doctor found no other injuries on this victim and determined the cause of death resulted from the stab wounds.

The third autopsy began at 3:00 p.m. the same day. This victim was identified as forty-seven-year-old Sherry Scheper, whose body was found in the dining room of her dwelling. The pathologist discovered that she had sustained blunt-force injuries to the entire top of her head and to the base of her skull. He also found three stab wounds in the back. Two wounds, each 2.3 cm in width, were located in the left midline of the back. Another wound on the left side of the lower back was 14.5 cm wide. The chest had one stab wound 44 cm in width. Two of the stab wounds punctured the victim's lungs and one damaged the right kidney. The postmortem examination also revealed that the victim had defensive wounds on her left hand. The pathologist determined that the cause of the woman's death was from massive head injuries and stab wounds.

Meanwhile, the investigators received the results of the ballistics test on the bullet found recovered from Randy Scheper's body and the other bullet found in the dining room wall of the victim's home. The bullets had clearly come from the same gun, but they had been fired from the .38-caliber revolver found at the crime scene.

In the course of their probe, the detectives contacted a relative of the Schepers, a man named Ted, who said that he had recently moved in with his kin on North Henderson Street. Ted said he left the residence on August 8 at about 8:30 p.m., picked up a friend of his, and they went to several local bars. About 1:30 a.m. on August 9, they went across the river to a bar in Illinois and stayed there until about 5:00 a.m. When they returned to Cape Girardeau, they stopped at a local restaurant for breakfast. Around

6:00 a.m., Ted took his friend home and then drove around himself for a while, trying to relax.

Ted finally drove by his family's home about 8:00 a.m. and was taken aback when he saw several police cars there. He thought they were raiding the house for drugs because young Randy had been selling marijuana. He decided to go back to his friend's house and stayed there until 9:30 a.m. Then he had his friend take him back to a local bar to see a girlfriend.

Ted told the police that he had not wanted to drive his own car because he was on parole and he was afraid that the police would stop him because he lived at a residence where there had been a raid. He and his friend returned to Cape Girardeau about 10:00 a.m. that same day and were shocked to learn that the members of his family had been murdered.

Ted told the investigators he didn't think that just one person had done the killings, because his family would have put up a fight. He also said that Sherry Scheper hadn't dated anyone since being divorced. She was a home person, always taking care of her sons.

The distraught relative told the detectives that Randy Scheper had been selling marijuana to high school kids and some black individuals. The information gave the probers a new avenue of investigation to follow. They turned up the names of three main dealers whom Randy dealt with and soon learned that one of those dealers sold crack to Randy in return for marijuana. According to Ted, the marijuana was stashed in Sherry's upstairs bedroom, unless she was awake, in which case, it was kept in the living room.

Ted told the detectives that whoever committed the murders had to know that there was dope and money inside the house. Also, the killer or killers would have to know the family, because neither Randy nor Sherry would ever let anyone in at that time of night. "Besides, Randy always looks out the window before he goes to the door," Ted pointed out.

The police learned from Ted that an individual named Chad Johnson stopped by the house on Saturday evening, August 8. He was driving a white Lincoln town car and had someone else in the car who would not show his face. Ted gave the police Johnson's address, along with a list of friends, enemies, drug dealers, and drug users who were acquainted with the Scheper family.

In the meantime, an individual named Gil, another relative who was interviewed by the probers, indicated that Randy wanted to be a "drug lord." Randy had dealings with drug dealers in Cape Girardeau and Cairo,

Illinois, Gil told the detectives, but he was only a small time dealer.

Gil emphasized that Sherry Scheper would not have been involved in any drug dealing. However, he said, she would have been fully aware of the dealing and would have kept a close watch on the situation. She might even have held money during the dealing, but that would have been the extent of her involvement. Most likely, she would have gone upstairs to her bedroom so she would not have to see or participate in what was going on. She often gave Randy money to buy drugs so he wouldn't steal to support his drug habit.

As for Curtis Scheper, Gil told the investigations, the twenty-two-year-old had a learning disability and was simply caught up in the drug activity at the household.

Gil went on to tell the detectives he had heard rumors that Randy was ripping off various drug dealers. With that in mind, Gil said he believed that a dealer or group of dealers had put a hit on the Schepers' home. He told the police of those drug dealers he knew who sold drugs to Randy.

Over the next few months, the detectives followed up on each lead in the investigation. One by one, the drug dealers were picked up and interrogated, friends were interviewed, and informants were contacted to see what they had heard on the street. After several months, however, the police still had no leads to the killer or killers.

The break in the case came on Tuesday, November 3, 1992, when Cape Girardeau City Police Detective Zeb Williams found an envelope in his department mailbox. The envelope was addressed to him by name only. He opened it and inside he found a hand printed message that read as follows:

> Gary Roll (177) killed Randy (Henderson) etc. Two witness to the murder live in fear of him. One other then I knows he is guilty and will not talk. I am Del Orfo. I will provide info and evidence for any reward money. There are conditions.
>
> I will not testify.
>
> If certain parties must not be questions–(they are in danger)
>
> III Certain parties were used by him may appear guilty, they are not, no matter what my evidence shows. (On my honor and word.)
>
> Del Orfo

A short time later, Detective Williams received a call from a man who identified himself as Del Orfo. He asked the lawman if he had received the message. Williams told Orfo that he had. He asked the mysterious informant to meet at a local restaurant.

Before leaving for the meeting, Detective Williams engaged two other officers to observe and to serve as possible backup in the event that something went wrong.

At the restaurant, Williams made contact with a man who identified himself as Del Orfo. The man showed his identification to the investigator and asked that his real identity be kept anonymous. The detective and the tipster mutually agreed that any further contacts or dealings were to be made under the name Del Orfo.

Del Orfo spoke, "All I have to say is: John Browne." He paused for a moment, then he went on to tell the investigator that Browne lived at a local trailer park in Cape Girardeau. David Rhodes, also from the Cape city, was involved in the murders, too, Orfo said, and the third party was Gary Roll. Orfo explained that he had become aware of the information recently when he was "doing acid" with his friend John Browne. Browne became depressed and told Orfo that David Rhodes, Gary Roll, and Browne himself were involved in the Scheper murders. Browne said that the gun used to kill Randy, along with the ammunition, had been buried behind Gary Roll's house. Orfo told Detective Williams that because he and Browne were both afraid of Roll, they managed to record a conversation with Gary Roll about the Scheper murders on October 25, 1992. Orfo said that Browne did the recording for "insurance," in case Roll tried to kill him to eliminate him as a witness. Roll was unaware of the taping and openly talked about his involvement in the slaying.

Continuing his narrative, Orfo said that Browne told him that he himself never went inside the Scheper house because the Schepers knew him. The purpose of going there was to get money and drugs.

The detectives left the restaurant with Orfo, who then gave them an audio tape cassette. As the officers listened to it, Orfo identified each voice for them.

"I've been around people who were talking about the Scheper homicides," Browne's voice could be heard saying.

"You act like you don't know nothing!" Roll ordered him.

"They say that Curtis had his tongue cut out," Browne said.

"I guarantee you, he didn't feel——," Roll shot back. "I heard people talk about the Scheper killings, too. I don't watch TV or read the newspaper. It didn't have to go down like that if they weren't so————stupid. I couldn't believe it. They tell me, 'I gonna do————!' Bip! Boom! No! No! No! Shut up, God damn it!"

"I was questioned by the police about selling a .38 pistol to Randy Scheper," Browne put in.

"They ain't no way—unless somebody says something—that they are going to believe I was involved in that...." Roll declared. "Besides, I ain't never going to say nothing. That's why I got rid of the ammo, when I come back, too. I got rid of the ammo, gun, and that badge."

The investigators knew they were on to something, but they wanted to make sure that they had a solid case before they made a move. They contacted Cape Girardeau County Prosecutor Morley Swingle to enlist his expertise in developing a plan of action. The investigative team decided that what they needed was another taped conversation with Browne about his involvement in the murders—only this time, it would be legal, authorized by the prosecutor. Del Orfo consented to wear a wire and engage John Browne in a conversation about the crime.

Although Orfo agreed to work with the detectives, he was concerned that Browne would be angry with him if he knew that Orfo turned the tape over to the police. In order to ensure Orfo's safety, therefore, the police came up with a diversionary operation to make it appear that the tape was seized from Orfo's house during a search. After he signed a consent-to-search form, the police did a "high visibility" search of Orfo's home, deployed several marked squad cars in his neighborhood.

Later that same day, the detectives fitted Orfo with a transmitting device. Then he met with John Browne and, in Orfo's own car, the two men drove around Cape Girardeau, discussing the murder. Meanwhile, a six-man police surveillance team followed Orfo's car, monitoring and recording the transmitted conversation. When Browne had said enough to incriminate himself in the Scheper murders, the police stopped the vehicle and asked both subjects to come to the police station for questioning.

Detective Williams told Browne that he was a suspect in the Scheper murders and asked him if he would answer a few questions. After being given his Miranda warning, Browne waived his rights and agreed to talk. He admitted that he was involved in the crime and began to tell the story. He said that on August 8, he, David Rhodes, and Gary Roll were doing acid and drinking beer at Roll's house. Then the trio decided that they needed more drugs and discussed where they could get some. They figured that Tim Anderson, a known drug dealer, always had a large quantity of marijuana on hand. With their decision made, Roll went into another room and came back with knives and guns for all of them. The three men left at about 1:00 a.m. on August 9 and drove to Anderson's house in Cape Girardeau. Browne said that their intent was to take any money and drugs they could find.

When they arrived at their target's home, Roll yanked out the phone wires from the junction box on the outside wall. The trio went up on the outside porch. Roll knocked on the door, but there was no answer. Next, he hit the door with his shoulder a couple of times, but it wouldn't budge. All at once, they heard a little girl's voice saying, "Daddy, there's somebody at the door!" Two of the trio froze.

"I'm not going in there!" Browne declared to his buddies. "Not with children!"

"Me either!" Rhodes chimed in.

"You wimps!" Roll snapped at them, and they hurriedly left the residence.

Browne said that they went back to Roll's house and mulled over another location where they might get drugs. Browne mentioned to his pals that he had seen Anderson delivering drugs to the Scheper house. He added that he had been inside the house and knew the layout.

Once again the trio's plan was set. Gary Roll was carrying a Smith & Wesson .357 revolver and a double-edged knife with a gray handle. Rhodes and Browne were each carrying .22 pistols. They parked in the front of the Scheper residence on Henderson Street at about 4:00 a.m. Browne said he was to stay outside because he knew the Schepers. So he went to the junction box, pulled out the phone wires, and then waited for his two chums.

According to Browne, Gary Roll had a Cape Girardeau police badge that he had found in a local park. Roll knocked on the front door. Sherry Scheper came to the door and looked out a small window. Roll held up the badge in front of the window. "I'm Lieutenant John Brown from the Cape Girardeau Police Department," he announced. "Open the door."

"Just a minute," Sherry responded.

"Now!" Roll ordered.

"Okay," she said as she opened the door.

Roll pushed his way in, Rhodes followed him. Roll pointed the gun at

Sherry and told her to get down on the floor. She did as she was told, her eyes widening in terror.

Browne said that even though he remained outside, he did look through one of the windows when he heard a gunshot. He was able to see Randy Scheper going into his bedroom. Then he heard a second shot. A short time later, Rhodes came outside carrying a Cheese Puff can and told Browne that it contained drugs and money. Browne took the can to Roll's truck while Rhodes went back into the house. A couple of minutes later, Rhodes came out again and they both waited in the truck. After a few more minutes, Roll came out, joined them, and they drove back to his house.

Once back inside Roll's home, Browne said, Roll washed the blood off his knife and off the Smith & Wesson .357 he had used in the deadly robbery. Then he noticed blood on the lower right pant leg of his blue jeans. He took a bottle of bleach and a towel and washed the jeans leg.

Browne told the detectives that he went out and buried the gun, knife, and police badge behind Roll's house.

When the detectives told Prosecutor Swingle what they had learned during the interrogation, he issued arrest warrants for twenty-one-year-old John Browne, eighteen-year-old David Rhodes, and forty-one-year-old Gary Roll. The prosecutor also issued a search warrant for Gary Roll's residence on Big Bend Road in Cape Girardeau.

About 5:00 a.m. on Wednesday, November 4, 1992, the Missouri Highway Patrol SWAT Team raided Roll's home. They took Roll into custody and began a search of his residence. The detectives seized several handguns and rifles, along with ammunition, a couple of knives, drugs, and a pair of blue jeans with a bleached-out right leg.

About fifty yards behind Roll's house, the cops recovered a Smith & Wesson Model 19 .357 Magnum, serial number 9K29981, and a box of .38 shells, a Gerber double-edged knife with a seven-inch blade, and a police badge.

Roll was taken to the police station and was read his Miranda warning. He agreed to waive his rights and to answer the lawmen's questions about the Scheper murders. Then he told the investigators that he did not know the people, he knew nothing about the homicides, and he had nothing to say about the incident.

The detectives continued their operation by arresting David Rhodes at his residence. They read him his Miranda rights and told him that they knew he was involved in the Scheper slayings.

Rhodes agreed to cooperate with the police. He corroborated Browne's story, but he had much more detail to offer about what took place inside the house on that fatal morning of August 9.

After the trio went into the house, Rhodes said, Curtis Scheper came into the living room. Roll ordered him to lie down next to his mother Sherry. Curtis did as he was told. At that moment, Randy rushed into the room.

"We want your money and your drugs!" Roll told the teenager.

"I ain't giving you——!" Randy snapped back.

Suddenly, Roll backhanded Randy across the face with his left hand, which held the gun. The gun unexpectedly went off and shot a hole in the wall. Randy fell to his knees screaming.

"I want your drugs and money!" Roll demanded.

"My dad will hear about this!" Randy responded defiantly.

At that point, Roll told Rhodes to watch Sherry and Curtis. Rhodes said he held the two on the floor at gunpoint while Roll took Randy into the bedroom. A minute or so passed, Rhodes told the detectives, and then he heard a gunshot.

Roll came back into the living room carrying some marijuana cigarettes in his hand. He stuffed them in his jeans pocket and knelt down next to Curtis. He stabbed Curtis in the back three times with the gray-handled knife.

"Curtis didn't even flinch or make a sound," Rhodes told the detectives. Then he said Roll turned to Sherry.

"We want your money and your drugs, and we want them now!" Roll thundered at her.

"They're upstairs," she said in a shaky voice.

Roll told Rhodes to take the woman upstairs and get the money and drugs. Rhodes said that he took Sherry up to her bedroom at gunpoint. She brought out the Cheese Puffs canister that had about twelve baggies of marijuana inside. She also took $214 out of her purse and gave that to him, too. Then they went back downstairs.

Rhodes told the investigators that when they got to the bottom of the stairs, Roll started beating the woman over the head with his gun. Rhodes himself took the canister outside and gave it to Browne. He went back inside the house and saw that Sherry had fallen to her knees and was clinging to Roll's leg as he continued to beat her.

"She was gagging and gurgling in her own blood," Rhodes said. "I got sick to my stomach and went outside." Rhodes and Browne waited in the truck for Roll. A couple of minutes later, Roll came out, and the trio drove away.

In due time, the crime lab sent the results of the ballistics tests to the investigators. The .357 Magnum found buried behind Roll's home matched the bullet found in the wall and the bullet taken from Randy Scheper's head. In addition, the hairs found clinging to the gun matched Sherry Scheper's hair.

David Rhodes and John Browne both pleaded guilty to three counts of murder, but Gary Roll stuck to his story that he knew nothing about the homicide. He pleaded not guilty and asked for a jury trial.

Prosecutor Swingle prepared the state's case and the trial began at the end of August 1992. In his opening statement, Swingle outlined the deadly events that took place on Sunday, August 9. He told the twelve-person jury of the eyewitness testimony and the physical evidence that would prove beyond a reasonable doubt that Gary Roll had committed the murders. Each piece of physical evidence would be presented to the jury—the ballistics, evidence, the knife, the hair fibers, the taped conversations between the defendants—until the prosecutor pieced together the complete puzzle of the triple homicide.

Testimony began with the prosecutor's first witness, Patrol Officer Roger Fields, the first lawman to arrive at the murder scene. Fields gave the jury a detailed account of what he saw and found at the crime scene.

Immediately after the officer's testimony, the judge called for a short recess. When the trial resumed, the defense attorney informed the judge that his client, Gary Roll, wanted to change his plea. Now Gary Roll pleaded guilty to three counts of murder.

A sentencing hearing for the defendants was scheduled in the Cape Girardeau County Circuit Court for Thursday, November 5, 1992. At that time, the prosecutor summarized the evidence. "Obviously this is an important case—a triple homicide—the murder of three people, almost a whole family," he told the jury. "The most serious crime there is. When you come back from the jury room, you will be sending a message to the community, to Gary Roll, and the other killers: you can't get away with murder." Then the prosecutor rested the state's case.

The defense's case rested on the cooperation of the defendants and the mercy of the court.

On Monday, November 16, 1992, after weighing the records of Rhodes and Browne, along with the pair's cooperation in the case, the jurors rendered their sentencing recommendations. As a result, John Browne received one life sentence for second-degree murder and David Rhodes received three life sentences for each count of murder, sentences to be served consecutively. As for Gary Roll, his cold-blooded acts led the judge to give him the death penalty.

David Rhodes and John Browne are now serving their sentences at the Jefferson City Penitentiary in Jefferson City, Missouri. Gary Roll is there on death row, awaiting execution.

Author's Note

Tim Anderson, Robert and Gail Marshall, Ted, Chad Johnson, Gil, Del Orfo, and Larry Woolard are not the real names of the persons so named in the foregoing story. Fictitious names have been used because there is no reason for public interest in the identities of these persons.

Case 17

Shotgun Killing

Ralph Thompson
August 12, 1992

Carrier Mills, Illinois

About 6:30 p.m. on Wednesday, August 12, 1992, Tom Harris was cruising on Smith Road in Carrier Mills, Illinois, when he drove past Ralph Thompson's residence. He looked toward the residence and noticed a red pickup truck in the yard at the far end of the outbuilding. Behind the truck, a quilt was lying on the ground with a pair of boots sticking out. Harris stopped and took another look. *That cannot be a body. Must be something thrown under a blanket,* he thought.

Harris pulled into the driveway and honked. No one responded. He noticed that Thompson's Ford Mustang was not in the garage, so he assumed that no one was home.

All night, Harris tossed and turned thinking about what he had seen. The next morning, he decided to drive back to the Thompson residence to take another look. He parked his car in the driveway and walked across the yard toward the blanket. When he got within a few feet of the quilt he stopped. "Jesus! It is a body!" he exclaimed out loud.

Harris rushed back to his car and drove down Smith Road to find someone who would go back to the scene with him. He and a neighbor returned shortly and walked to the back of the truck. Harris lifted the blanket. It was Ralph Thompson.

Illinois's Saline County Sheriff's central dispatcher received the call on Thursday, August 13, logging it in at 8:32 a.m. "Sheriff's office, may I help you?" asked the dispatcher.

"Yes—we have found a body! A dead body!" The caller shouted over the phone.

Captain James Wheatcroft and Deputy Jerry Lindsay sped down the

213

Carrier Mills blacktop, took a left at the first "T," a right on Smith Road, and arrived at the scene in ten minutes.

The lawmen found a red pickup truck parked at the north end of the outbuilding. Near the front of the truck, a ball cap and an upper plate of false teeth were lying in a large pool of blood. On the ground at the rear of the truck on the passenger side, a human body was lying face down. The body was covered with a quilt. The lawmen lifted the blanket and discovered that the victim, in full rigor mortis, was a middle-aged white male. He was naked from the waist up. A mass of congealed blood covered the lower part of his back and he had a severe wound to his upper left arm.

The lawmen secured the crime scene and put in a call requesting the assistance of a crime lab technician from the Illinois State Police Department of Criminal Investigation (DCI).

Meanwhile, Sheriff George Henley arrived at the scene and ordered the lawmen to search Thompson's residence for his relative. Deputy Lindsey walked briskly toward the house. Suddenly, as he rounded the corner of the house and found a trail of blood at the entrance of the garage, the officer's stomach churned and his mind raced with thoughts of finding another dead body.

The deputy continued around the house and noticed that a screen had been pulled from a window on the north side. Upon entering, he quickly went from room to room in hopes of finding the relative alive. Lindsay sighed with relief as he entered the last room and realized the house was empty.

Continuing with the on-scene investigation, the police learned that Thompson's Ford Mustang convertible was missing. They had ample reason to believe that it had been taken by whoever had committed the homicide.

Sheriff Henley called central dispatch and put a "stop and hold" alert on Thompson's vehicle and had a missing person report filed on Thompson's relative.

Meanwhile, crime scene technician Gary Otey and Frank Cooper arrived at the crime scene. Upon entering the residence, they found blood on the stereo and pool table in the game room, blood on the garage flood, and a trail of blood leading out of the garage entrance. The officers discovered one Winchester .30-30 caliber cartridge casing and a .30-30 slug lodged under a stack of magazines inside the garage. They removed several shotgun pellets from the door facing and the wall in the game room.

The lawmen search the outside area around the residence and found a large puddle of blood next to the garage.

Technician Otey and Cooper then moved in the outbuilding, which was to the west of Thompson's house, and recovered a Smith & Weston .357 handgun, model 19-5, serial number 194K965. The gun had been wrapped in a T-Shirt and placed in a bag underneath the window.

In Thompson's pickup truck, the police found a small notebook. It contained a list of guns: one Voluntary Arms 16-gauge single-shot shotgun, serial number 70491XE, and one .30-30 caliber Martin Glenfill Model 30A lever-action rifle, serial number 18020768.

At 6:30 p.m. that same day, a forensic pathologist Dr. John A. Heidingsfelder, performed the autopsy on Thompson's body. The pathologist concluded that the victim had initially sustained a shotgun wound to the upper arm with subsequent destruction of skin, skeletal muscle, and the left humorous and upper arm bones. Based on the clinical evidence provided by the crime scene technicians, the doctor determined that Thompson mostly likely received a second gunshot wound from a .30-30 caliber rifle between the game room and the garage entrance. The wound was a grazing shot in a downward direction. The crime action then apparently moved from the garage to an adjacent area, where a large quantity of blood was found. The third shot was also a .30-30 in the right lower back. The damage to the aorta and surrounding parts of the body caused by the last shot resulted in rapid death.

The officers continued the probe by canvassing the neighborhood. From one neighbor, they learned that Thompson had backed his truck up to the outbuilding between noon and half past one o'clock on the afternoon of August 12. A little while later, the neighbor thought she heard Thompson hammering, but she did not think anything of it because Thompson was always hammering on something. No one else in the area had seen or heard anything unusual.

Meanwhile, the police found out that Thompson's missing relative was staying with friends in Harrisburg, Illinois. The relative told the police that she had no idea who might have killed Ralph, but she did tell them that Ralph had a friend named Bruce Smith who had lived with him for several months. Recently, Bruce had moved to Florida.

The deputies contacted Bruce Smith by phone. Smith told them that he had been good friends with Thompson for the past sixteen years. He had lived with Thompson until about a month earlier when he moved to Florida. Smith confirmed that Thompson owned a 16-guage shotgun, a .30-30 rifle, a .22-caliber rifle, a .22-caliber pistol, and a BB-gun. Thompson kept the rifles in a gun rack located on the wall in the bedroom.

Smith went on to say that in the summer of 1991, while attending a party, Thompson had introduced him to another acquaintance named Joseph Jordan. Later that same evening, Smith overheard Thompson talking to Jordan about a $500 or $600 loan. He came to understand that Jordan had borrowed the money from Thompson for a car. The conversation was calm, Smith said, but Thompson did remind Jordan that he still owed him the money.

In December 1991, Smith told the police Thompson and Jordan came to a lounge where Smith himself worked. They wanted Smith to go with them when they got off work. When the trio left, Jordan was driving Thompson's Mustang convertible. Thompson was sitting in the front passenger seat and Smith was in the back. They stopped at a package liquor store where they purchased two cases of beer and then drove to Thompson's residence. The three sat around the table drinking beer. A short time later, Thompson went to bed.

Smith told the police that he and Jordan continued drinking beer. Then Jordan asked Smith if he had any money. Smith told him he had a couple of dollars. Jordan said that he wanted to get a bottle of whiskey but that would not be enough. He said he would get the money from Thompson without his knowledge. Smith warned Jordan that he better not take the money. Jordan walked into the living room while Smith went to check on Thompson. They both retuned to the kitchen where Jordan suggested they steal something they could sell to get money. According to Smith, Jordan was not specific about what he wanted to steal.

The next morning at about six o'clock, Smith said his sleep was disrupted by shouts from the kitchen. He walked into the kitchen and found Thompson and Jordan sitting at the kitchen table drinking beer. Thompson was shouting at Jordan because he had caught Jordan trying to take money from his billfold. The two continued to argue for a few minutes, then suddenly, Thompson stood up and told Smith that he was going to take Jordan home. Thompson and Jordan walked out of the door.

For several months after that incident, Smith said, Thompson complained about Jordan owing him money. Thompson even contacted some of Jordan's relatives trying to collect money. When Jordan found out, he got angry, called Thompson, and threatened to beat the hell out of him if he ever did that again.

After the call, Smith said, Jordan called Thompson about two or three times. Thompson sounded calm when he talked with Jordan during those later phone conversations.

Further investigation revealed that Jordan had been seen on the afternoon of August 12 driving Thompson's Ford Mustang. Jordan was flashing money and wanted to have a party with some of his friends. Jordan's friends said he told then he was going to leave the area. They also noted Jordan was accompanied by a friend, Terry Olsen from Arkansas.

The sheriff immediately issued arrest warrants for Joseph Jordan and Terry Olsen for the theft of Thompson's vehicle and entered the information into the National Crime Information Center (NCIC) computer network.

Three days later, on August 17, Sheriff Henley received a call from Missouri's East Prairie City Police Department. Terry Olsen had turned himself in. Olsen told the East Prairie cops that he thought Jordan was still in the area. He also said that Jordan had pawned two guns at a pawnshop in Sikeston, Missouri.

That same day, a team of Illinois and Missouri police hurried to that pawn shop. The investigators recovered a Volunteer Arms 16-gauge shotgun, serial number 70491WE, and a pawn ticket signed by Joseph Jordan.

The detectives returned to the police station with the weapons and then probed Terry Olsen to spell out everything that happened. Olsen told them that he had first met Joseph Jordan in Bald Knob, Arkansas, in June 1992. He and Jordan became friends and often played pool at a local recreation center there. During the first part of August, Jordan told Olsen that he had a sick uncle in Carrier Mills, Illinois. He said that if he had a way to get to his uncle's place, he would have a car to come back in. Olsen said he felt sorry for Jordan, so he drove him to Illinois around August 6. The duo arrived at a friend's house in Harrisburg, Illinois, at about eleven thirty that same night. Olsen took Jordan to his uncle's a couple of times, but never got out of the car, nor did he ever meet his uncle. Olsen said that on the afternoon of August 12, Jordan showed up with a Ford Mustang. The car had no plates. Jordan told Olsen that his uncle had dropped the vehicle registration and insurance. Figuring that Jordan would get the proper registration for the vehicle soon, he took his plates off his old truck and put them on the car so Jordan would not get stopped by the police. Olsen said that he and Jordan drove to Myrtle Beach, North Carolina, stayed for a day, and then went to Olsen's grandmother's home in East Prairie, Missouri.

Olsen told the lawmen that Jordan took a couple of guns he said his

217

uncle had given him to a pawnshop in Sikeston. He returned that evening. They went to bed early. The next morning, Monday, August 17, when Olsen woke up, Jordan was gone. Later that day, Olsen heard on the news that Ralph Thompson had been murdered and that himself and Jordan were wanted for car theft.

Four days later, on Friday, August 21, Nevada's Lander County Sheriff's dispatcher received a call from a local motel by an out-of-state motorist in need of gas.

Deputy Myron True was sent to the motel. As Deputy True got out of his vehicle, a motorist approached him and told him that he was the person who called. He told the officer his name was Terry Olsen.

True asked for identification and the motorist told the officer that his wallet and money had been stolen a few days earlier. He said that he had been traveling from Arkansas and was willing to work for some gasoline. True asked where his car was located and the motorist pointed out a light-colored Mustang with Arkansas plate number TMB593.

Deputy True asked for the vehicle registration and the driver told him that it was in the glove compartment. The officer opened the compartment and found a chrome knife inside.

Then the motorist handed the officer an insurance form made out to Shirley Olsen, but True still could not find any registration in the compartment.

True ran a vehicle registration check by VIN number and learned that the car was registered to Ralph Thompson and the car had been reported stolen. The deputy placed the motorist claiming to be Terry Olsen under arrest for grand larceny auto and read him his Miranda rights.

At that point, the motorist told Deputy True that his real name was Joseph Jordan and that his billfold was under the front seat. Later, the police recovered the billfold and conducted a thorough search of the vehicle. In the trunk, they found a Panasonic laptop computer; a pawn slip from Sikeston, Missouri, for a 16-gauge shotgun; a .30-30 rifle; and a pawn slip from Myrtle Beach, South Carolina, for an Emerson cassette player. The lawmen also discovered an Arkansas license plate TMB593, two Illinois license plates AL6035, and four rounds of live .30-30 ammunition stuffed under the front seat.

Meanwhile, the Illinois police received a billfold which they learned belonged to Ralph Thompson. The Carrier Mills resident who turned the billfold over to police reported that their children had found it under a bridge on Butler Road while they were playing.

In addition, the police were contacted by the crime lab, which had concluded ballistics test on the bullets found in Thompson's body came from his own .30-30 rifle.

On Monday, August 23, the police presented their evidence to the prosecutor who then ordered arrest warrants issued on Joseph Jordan for five counts of first-degree murder, two counts of armed robbery, one count of residential burglary, and two counts of theft. Joseph Jordan waived extradition and on Wednesday, August 26, Sheriff Henley returned from Battle Mountain, Nevada, with Jordan in tow. The detectives read Jordan his Miranda rights. He waived his rights to an attorney and told the police that he wanted to give a voluntary statement.

Jordan told the investigators that on August 11, at about 2:30 p.m., he had a friend drop him off at Thompson's house. Jordan said he went to the back door, but it was locked. He turned a couple of nails and pulled the screen from the kitchen window. He got inside, where he sat on the couch and watched a couple of soap operas and drank beer.

About fifteen minutes later, Ralph Thompson came home. He was surprised, but not mad. Jordan said the two sat on the couch and drank beer and talked for about thirty minutes. Then they got into an argument over the money Jordan owed. Jordan said he went into the bedroom and took the 16-gauge shotgun from the rack. When Thompson went to the kitchen to get a beer, Jordan said that he shot Thompson. Thompson screamed and grabbed his shoulder as he ran for the door leading to the garage. Jordan said that he grabbed the .30-30 from beneath the bed and fired another shot at Thompson as he went out the door. Then he ran after Thompson.

Suddenly, Jordan stopped talking to the detectives. His body began to shake uncontrollably as he stared silently at the floor.

"Then what happened?" the detective asked. "Where were you when you fired the third shot?"

Jordan looked up at the detective, then back down at the floor, then at the detective again. "I was standing at the end of the garage. I aimed on that one. I aimed for his back. He was next to the truck when I fired. I saw him fall and I ran out where he was. He was bleeding. I ran inside and grabbed a blanket off the bed. I draped it over him. Then I took him by the feet and dragged him to the far side of the truck."

Jordan told the lawmen he took the victim's wallet and car keys. He grabbed the two guns and put them in the back of the car. In the process, he noticed blood on the car and on both his pant legs. He jumped in the car, drove to a local car wash, and hosed the blood from the car and his pants.

Then, Jordan said, he headed for a friend's house in Vienna, Illinois, and along the way, he took $125 from Thompson's billfold and threw the billfold under a bridge. Jordan said he stayed at a friend's house that night, went to Myrtle Beach for a day and pawned a stereo, then returned to Missouri the next day.

While Jordan was at the home of Terry Olsen's relatives, he said, he could not sleep. He got up and turned the television on and found out that Thompson's body had been discovered. He left while Olsen was still sleeping. He stopped in Poplar Bluff, Missouri, and got a motel room. While watching TV, he learned that Olsen had turned himself in, so he decided to head west, obviously hoping to elude the law.

"When I got to Nevada, I ran out of gas and money. That is when I ran out of help. That is when I got caught."

With Jordan's statement, the detectives concluded their investigation. The facts showed that Terry Olsen had nothing to do with the crime, so they arranged for all charges against him to be dropped.

On December 1, 1992, in the First Circuit Court in Harrisburg, Illinois, Joseph Jordan pleaded guilty to the first-degree murder of Ralph Thompson. He was sentenced to forty years and is now serving his sentence in Menard Prison in Chester, Illinois.

Author's Note

Tom Harris, Bruce Smith, and Terry and Shirley Olsen are not the real names of the persons so named in the foregoing story. Fictitious names have been used because there is no reason for public interest in the identities of these persons.

Case 18

The Strangled Teen

Patricia Kay Johnson
September 14, 1992

Morganfield, Kentucky

Kentucky's Morganfield City Police were enjoying a relatively quiet afternoon on Monday, September 14, 1992, until a disturbing telephone call came in from a frantic woman who said she was a relative of Patricia Kay Johnson. The relative told the dispatcher that Patricia, described as being sixteen years old; five feet, eleven inches tall; 130 pounds; with long brown hair; was missing. "She was wearing a navy-colored ribbed cotton top, blue jeans, and white tennis shoes," the caller said.

The dispatcher attempted to calm the caller, recorded the time at 2:15 p.m., then tried to get further information.

The relative said that Patricia left their mobile home at about seven thirty that same morning. She stopped a few trailers down at another residence to pick up a little girl for the day care. The child's father told the relative that he had already sent the girl to day care when Patricia arrived. He said that he heard a car pull away, but he was too sick to look out the window. He fell asleep and woke up in the afternoon, the father said, and when he looked outside, he saw Patricia's car in the driveway. He became concerned and decided to call Patricia's family.

The caller told the police that Patricia, a high school senior, planned to pick up two of her friends on the way to school, but she had failed to do so. Also, "We had definite plans for this afternoon," he said, "and she would not have stood me up."

Detective Jeffery Hart headed out to meet with Patricia's relatives at the residence where her light-blue 1984 Ford Escort hatchback was parked in the driveway. One of its windows was rolled down, the keys were in the ignition, and Patricia's purse lay on the front seat with the billfold spilled onto the floor board. "She always rolls up the window and locks the door, even when she pulls up at home," one of the relatives told the investigator.

Figuring that the circumstances surrounding Patricia's disappearance were suspicious, Detective Hart decided to treat the incident as a possible abduction. If a crime had indeed been committed, the car was the only piece of physical evidence he had. The detective wasn't taking any chances. He took photographs of the vehicle, dusted it for latent fingerprints, and collected whatever items it contained. Then he had the car towed to the police station to be impounded as physical evidence.

Meanwhile, other officers continued the investigation by canvassing the neighborhood. They were hoping to find a witness who might have seen a stranger or strange vehicle near the residence where Patricia was last seen, or someone who might have been alarmed by a woman's screams. One by one, however, the neighbors told the police that they had not seen anything unusual or head anything that aroused suspicion.

The probe continued through the night with the questioning of friends, teachers, and Patricia's boyfriend. Even so, whatever information the police gathered was of little help.

The next morning, Tuesday, September 15, the police officially listed Patricia as missing and entered the information in the National Crime Information Center (NCIC) computer network. Then they had more than two hundred posters printed with Patricia's picture and description and distributed them throughout the county.

On Wednesday, September 26, with still no trace found of the missing teenager, the local newspaper carried a plea from the Morganfield PD urging anyone with information about the whereabouts of Patricia K. Johnson to notify the police immediately.

Despair began to grow in the community as days passed and, one by one, the leads and rumors begin to dwindle, with little information being developed regarding the missing sixteen-year-old.

Volunteers joined the police to plan a search of Union County, section by section. They decided to search the most remote area of the county first—the Higginson-Henry Wildlife Refuge.

Three days later, on Saturday, September 19, about fifty volunteers and police officers began search of the twenty-thousand-acre refuge located southwest of Morganfield. For next forty-eight hours, the searchers struggled through dense woods, brush, and scrubs looking for tire tracks, clothing, an abandoned car, or anything else that might help in finding the girl. The search was fruitless.

Still, the search attracted so much attention that one national trucking firm had their drivers distributing posters bearing Patricia's photo and description in truck stops across the country.

By now, the volunteer force had grown to five hundred people. "I've been here for seven years, and there's never been anything to this effect," Detective Hart remarked. "We'll try to tie some leads together and come up with her." Unfortunately, the probers had to face some delays. Rain and fog moved into the area, with more than half the spacious county still left to be searched. The Morganfield police, the volunteers, and a Kentucky State Police helicopter anxiously waited for a break in the weather so they could resume the search.

Meanwhile, about one hundred relatives and friends gathered to pray for Patricia's safe return. At one minute past midnight on September 22, they wished her a happy seventeenth birthday. One of her relatives told friends how, one year ago that day, she had rented a sign outside the local flower shop to wish Patricia a happy sixteenth birthday. The relative had sent flowers and balloons for "Sweet 16." Now, on her seventeenth birthday, relatives and friends who had planned to take her out for dinner were carrying light-blue candles, the victim's favorite color, in honor of Patricia and for her safe return. All night, community members took turns at the local church praying for the missing girl.

The next morning, the weather cleared and the massive search resumed. For days, the volunteers combed the fields and searched the forest. Section by section, the searchers on foot struggled through heavy brush and rugged terrain, hoping to find a clue to Patricia's whereabouts. The state police helicopter crisscrossed the area from the air. A group on horseback searched the forests for the missing young woman.

At the end of the search, they had found not a piece of evidence that would lead to Patricia Johnson. At this point, she had been missing for ten days.

The break in the case came on Monday, September 28, when the police received a tip from a caller who reported having seen a man in his twenties, with light-brown hair, driving Patricia's car at 1:00 p.m. on the same day she was reported missing.

All this time, Detective Hart had been mulling over a theory and now it seemed that it might have been on the mark. He hadn't told anyone about it, but he had always suspected the man whose daughter Patricia had gone to pick up for day care. The man worked as a part-time contractor for Patricia's father. The first time police interrogated that individual, he told them that he'd seen Patricia at 7:45 a.m. on the day she disappeared. Then he changed his story, saying that he saw her at 10:00 a.m. The detectives learned that he had gone to a relative's house to change his clothes hours after the victim disappeared, a fact which he never mentioned to the detectives.

Even without his inconsistent story about his last sighting of the victim, the police already had ample reason to suspect this man, whose name was Toni Lee Parrish. He had an arrest record with the Morganfield PD, and a review of that record was illuminating. Parrish had plenty of brushes with the law over the past eight years. The reports contained a prefacing note stating, "He is mentally ill and a danger to himself and others." They continued with listing a series of offenses. On November 14, 1984, he was arrested for attempting to break into a Union County home. He pleaded guilty to the charges and was sentenced to ten days in jail, fined one hundred dollars, ordered to make restitution, and given a year's probation.

Eleven days after that arrest and just after his release from jail, Parrish and a friend of his were charged with car theft. Through a plea bargain, Parrish received five years in prison, suspended to probation, and had to pay restitution.

On January 11, 1991, he had another brush with the law. He was alleged to have threatened to kill a relative, and he wound up being charged with wanton endangerment. That incident prompted the district court to have Parrish referred to an alcohol-abuse center for treatment. He stayed only one day and then left, against the advice of the center staff.

Later, he was a suspect in an attempted abduction in a department store parking lot at Henderson, Kentucky. In that case, a woman in her mid-twenties who was going to her car was grabbed by a man and pushed into the car. She screamed and the man fled. Parrish was never charged, but the police definitely considered him a suspect.

Then on Thursday, January 9, 1992, police were called out when Parrish walked into a care center in Morganfield with three suicide notes—one for the psychiatric center, one for the police, and one for his wife. After passing the notes out, he walked outside carrying a .22-caliber rifle and waited for the cops to a arrive. For the next twenty-five minutes, officers tried to convince Parrish to lay down his rifle. "I thought he was going to put it down," one lawman later reported. "He started to go down with it, and then all of a sudden, he turned around and smiled at me and pulled the trigger."

Parrish shot himself in the left side of the chest. He later told a psychiatrist that he'd wanted the police to kill him that day.

On Saturday, September 26, Detective Hart headed for Toni Parrish's home to interview the man. When he got there, the detectives learned that Parrish had moved out four days earlier on September 22.

That same afternoon, when Detective Hart returned to his office, a man named Carl Young came to the police station. Young informed Hart that Parrish had moved into Young's house four days earlier. Young said that Parrish told him he'd had a big fight with his wife and wanted to stay with him for a while. Over the next four days, Parrish kept talking about Patricia all the time. From Young's viewpoint, it was as if Parrish knew where she was and wanted to tell someone, but he just couldn't get it out.

Young said he began to question Parrish about Patricia. Did he know where she is? Finally, Young told the detective, Parrish broke down and told a startling story. Parrish said that after his wife had gone to work, he called in sick, and then he sent his daughter to day care fifteen minutes early. When Patricia Johnson arrived, he was waiting. As soon as she came inside, he attacked her. She got away from him and ran for her car, but he ran after her, caught her, and forced her back inside the trailer, where he killed the pretty teenager.

"I asked Toni outright," Young said. "'You raped her in the trailer, she ran away from you, you took her back inside and strangled her?'"

He said that Parrish replied, "Carl, you're about right."

Then, Parrish told Young that he placed Patricia's body in the trunk of her car and drove to a spot neat the Ohio River where he disposed of the body.

Young went on to tell the lawman that Parrish wanted him to help bury the body. Together, they drove fifteen miles southwest of Morganfield to a location about two miles north of Kentucky 1508, near Dekoven, in the Dennis O'nam Ditch. The first time, he said, they could not find the body. The second time they went back, they saw a body, but it was too far out to reach without a boat.

The Morganfield investigators sped to the location given by Young. At 1:30 p.m., they found the body. Not readily visible due to the dense vegetation, it was floating about fifteen feet from the bank of the ditch. The police figured that the heavy rains had washed the corpse from where it had been hidden initially.

The body was partially decomposed. Its condition led the coroner to the conclusion that the victim could have been dead for about twelve days. The body was removed to a local hospital for an autopsy.

That same evening, Dr. Mark LeVaugh, a forensic pathologist, performed the required autopsy on the body after it was positively identified as Patricia K. Johnson. The postmortem examination revealed that the victim had died of manual strangulation. Her face bore numerous blunt trauma injuries and bruises. There were no stab wounds or gunshot wounds. The pathologist determined that the victim had been sexually assaulted and that she had put up a struggle as she was being strangled. The pathologist further determined that the blunt trauma was probably caused by a fist. The time of death was consistent with the time that the victim was reported missing.

The police went looking for Toni Parrish and found him a few hours later. They arrested him without incident and charged him with the kidnapping, murder, and rape of Patricia K. Johnson. Parrish asked for a lawyer and said that he had nothing to say to the police.

Next, the investigators obtained authorization and went to the suspect's home where the sexual assault allegedly took place. They processed the dwelling for physical evidence, but they found nothing that would serve as evidence of the crime.

A week later, on Wednesday, October 7, a Union County grand jury heard testimony in the Johnson case. Detective Jeff Hart was the only witness. He gave the account of events leading up to Patricia Johnson's disappearance. He explained that after the arrest of Toni Parrish, the police learned that a relative heard screams of pain outside his mobile home on September 14. The man went out into the driveway in time to see Parrish carrying Patricia into the trailer.

The presence of a dog nearby, coupled with the fact that Patricia was holding her back, led the relative to believe that Patricia had been bitten by the dog. The man told the police that Parrish came back outside and quieted his concerns. Parrish told him, "She is shaken up, but all right."

The relative explained that he'd never said anything about that incident because he didn't believe it had anything to do with Patricia's disappearance.

Continuing his testimony before the grand jury, Detective Hart said that Carl Young led him to the body after Young came to police headquarters to report that Toni Parrish had admitted to killing Patricia and had asked him to help bury her.

On Friday, October 9, 1992, the Union County grand jury indicted Toni Parrish on charges of kidnapping, first-degree murder, and the first-degree rape of Patricia K. Johnson.

Toni Parrish appeared before Judge Tommy Vhandler for arraignment October 12. The accused man pleaded not guilty to all the charges. Then the judge ordered that a psychiatric evaluation be made of the defendant by the Kentucky State Reformatory. A series of court appearances followed over the next several months.

During a pretrial hearing on March 10, 1993, Defense Attorneys Leah Cooper and Jill Giordano argued that the state had no evidence to support the charges against their client, Toni Parrish, for kidnapping and rape. They moved that the charges be dropped. In addition, the attorneys filed for a change of venue to guarantee that their client would receive a fair trial. Finally, they filed a motion to suppress the statements Carl Young made to police about Parrish's involvement in the murder.

Judge Chandler denied the request to drop the charges, but he did grant a change of venue to Marion, Kentucky.

Eight months later, on November 4, 1993, another pretrial hearing was held. At that time, the court heard the results of Parrish's psychiatric testing, which determined that he was mentally competent to stand trial.

The prosecution then called Union County Kentucky Sheriff Ron Girten to the stand. He told the court that three days after the defendant's arrest, Parrish had asked to talk to the sheriff himself. Parrish told the lawman that he and Patricia had gotten into a fight and he'd put his hands to Patricia's throat after she told him that she was going to tell his family that they'd had an affair. Parrish said he hit her a couple of times in the face because she kept screaming and fighting. Parrish told the sheriff that he was scared, that he didn't mean to kill her.

The prosecution was suspicious of Parrish's declared motive for killing Patricia Johnson. Nevertheless, he had admitted to the sheriff that he committed the murder.

Then the defense proceeded with arguments to suppress Carl Young's statement. The defense argued that Young had numerous criminal charges pending against him in court and he therefore had ample reason to make a deal with the state. Young himself testified that he would have told the police regardless of whether he had charges on file against him. "He killed a sixteen-year-old girl, that I know," Young said about Parrish. I would have told on him. I would do it right now if I wasn't in at all. I don't want to go to prison and I thought that it would help. Besides, he took me to the body. I would say that pretty much p.. ...s he killed her."

Judge Chandler denied the motion to suppress Young's statements. He set a jury trial date for February 28, 1994.

After Judge Chandler recessed court, a reporter interviewed a relative of the victim's. The relative told the reporter that Parrish's statement about having an affair with the victim was totally untrue, and he asserted that the confession was fabricated so that Parrish could get a lesser sentence. "Patricia got along with everybody, but she despised Parrish," the man declared. "That's the reason we know it is a fabricated confession."

The family was coping with their loss, the relative said, but their outlook on life had changed over the last fifteen months. "You're used to coming home and having her here, but now you look over and don't have her there anymore. Everyday, every night—you miss that, you know." The man swallowed hard and glanced at the reporter. "There'll definitely be a trial. I don't care if it takes ten years to settle, I've got the time to wait."

Four months later, on Thursday, April 14, 1994, bailiffs escorted Toni Parrish from the jail across the street to the Union County Courthouse, a sprawling historical structure near the heart of downtown Morganfield. Parrish's lawyers had entered into a plea agreement with the prosecution.

Parrish plead guilty to first-degree murder in return for having the charges of kidnapping and rape dropped.

On Thursday, May 12, 1994, Judge Chandler sentenced Toni Parrish to life in Prison. Parrish is now serving his term in the Kentucky State Prison at Eddyville.

Author's Note

Carl Young is not the real name of the person so named in the foregoing story. A fictitious name has been used because there is no reason for the public interest in the identity of this person.

Case 19

Murder By Home Invasion

Velma Carter
June 30, 1993

Herrin, Illinois

Chief of Police Tom Cundiff of Herrin, Illinois, received the disquieting call at headquarters about 11:30 a.m. on Thursday, July 1, 1993. The frantic caller identified himself as Jack Harris and expressed his concern about his neighbor, Velma Carter. She was usually out in her yard every morning, he said, but today he hadn't seen her. Worried about her, Harris said that he'd gone over to check on Velma and discovered her kitchen window open and its wood-frame screen leaning against the exterior wall of the house.

Harris told the chief that he called out for Velma, but he'd gotten no answer. Then he looked through the kitchen window and was able to see through to the bedroom. He discerned what appeared to be the form of legs and feet under the bedspread at the end of the bed.

Upon hanging up, Chief Cundiff rushed to Velma Carter's residence on West Maple Street. He checked all the doors and found them locked. Seeing no other alternative, the lawman climbed through the open kitchen window. He walked to the bedroom and discovered a body covered with a bedspread.

At first, Cundiff thought that Velma C. Carter, an eighty-six-year-old retired kindergarten teacher, had died in her sleep of natural causes. Then he pulled the bedspread down from the upper part of the body and immediately realized he was wrong. Velma was lying on her back, covered with a sheet, with a pillow over her face. Upon removing the sheet and pillow, the chief discovered that both of Velma's arms were extended upward, with each hand placed at the sides of her head. Abrasions were visible on her chin and around her nose. Chief Cundiff immediately called for the assistance of the crime lab and the major case squad.

At 11:15 a.m., crime scene technician Jerry Rea from the Illinois State Police Division of Forensic Services and Identification arrived at the apparent crime scene. He began processing the interior of the single-story residence with the assistance of members of Illinois's Williamson County Major Case Squad, which included Herrin Detective Mark Brown, Williamson County Detective Eric Frattini, Energy Chief of Police H. L. Pulley, Illinois State Police Field Supervisor Frank Cooper, Marion Detective Les Snyder, Carterville Detective Oren Drew, and Williamson County Coroner Monte Blue.

Technician Rea photographed and measured the crime scene while other investigators examined the doors and windows of the home. The double kitchen window on the south side of the house was the only open window. A closer examination of the window revealed that the nails which were used to secure the window screen were bent.

The probers discovered the back interior door ajar. The door was equipped with a key latch lock which was now in the open position; yet, the exterior door was closed and locked. An examination of the door for latent fingerprints proved to be fruitless.

The detectives then moved to the kitchen in search of further evidence. The kitchen was orderly, with papers neatly stacked on the table. A Bible opened to Revelations was lying next to the papers. The investigators carefully scanned the room and discovered two partial footwear impressions on the edge of the counter and sink which were located just below the kitchen window.

Next, the east bedroom was processed. It, too, was quite orderly, with miscellaneous items neatly arranged on top of the bed. The bedspread was pushed inward between the mattress and box springs. On the floor along the south side of the bed, the police found a pink robe.

In the west bedroom, where the body was lying, the investigators noted that the bed was located in the northwest corner of the room. They noticed a bed leg indentation in the carpet and determined that the northeast corner of the bed had been moved three inches in a northwest direction. On a night table next to the bed was an alarm clock displaying the correct time. Next to the clock, the victim's eyeglasses were lying upside down, neatly placed.

When the probers removed the sheets and pillow from the victim, they saw that she was dressed in a mid-thigh-length nightgown. Her body was cold to the touch. Rigor mortis had set in at the major joints and lividity was present in the neck area. The abrasions on her nose and chin had a purplish color, as did her lips and fingernails.

From relatives at the scene, the investigators learned that the victim had a plastic container which she used to store miscellaneous papers and money. She usually kept that container in the kitchen cabinet. When the police found it, the container was empty. They had ample reason to believe that any money which might have been in the jar had been taken by whoever had committed the homicide.

The police collected the pillow and bed sheets, a fabric impression on the kitchen counter, hair fibers from the victim and her clothing, fingernail scrapings from her hands, and the robe from the east bedroom. They submitted these items to the Illinois Forensic Lab in Carbondale, Illinois, for examination.

At nine o'clock that evening, a forensic pathologist, Dr. Jon A. Heidingsfelder, performed the autopsy on Velma Carter's body. The examination revealed intense cyanosis of the fingernail beds—that is, they had turned blue. The abrasions on the front of her chin and both sides of her nose and the bruising of the skin on the nose were recent. Based on the crime scene, the circumstances, and the external injuries, the pathologist concluded that the victim died of asphyxiation due to smothering or due to compression of the nose and mouth. This might have been accomplished with a pillow, possibly a robe, but also by placing the hands over the mouth or nose.

Meanwhile, Chief Cundiff questioned Jack Harris, the neighbor. Harris said that he'd last seen Velma alive on Wednesday, June 30. He'd brought her home from a church function around 9:00 p.m. He had remained in her driveway until she turned on her kitchen light and then he left. He returned this morning to check on her and then called the police.

Other investigators continued the probe by canvassing the neighborhood. They were hoping to find some witness who might have seen a stranger or strangers near Velma Carter's residence or perhaps someone who might have been briefly awakened by a woman's scream in the night. One by one, however, the neighbors told the detectives that they had not seen anything unusual or heard anything that aroused their suspicions.

The police were baffled. It seemed that the motive for the homicide was burglary. Yet the police were not sure if anything at all had been taken. Although relatives said that Velma kept money in her jar, it would have been only a few dollars at the most, and one of the neighbors told the police about having seen the jar a few days before. "It had papers in it—no money," the friend declared. "Why would someone want to kill such a harmless, sweet lady?"

The day after the murder—Friday, July 2—the police got a break. Detective Mike Wiseman of the Marion Police Department telephoned Herrin Detective Brown to convey an intriguing bit of information. A confidential source had revealed that an individual named Bruce once was telling people that he had killed Velma Carter and that two other men, Tom and Gary Adams, were his accomplices. The trio had been to a local store, spending a large amount of money on the evening of the homicide.

Detective Brown found Bruce Jones at his home in Herrin that same day and brought him to the police station for interrogation. The lawman read the suspect his Miranda rights and explained that he wanted to question him about the murder of Velma Carter. The suspect's hands began to shake as he signed a waiver stating that he understood his rights and that he would voluntarily talk to the police.

Then Detective Brown asked Jones if he had spent a large amount of money on Thursday evening, July 1.

Jones said that he and a friend had gone to the store and purchased a stereo CD player and a CD record. The total amount of the purchase was about $130. Smith told the lawman that his friend had received a check in the mail—that was the money used for the purchase.

"Who have you been hanging out with?" the police asked.

Jones said that he had been hanging out with Bill Wagner, Gary Adams, and Tom Adams.

"What were your activities on Wednesday night, June 30, up to July 1?" the detective inquired.

Jones said he'd been at Bill Wagner's house until about 8:30 p.m. Then he and his friend rode their bikes out through the woods for about ten or fifteen minutes. They rode past Velma Carter's house about 9:30 p.m. and saw a light on inside. They arrived at the friend's house and stayed there until about 10:30 p.m. when a relative of his came by, loaded the bike on a trunk of the car, and the two went home. Jones said that he went to bed when he got home and didn't get up until ten o'clock the next morning.

"Who was at the Wagner residence on Wednesday night when you were there?" Brown asked.

"Gary Adams, Bill Wagner, and Jason Jackson," Jones replied.

"Who do you think might have killed Velma Carter?" the police asked.

"I think Jason Jackson might have committed the murder," Jones responded somewhat nervously.

"You've been telling people that you, Gary Adams, and Tom Adams committed the murder," Detective Brown said suddenly.

Jones turned pale. "No! No! I didn't do it! I didn't have anything to do with it, and neither did they. I believe Jason Jackson did commit the murder!"

Jones took a deep breath to regain his composure and then continued his story. He told the detectives that while he was at the Wagner residence on Wednesday night, June 30, Jason Jackson threw a green duffel bag out the window of the Wagner home. The bag contained a black suit jacket.

Then, Jones said, he himself rode his bike to the alley behind Velma Cater's residence and witnessed Jason Jackson hiding the bag in some bushes. Jackson told Jones that he was going to break into the house and take the elderly woman's money. Jackson said that he was going to wear the black suit jacket so he wouldn't be seen and a pair of socks over his hands because he did not have gloves. He planned to carry out the burglary at about two thirty on Thursday morning. Jackson told Jones that if he would keep quiet about the burglary, he would give Jones three thousand dollars. After they left the area, Jones said, he went to his friend's house, as he had told police earlier.

The next morning, Jones went to the Wagner residence and found Jason Jackson there. Jason told Jones that he had killed Velma, but there was no money to be found in the house.

Next, the police questioned Bill Wagner, who told them that the whole situation started about a week earlier. Wagner, Jackson, and several of their friends were sitting around talking. Wagner told the police that Velma Carter came up during the conversation and a relative who lived near her said that Velma had hundred dollar bills stashed under the mattress in the spare bedroom. The relative said that she had watched Velma count the money before.

According to Wagner, several days later, Jackson said that he wanted to break into the house and get some quick money, because he was concerned about a friend who was about to be evicted. Wagner said he didn't believe that Jackson was really serious about the break-in, but he did tell Jackson that it would be a stupid thing to do.

Continuing his story, Bill Wagner said that on the night of June 30,

Jackson was at Wagner's house. Jackson left around 8:30 p.m. and told Wagner that he was going to get a pack of cigarettes. He returned about an hour later. Wagner said that when he went to bed around 1:30 a.m., Jackson was still at his house.

The next morning, about ten o'clock, Jackson came to Wagner's home again. He started laughing and joking around about the break-in. First he said that he didn't do it; then he said that he had gotten into the house, but he had found no cash. During the burglary, he said, the woman had sat up on the edge of the bed and scared him.

Meanwhile, the police found Larry Jason Jackson at his residence and escorted him to the police station for interrogation. At 6:02 p.m., Detective Brown and Carterville Detective Oren Drew read Jackson his Miranda rights. Jackson told them that he understood his rights and agreed to talk.

The police informed Jackson that they had information that he had been involved in a burglary at Velma Carter's residence and then murdered the victim. Jackson denied any involvement in the burglary or the homicide. The detectives went on to tell him that there was information that he had planned the burglary and other people knew about it. Jackson continued to profess his innocence, but after fifteen minutes of intense questioning, the detective began to wear him down.

The police stopped the questioning for a few moments. Then Detective Brown looked at Jackson and told him that it was important that he tell the truth. Jackson dropped his head and took a deep breath. "I'll tell you what happened," he said, finally. The investigators listened closely as the suspect told how he'd hidden the duffel bag in the alley behind the victim's house and then returned later. "Around two in the morning, or three, possibly, I went back. I put that jacket on and I put socks on my hands and then I walked up to the house and took the back screen out of the window. I climbed in. I went there to see if there was money underneath this one bed that she was not sleeping on and I didn't find none.

"I was in the process of leavin' and she woke up. I turned my head, just walked over to her, and pushed her down. I left and I did not know I harmed her in any way, but then I just went out the door and I went back to the house.

"After I changed clothes there, I put the clothes I had on inside the bag and I dumped it out there in a little swamp behind the house that I was staying at."

The police knew from the evidence found at the crime scene that

Jackson was not telling everything. They continued questioning him for more details.

"So there was supposedly money in the bedroom where she wasn't sleeping?" Detective Drew asked.

"Yes. In between the mattresses," Jackson replied.

"So you went in the house and went directly to the bed that she wasn't sleeping in?" Drew asked.

"Yes." Jackson answered.

"What did you do when you didn't find anything?" Drew asked.

"I was in the process of leaving the house at that time. I was trying to get out of there real quick before she woke up," Jackson explained.

"And that's when she woke up?"

"Yeah."

"Where did you get the pillow that you pushed her down with?"

"I put one leg on the bed, reached over her, grabbed the pillow, and I just pushed her down, hoping she wouldn't see me. The pillow was over her face. I held it there until she quit moving. Then I left."

At the conclusion of the interrogation, the detectives arrested Larry Jason Jackson for the murder of Velma Carter. At seven o'clock that same night, the lawmen asked Jackson to show them the exact place where he'd placed the duffel bag. Jackson took them to the swamp area. The duffel bag was still floating there, although Jackson told the police that he had placed bricks inside so that it would sink.

The police recovered the duffel bag as well as a black sport coat, a pair of white socks, and three bricks. They returned to the police station and took Jackson's clothing into evidence. They submitted everything to the crime lab for examination and testing. The results showed that five acrylic fibers recovered from the kitchen cabinet were consistent with the suspect's white socks. Furthermore, the evidence collected from the victim contained numerous hairs, fibers, soil particles, and botanical material similar to what was found on the suspect's clothing.

The physical evidence found at the scene could only be used as supportive evidence in court, and the state's attorney knew he would not get a conviction on the physical evidence alone. However, that concern was soon allayed at Larry Jason Jackson's first court appearance, when the accused man pled guilty to the murder of Velma Carter.

Over the next several months, a series of sentencing hearings for Jackson were conducted in the First Circuit Court of Williamson County, Illinois.

Meanwhile, for the first time in his nine-year career, State's Attorney Charles Garnati experienced the pain of prosecuting a murder case involving a long-time friend. Velma Carter had been his kindergarten teacher. Garnati wanted the death penalty for Jackson, not because of the friendship, but because, as he argued, the defendant planned the crime for two weeks before he finally murdered the eighty-six-year-old victim.

Defense Attorney Larry Broeking argued that Jackson had grown up in a dysfunctional family. The now convicted man had received little care, guidance, or love as a child, the lawyer contended, and therefore deserved the mercy of the court.

On Monday, December 29, 1993, back in the First Circuit Court of Williamson County, Judge Donald Lowery asked Jackson if he had anything to say before sentence was passed.

Jackson hung his head and said, "I want everyone to know, I'm sorry. I didn't mean to hurt anyone."

Judge Lowery then sentenced Larry Jason Jackson to seventy-five years for the murder of Velma Carter. Jackson is now serving his sentence at Menard Penitentiary in Chester, Illinois.

Author's Note
Jack Harris, Bruce Jones, Tom Adams, Gary Adams, and Bill Wagner are not the real names of the persons so named in the foregoing story. Fictitious names have been used because there is no reason for public interest in the identities of these persons.

Case 20

The Life and Death Struggle

Jane James
October 22, 1993

Carbondale, Illinois

About 8:40 p.m. on Sunday, October 24, 1993, Illinois's Jackson County Sheriff's Department received a disquieting phone call.

"There's been some violence at Jane James's trailer," the male caller blurted out in a frantic voice. "Someone may be hurt."

The dispatcher attempted to calm the caller, took directions to the residence, then immediately directed a patrol car to the scene.

The patrol officer arrived at the scene minutes later.

Upon entering, the lawman immediately realized that a life-and-death struggle had taken place in the residence. Several pieces of furniture had been knocked over, and blood was all over the room—on the furniture, on the floor, and on the walls. The officers noticed a trail of blood that led down the hallway into another room. Stepping carefully to avoid disturbing any possible evidence, the officers followed the trail of blood down the hallway and into the back bedroom. There on the floor beside the bed, they found a body, covered by a blanket, in a large pool of blood.

The officers carefully lifted the blanket and discovered the nude body of Jane James. Her throat was slashed and she had what appeared to be several stab wounds in her chest.

The odor in the room was nauseating. The victim's body was in the early stages of decomposition. Were it not for the positive identification by the police, it would have been difficult to make out the victim's features.

The officers went from room to room, but they found no other bodies or any weapons that might have been used in the murder. After checking all the doors and windows, they determined that there was no forced entry.

A short time later, crime scene technicians from the Illinois State Police Division of Forensic Services and Identification arrived and began processing the crime scene. They photographed the scene, dusted for fingerprints, and collected physical evidence. The processing lasted throughout the night. Numerous pieces of evidence were recovered, including fingerprints, hair fibers, blood samples, and fingernail scrapings from the victim.

Meanwhile, homicide detectives took the investigation into the neighborhood with a door-to-door canvass. They were hoping to find someone who had seen or heard something unusual. Most of the neighbors had gone to work. One neighbor, however, said that on Friday, October 22, around five o'clock in the morning she heard a scream and thumping sounds coming from the direction of the James residence. It didn't alarm her, though, because there were always a lot of noise in the area. No other neighbors had seen or heard anything unusual.

Police contacted the rehabilitation center where Jane James worked as a personal care assistant. The probers learned from female client that she had last seen James on Monday, October 18, at about 11:30 a.m. Later that same day, James did not show up for a 5:00 p.m. appointment with the client. The client said she tried to contact James by phone but was never able to reach her.

Probers also found out that another friend of the victim's, who was trying to reach her, had called James's residence. She never got any response, either.

That same day, forensic pathologist Dr. John A. Heidingsfelder performed an autopsy on James's body. The examination revealed that the thirty-four-year-old victim had been stabbed five times around the heart. Three of the wounds went into the heart and all five wounds were within three or four inches of each other. The victim had also suffered a slash wound across the front of her neck that cut into the wind pipe. There were two other cuts on her neck. The pathologist concluded that a knife blade of at least four and a half inches was used in the attack. The doctor reported that the victim had been dead from three to five days.

Detectives pushed forward with the investigation by questioning Susan Vancil, a friend of the victim's. Vancil told the police that Brian Gillin, James's boyfriend, had lived on and off with James for some time. According to Vancil, the relationship had deteriorated and Gillin had moved out. Vancil said she had tried to reach James by phone but was never able to. Later, Vancil said she saw Gillin in town and asked about James. Gillin told her that he had not seen James for several days.

The detectives next interviewed Brian Gillin, who told them that at one time he and James had a relationship. He had lived with James for a while, but several months before, they broke up and Gillin moved out. James and Gillin remained friends, he said. He would visit her frequently and do odd jobs for her, but that was the extent of their friendship. Gillin said he could not give an exact date, but he had not seen James for several days.

Meanwhile, detectives mulled over the possible motives for the murder. *Whose fingerprints were in the house,* they wondered. *Had James been killed by somebody she knew or by a stranger?* The sleuths had learned in the course of the investigation that several items were missing from the residence. Maybe the victim had surprised someone who was breaking into her home and, during the struggle, the victim was murdered. The detectives were hopeful that the crime scene would be able to come up with some usable information. Aside from the obvious cause of death, there was precious little other evidence in the case.

Then probers learned from the crime lab that the physical evidence gathered at the crime scene would be of little help to them in locating a suspect. Apparently, the blood and hair found in the house belonged to the victim.

As the hours of investigating wore on, several key developments cropped up. One female witness said that she had tried to contact Jane James several times. Each time she called the residence, Brian Gillin answered. He kept telling the witness something different. Once he said James was at the store, then he said she was at work , and yet another time, he said James was sleeping.

Another witness, John Holmes, told the police that the victim was friends with his wife. He said that on the night of Saturday, October 23, Gillin called him to say that he was scared because he thought he had killed James. Gillin said that deputies were outside the mobile home but that he would only surrender to Holmes. Holmes said that he checked with the sheriff's department and learned that there were no deputies at the mobile home, so he discarded Gillin's phone call.

Gillin called Holmes the next day and apologized for the previous phone call. He now told the friend that he had been hallucinating and that James was asleep in the bedroom.

Police leaned from a female friend of the victim's that Gillin had moved out of James's residence a few months back, but when she talked with James on October 17, James told her that Gillin had moved back in.

A neighbor told the police that she saw Gillin on Sunday, October 24, washing James's car outside the mobile home.

Then police discovered a couple of days before they found the body, Gillin tired to sell the victim's car at three different car dealers and to open a bank account with a check drawn on the victim's checking account.

Brian Gillin was now the prime suspect in the James murder. But even without his contradictory stories about when he had last seen Jane James and where he was the day she was killed, the police had ample reason to suspect Gillin. They found out that Gillin had an arrest record in Illinois. In 1980, Gillin was convicted of felony theft. Then in 1981, Gillin was convicted of attempted murder and armed violence in Cook County. He received concurrent sentences of twenty years for each charge and he was released from prison in July 1991. He was discharged from parole three months before James was murdered.

The police found Gillin at a local bar in Carbondale and escorted him to the police station. The police told Gillin that they had new information that was inconsistent with his previous statement to them. Gillin denied knowing anything about the murder. "I have nothing else to say," he said.

On October 25, Brian Gillin was arrested and charged with the murder of Jane James. Detectives took the suspect through the booking process, taking fingerprints and mugshots and filling out arrest reports. After completing the booking process, the detectives transported Gillin to the Jackson County Jail.

Two months later, a pretrial hearing was conducted at the state's request. Jackson County State's Attorney Mike Wepsiec made a motion requesting the court's approval to obtain the psychologist records of Brian Gillin from court in Cook County, Illinois. The prosecutor told the judge that he wanted the records because he anticipated that Gillin's attorney would plead that Gillin was not guilty by reason of insanity. Defense Attorney Tim Capps said that because he had not decided on a strategy, the motion might be premature. The judge approved the motion but said that he would seal the records. The judge said he would review it if the insanity defense was raised in court and, at that time, determine what parts of the evaluation might be relevant to the attorneys.

The jury trial before Judge David W. Watt Jr. began on Monday, September 12, 1994.

The state's case rested on several witnesses who would testify about Brian Gillin's behavior. Prosecutor Wepsiec said that testimony from a forensic pathologist would be presented to support that Gillin knew of James's death days before he was questioned by the police.

A female witness testified that Gillin told her a different story each time she asked Gillin if he had seen James. Three different witnesses testified that Gillin told them he had killed or thought he had killed James. Another witness testified that Gillin was at James's residence washing her car just hours before the body was found. Witnesses also testified about Gillin's attempts to sell the victim's car three times and the attempts by Gillin to open a checking account with a check from the victim's account.

The defense's case rested on the testimony of the defendant himself, who now admitted that he had killed James. However, Defense Attorney Capps argued that the evidence would show that Gillin was acting in self-defense when James was slain.

Gillin told the court that the victim returned home early one morning intoxicated and accused him of having an affair. After arguing with James, Gillin said he went to sleep on the couch in the living room. A short time later, he woke up when something hit him in the head. According to Gillin, James was standing in front of him. He got up off the couch and as he stood up, James stabbed him in the wrist with a steak knife.

Gillin said that James was waving the knife at him and was challenging him to take it away from her as the argument moved from the living room into the kitchen. Gillin testified that he fell backwards into the kitchen after tripping. He scrambled to his feet and picked up a knife from the kitchen sink. At that time, James was about three feet away. She had her arm raised with the steak knife in her hand. Gillin told the court he recalled stabbing James twice, but then he went into a state of shock and just lost it.

The defense case suffered a setback when the prosecutor began his cross-examination. He questioned Gillin for several hours about his statements to the police, friends, and his activities after the murder. Gillin told Prosecutor Wepsiec that he didn't remember saying anything that the prosecution witnesses had claimed he said about the victim's whereabouts in the days before her body was found. Gillin also testified that he did not remember trying to sell James's car at three used car dealerships or trying to open a bank account with a check drawn from her account.

Prosecutor Wepsiec asked Gillin why he didn't try leaving the mobile home through a nearby door after he was first stabbed. "I was shocked and more worried about taking the knife away from her," Gillin replied.

Gillin said that he didn't intend to kill James when he stabbed her. He testified that he loved her and said that she would only become violent after she drank alcohol.

"She had a big heart. When she wasn't drinking, she was a totally different person," Gillin told the court.

The five-day trial ended on October 3, 1994, with the state's attorney and the defense attorney making their closing arguments before Judge Watt. Prosecutor Wepsiec compared Gillin's testimony to a movie. "If this were a movie script, it would win an Academy Award. It has drama, tension, violence. It even had our hero over here," the prosecutor said, pointing to the defendant, "escaping death from a madwoman." Prosecutor Wepsiec theorized that James had been killed after arguing with Gillin because he pawned a television set. She was stabbed five times around her heart and her throat was slashed. The prosecutor also reminded the jury that James was nude during the attack and questioned the realty of Gillin's claim that he was acting in self-defense. "The evidence is overwhelming. Gillin has hung himself with his own testimony."

In closing, Defense Attorney Camps argued that in the days after James's death, Gillin had wandered around Carbondale fighting an inner battle because of trauma. "Whatever happened on the night James died had been sudden and unexpected," Camps told the jury, adding that Gillin was afraid and "knew what she was capable of."

"Self-defense is gender-neutral," Camps argued. "Because a woman is the aggressor doesn't make it funny or cute or any less dangerous."

The defense then rested. Deciding the defendant's guilt of a lesser charge of second-degree murder because of the defendant's self-defense claim now rested in the hands of the jury. Did the state present evidence that gave proof beyond a reasonable doubt or were there other plausible possibilities?

The jury deliberated for four and a half hours before reaching a verdict at 2:30 p.m. on September 15, 1994. They found Brian Gillin guilty of first-degree murder. Gillin bowed his head but showed no other emotion when Judge Watt read the verdict.

Defense Attorney Camps asked for a poll of the jurors. Gillin, still with his head bowed, shook his head from side to side as one by one the nine men and three women confirmed the guilty verdict.

The prosecutor concluded with testimony from a relative of Jane

James who said she favored a sentence of natural life in prison. She testified that she didn't know if Gillin would live until he was in his mid-seventies. "At that age, he probably won't be able to kill another one. He tried twice; he succeeded the second time. Don't give him the chance, not again. I don't want another relative to go through this. It's too much. He has to be stopped," the relative said.

Public Defender Camps argued that the attack on James was not premeditated and Gullin believed he had to defend himself.

Next, Camps put Gillin on the stand. Gillin once again testified that he acted in self-defense. He told the judge that he would accept whatever sentence was imposed, but he did not feel that he should have been found guilty of first-degree murder. Gillin told the judge that he loved James and "never did anything to hurt her." He apologized to James's family and friends, and also to the relatives of the 1981 victim. Gillin said, "With God's grace, I hope both families will forgive me."

The judge considered the arguments and then made his decision. The judge noted that Gillin had been sentenced to twenty years in prison in 1983 for attempted murder and armed violence in Cook County and served little more than eight years of the sentence before being released.

Watt said he found that the attack on James was "deja vu" all over again, except in this case, the victim died.

Watt told Gillin he found no potential for rehabilitation in him. "I'm going to do my job and the public better hope the rest of the state agencies do theirs," Watt said. Judge Watt Jr. then sentenced Brian Gillin to eighty years in prison for the stabbing death of Jane James.

Gilli sat slumped in his chair and showed no emotion when the sentence was passed.

After the hearing, State's Attorney Wepsiec told reporters that the extended sentence will ensure that Gillin will be "a very, very old man most likely unable to commit another murder." He will be at least seventy-five years old before he is eligible for parole.

CPSIA information can be obtained
at www.ICGtesting.com
Printed in the USA
JSHW031736200323
39185JS00001B/106